MOTION PICTURE

AND VIDEO LIGHTING

MOTION PICTURE
AND VIDEO LIGHTING

Second Edition

Blain Brown

Focal Press
Taylor & Francis Group

NEW YORK AND LONDON

First published 1995
This edition published 2013 by Focal Press
70 Blanchard Road, Suite 402, Burlington, MA 01803

and by Focal Press
2 Park Square, Milton Park, Abingdon, Oxon OX14 4RN

Focal Press is an imprint of the Taylor & Francis Group, an informa business

Library of Congress Cataloging-in-Publication Data
Brown, Blain.
    Motion picture and video lighting / Blain Brown. — 2nd ed.
        p. cm.
    Includes index.
    ISBN-13: 978-0-240-80763-8 (pbk. : alk. paper) 1. Cinematography–Lighting. 2. Video recording–Lighting.   I. Title.
    TR891.B76 2007
    778.5'343–dc22

                                                    2007010633

ISBN-13: 978-0-240-80763-8 (pbk)
ISBN-13: 978-0-080-55107-4 (ebk)
ISBN-13: 978-0-240-80981-6 (dvd)

Typeset by Charon Tec Ltd (A Macmillan Company)
www.charontec.com

Printed and bound in the United States of America by Sheridan

To my wife, Ada Pullini Brown, without whom nothing would ever get done.

Table of contents

Preface to the Second Edition

Since the first edition of this book, there have been significant advances in motion picture and video lighting technology, and we have tried to include as many of them here as possible. However, despite the advances in lighting equipment, film stocks, and lenses, and, of course, the introduction of DV and HD video technology and its acceptance in the professional world, the fundamentals of lighting remain the same. Good lighting is eternal; the basic concepts of lighting have not changed since they were explored by Rembrandt, Caravaggio, and other masters.

In this book we attempt to cover both the technology of lighting as well as the aesthetics, the techniques, and the "process"—the thinking and methodology by which a scene gets lit and made ready to shoot.

One factor will never change in motion picture, video, and HD production: time is always of the essence. Production costs money—usually a lot of money. As a result, the ability to be fast is always as important as any other aspect of your performance. This is true whether it is a no-budget film or a large studio film. Ask any Director of Photography; he or she will tell you that the ability to achieve good results quickly is crucial to getting and keeping the job.

Understanding the process is critical to being fast, but knowing the capabilities of the equipment and being well versed in how other people have done it before is also important.

On the set, we often tend to work intuitively. As you learn lighting, however, it is important for you to think carefully about what you are doing and why you are doing it. This will lay a solid ground under your intuitive decisions later on and will ultimately give you more confidence. As you work, others will be watching you: the director, the AD, the producer, your crew. The more confident you are in what you are doing and the approach you are taking, the smoother things will go.

Learning lighting is a life-long pursuit. Few people ever feel they know it all. The chance to constantly learn, get better, and find new ways of doing things is one of the attractions of lighting; if it were done by formula time after time, it would be a boring job.

Whether you are just beginning in the field of motion picture and video lighting or if you have been doing it a while, I hope this book will help you continue in your pursuit of better lighting.

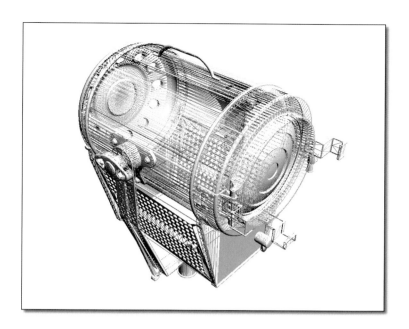

THE HISTORY OF LIGHTING

Lighting is to film what music is to opera.

- C.B. DeMille

Lighting creates the environment for storytelling and we must never forget that, at its heart, filmmaking is telling stories with pictures.

The first lighting for storytelling was fire. For some purposes, it is still nearly perfect. Firelight is warm and glowing, associated in the mind with safety, heat, and protection from nature. It draws people toward it; they automatically arrange themselves into a circle at a comfortable conversational distance. It flickers gently and provides a visual focus that prevents one's attention from wandering. It starts out bright and blazing, then gradually dims as the mood turns inward and eyes grow heavy; it fades away to darkness just about the time the audience is ready to go home. For the hunter returned from the hunt, the village shaman performing a ritual, or an elder recounting the story of the tribe, it was ideal.

As theater became more formalized, with written scripts and larger audiences, daylight performance became the norm: more light was necessary so that everyone could see

FIGURE 1.1 Motivated, dramatic lighting for *The Thread of Destiny* (1910).

clearly. Classical Greek plays were performed at festivals, which ordinarily began at dawn and continued through most of the day. With little emphasis on costumes (other than masks), staging, sets, or effects, the theater subsisted almost entirely on the power of the spoken word. (Some purists feel it's all been downhill from there.) Even up to the time of Shakespeare and the Globe, daylight performances were the standard for the mass market.

Increasingly, though, works were also performed in the houses of nobility and for smaller audiences. These indoor and evening performances were lit with candles and torches, which doubtless had a simple and powerful effect. Staging as we know it today came of age with the great spectacles of Inigo Jones, the seventeenth-century British architect who produced elaborate festival pieces with sumptuous costumes and sets.

Controllable Light

Controllable, directional lighting for the theater is not a new idea. In fact, it dates back to the French chemist Lavoisier, who in 1781 suggested that movable reflectors be added to oil lanterns. With such innovations French theater led the way in lighting during this period, but there was always a division of opinion in European drama between those who wanted simple illumination of the elaborate sets and drops and those who wanted to develop a more theatrical and expressive lighting art.

The first technological advance came with the introduction of gaslight, which was more reliable and less smoky, but only slightly less hazardous. The next advance was the introduction of limelight, which burned natural gas and oxygen in a filament of calcium oxide (limestone). This significant advance, which produced a beautiful warm light that complimented the actors' skin tone, is still commemorated in our everyday language with the phrase, "step into the limelight." At about the same time, this smaller, more concentrated source was combined with simple plano-convex lenses and spherical reflectors to provide the basis for one of the most important elements of modern lighting control: directional and focusable units.

The great theater pioneers Adolphe Appia (1862–1928) and David Belasco (1853–1931) were revolutionary figures in the realm of expressionistic staging. Appia was perhaps the first to argue that shadows were as important as the light, and the first for whom the manipulation of light and shadow was a means of expressing ideas. In opposition to the "naturalism" of the time (which was, in fact, a very artificial broad, flat lighting), Appia created bold expressionist lighting full of *sturm und drang.*

Belasco emphasized realistic effects to underscore the drama. He foreshadowed the private thoughts of many a modern cinematographer when he stated, in 1901, that the actors were secondary to the lighting. His electrician Louis Hartmann is credited by some as inventing the first incandescent spotlight (Appia, Gordon Craig, and Max Reinhardt are also contenders), the forerunner of most of the lights we use today. To counteract the harsh theatrical hardness, Belasco and Hartmann also developed a row of overhead reflected soft lights, which were useful for naturalistic daylight scenes. (To this day there is no such thing as a true soft light in theater lighting.) Laudably, Belasco gave Hartmann credit on the billboards for the shows.

Carbon arcs, which use electrodes to produce an intense flame, were also employed in theatrical applications beginning in 1849. They were widely used, particularly in high-intensity follow spots.

Early Film Production

With the advent of motion pictures in 1888, the earliest emulsions were so slow that nothing but daylight was powerful enough to get a decent exposure. Filmmaking was largely an outdoor activity until Thomas Edison (1847–1931) unveiled his famous "Black Maria." Built in 1893 by Edison's associate William K.L. Dickson (co-creator of early motion picture technology), the Black Maria was not only open to the sky but could be rotated on a base to maintain orientation to the sun.

As the motion picture industry developed, early studios in New York City and Ft. Lee, New Jersey, were open to the sky as well, usually with huge skylights. Some control was possible, with muslins stretched under the skylights to provide diffusion of the light and control contrast. Because these were silent films and noise was not an issue, less space was needed in the studios since two or more production units could work within a few feet of each other.

The first artificial sources used in film production were Cooper–Hewitt mercury vapor tubes, which were suspended under the glass roof of the Biograph Studio on 14th Street in New York City around 1905. These were followed soon after by the introduction of arc lamps, which were adaptations of typical street lights of the time. The long-exposure requirements, the lack of adequate equipment, and the still slender economics of the business made anything but flat, overall lighting nearly impossible to attain.

As artificial sources were developed, the controlling factor was the spectral receptivity of the emulsions. Before 1927, black-and-white film was orthochromatic; it was not

FIGURE 1.2 Arc lights in use on an exterior set with rain effects. (Photo courtesy of Mole–Richardson Co.)

sensitive to red light. Tungsten lights were almost useless because of their large component of red.

Another adaptation of contemporary industrial equipment to motion picture use was the introduction in 1912 of white-flame carbon arcs, which had previously been used primarily in photoengraving. As with arcs today, these new units (called broadsides) were characterized by very high output and a spectral curve compatible with orthochromatic film. Carbon-arc spotlights were purchased from theater lighting companies such as Kliegl Brothers of New York (whose name still survives in the term *klieg* lights).

Another legacy of Belasco's illustrious career was carried on by a young man who worked as an actor for him, Cecil B. DeMille. DeMille rebelled against the flat illumination characteristic of the open-to-the-sky film stages. In the film *The Warrens of Virginia*, director DeMille and cameraman Alvin Wyckoff used a startlingly modern concept: they used sunlight reflected through windows as the sole source of light.

At the time, only a few American filmmakers, DeMille, Edwin Porter, and D.W. Griffith's cameraman Billy Bitzer, fought the stylistic preference for broad, flat lighting. Bitzer had used firelight effects in *The Drunkard's Reformation* in 1908, and the next year Pippa Passes evoked the changing time of day with directional lighting simulating the passage of the sun. *The Thread of Destiny* contained scenes lit solely by slanting rays of sunlight and may be the first truly effective use of chiaroscuro (dubbed "Rembrandt" lighting by Wyckoff).

FIGURE 1.3 Early tungsten units in use on the set of *Broadway*. The dome-shaped units were called "rifles" for their ability to project light at a distance. The open-face units were called "Solar Spots". Films were "slow" back then (meaning they needed large amounts of light to get a good exposure). Lenses were also slow; the result was that sets had to be lit to a very high lighting level. (Photo courtesy of Mole–Richardson Co.)

Introduction of Tungsten Lighting

For years, cameramen looked longingly at the compact, versatile tungsten lamps that were then available (called Mazda lamps at the time), but attempts to use them were foiled by the spectral sensitivity of the film stocks in use at the time; they were almost completely blind to red light—even slightly red objects would photograph as black. The tungsten incandescent bulbs were (as they are today) heavily weighted in the red end of the spectrum.

In 1927, the introduction of a film stock sensitive to all visible wavelengths (hence its name, *panchromatic*) altered lighting capabilities radically. The new stock was compatible with tungsten incandescent sources, which offered many advantages, including reduced cost. *Broadway*, produced in 1929 by Universal and shot by Hal Mohr, was the first film lit entirely with tungsten.

Studio management saw in the new technology an economical means by which set lighting could be accomplished by the push of a button. The "bean counters" in the head office (they had them even then) responded enthusiastically to the economics of incandescent lighting, so much so that in some studios the use of arc lighting was banned except by special permission. With sound technology confining the cameras to immobile sound-proof "ice boxes" and the resulting lack of the powerful arcs to create strong effects, together with very static camera work, the outcome was many a visually dull picture and one of the low points of studio cinematography.

(a)

(b)

FIGURE 1.4 (**a**) Before the invention of halogen bulbs, a typical large tungsten lamp (in this case a 5K bulb in a Mole Skypan) was enormous. (Photo courtesy of Mole–Richardson Co.) (**b**) Tungsten halogen bulbs allowed the invention of "baby" units—much more compact than the normal units. Shown here is a Mole "Baby-Baby"—a "baby" size 1000-watt light, which is commonly called a baby light.

The makers of carbon arcs responded to this challenge by developing carbons that were compatible with panchromatic film. Even with the new carbons, arcs remained (as they do to this day) more labor-intensive and bulky. The death blow was dealt by the advent of HMIs, which are more efficient in their use of power and don't require a dedicated operator.

The drawback of incandescent lights was (and still is) that they are inherently far less powerful than carbon arcs. The need to achieve maximum output from the incandescent lamps resulted in the introduction of an improved reflector made of highly polished, mirrored glass. Lights based on this technology were sometimes called rifles, for their capacity to project sharp beams long distances. They were efficient but hard to control; they were hardly more than a raw source of light. What cinematographers yearned for was a light of even greater intensity, but with controllable beam spread and distribution. In 1934, the introduction of the fresnel lens led to the development of lighting units that are almost indistinguishable from those we use today.

Following the introduction of three-strip Technicolor with the film *Becky Sharp* in 1935, arcs came back into favor. Technicolor required a spectral distribution close to that of natural daylight, which made tungsten lighting difficult. In the intervening years, manufacturers had managed to make arcs quieter and so white-flame carbons, which produce daylight blue with very high output, were just the ticket for the new process. The addition of the fresnel lens also made them more controllable.

This was the heyday of the carbon arc. Not only did they have the correct color balance, but the fact that Technicolor is a process where the image formed by the lens is split by prisms into three different film strips meant that enormous quantities of light were needed. Some early Technicolor films were lit to such intensity that piano lids warped and child performers (most notably Shirley Temple) were barely able to withstand the heat on the set.

To use tungsten lights with color, it was necessary to lose almost half of the light to filtration, so their use on color sets was very limited; they still found wide use in black-and-white filmmaking and later in television.

The Technicolor Era

As with the advent of sound, Technicolor imposed severe restrictions on cinematographers. Until color came along, the use of light meters was almost unknown: cameramen used film tests, experience, and guesswork to establish exposure. The precise engineering needs of the three-strip process made it necessary to impose rigid standards. In the early days, cameramen were not trusted to handle the job alone. The licensing of the Technicolor process carried with it the obligation to employ one of Technicolor's advisory cameramen to oversee color balance and exposure. Films of this period are distinguished by having two cameramen listed in the credits.

The constant supervision of the Technicolor cameramen, along with the employment of color advisors, gave rise to the still current myth of the "Technicolor look." Contrary to popular belief, the Technicolor process and the film stock then available did not necessarily lead to bright, intense color completely lacking in subtlety. What we think of as the Technicolor look is in fact a reflection of the desire to show off the new technology, coupled with the somewhat primitive artistic tastes of the studio chiefs of the period. Since the process gave engineers and advisors as much input into the look of the film as the cameramen and directors, the dictates of the head office could be implemented in an orderly, bureaucratic way, thereby bypassing the age-old film tradition according to which directors and cameramen would agree to ridiculous demands in the conference room, then follow the dictates of conscience and art while on the set.

The pendulum swung back to tungsten with the introduction of high-speed Technicolor film balanced for incandescent light in 1951. Other companies such as Kodak and Ansco also made tungsten-balance films available. This established the standard that now prevails: color films balanced for tungsten light but usable in daylight with filtration. Only recently have Kodak and Fuji introduced excellent lines of daylight balance negative films. In 1955, yellow-flame carbons (tungsten balance) were invented, which made arcs usable with the new tungsten-balanced films without the use of color correction.

One major obstacle remained for incandescent lamps: the vaporized tungsten metal that burned off the filament tended to condense on the relatively cooler glass envelope of the bulb. As a result, the output of the lamp steadily decreased as the lamp burned; in addition, the color balance shifted as the bulb blackened.

A far more practical solution was the invention of the tungsten–halogen bulb in the early 1960s. Employing a gas cycle to return the boiled-off metal to the filament, the design resulted in lamps with longer life spans and more efficient output. Another advantage of the smaller quartz lamps is their capacity to fit into smaller housings than could a conventional tungsten incandescent. The result has been more compact lights (baby babies, baby deuces) and smaller lights, such as the popular Tweenie 650-watt size.

(a)

(b)

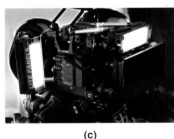

(c)

FIGURE 1.5 (**a**) Kino Flo color-correct fluorescent lamps on a set. (Photo courtesy of Kino Flo, Inc.) (**b**) Mole–Richardson 12K fresnel HMI. (**c**) LED panel lights mounted on a camera. (Photos courtesy of Lite Panels, Inc.)

HMI, Xenon, Fluorescent, and LED Sources

A revolution in lighting came in the late 1960s when enclosed metal arcs (HMIs) were developed for German television. Their main features are the tremendous advantage in lumens-per-watt output over conventional sources and the fact that they are daylight–color-balanced without the need for filtration.

HMIs have changed the lighting business by allowing more powerful sources with less electrical input, which translates into smaller generators and smaller cables. The largest sources (12K and 18K) have output that equals and exceeds the output of the power-hungry carbon arcs, but don't require direct current (DC) or a full-time operator.

Although these stable, efficient sources were originally developed for television, filmmakers were quick to recognize their advantages. When the first film was shot using the new lights, everyone was horrified when the exposure varied constantly. Research quickly revealed the cause of the notorious flicker effect: HMIs are arc sources just like the old Brutes, but while Brutes were DC, HMIs are alternating current (AC). The light output varies as the AC cycle goes up and down; as a result, the output of the light varies as well.

With a few exceptions (such as using PAL equipment in a NTSC country or running the lights off of a noncrystal sync generator), in video this is no problem, since both are synchronized to the same AC cycle. In film, however, there are many conditions in which the two are not synchronized. We now know the conditions that must be met for HMIs to be used successfully, but the problem has added new considerations to filming and imposed limitations on many types of filming, particularly high-speed photography and working with live monitors.

Meanwhile, 1982's *Blade Runner*, with its stunning cinematography by Jordan Cronenweth, popularized a new player—xenons. A gas-discharge arc, the xenon is a cousin to the HMI and big brother to the xenon gas projector lamps used in theaters. A highly efficient source coupled with a polished parabolic reflector gives xenon the capability of extraordinary output in an extremely narrow, focused beam. Although very specific in application, xenon has proved a useful and powerful tool for the image maker.

The development of flicker-free HMIs that feature electronic rather than magnetic ballasts eliminated most of the technical problems involved in using HMIs in off-speed filming. One drawback is that in flicker-free mode, some units emit a loud hum, which may be objectionable to the sound department.

Kino Flo and LED

Other developments include the creation of fluorescent tubes with color rendition good enough for color filming applications. Pioneered by Kino Flo, color-corrected, high-frequency fluorescent sources (to eliminate flicker problems) have been extremely popular in all types of applications.

A more recent development is LED panel lights, which are extremely compact and can be made very small; they have become very popular for applications such as car interiors and when it is important to hide lighting units throughout the set.

Today's image maker has a wide variety of powerful and flexible tools available for lighting in film and video. The history of lighting is the story of adapting new technology and new techniques to the demands of art and visual storytelling. The same concerns still face us every day on the set, and we can draw on the rich experience of those who have gone before us.

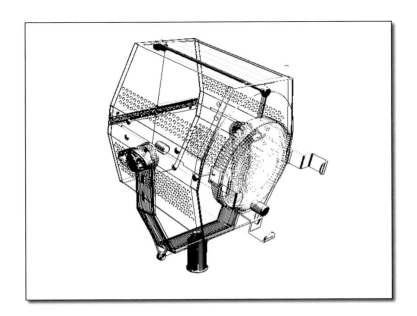

LIGHTING SOURCES

Lighting instruments are the tools of our trade. Just as a mechanic must know what his tools are capable of, we must understand the capacity of our resources in order to use them to their potential. Here we will examine them classified in their major groups: tungsten fresnels, HMIs, carbon arcs, open-faced units, PARs, softs, broads, and miscellaneous.

Fresnels

With very few exceptions (such as the Dedo light), most lights that have a lens use the fresnel lens. Developed in the 19th century for lighthouses by Augustin-Jean Fresnel, the lens was further refined to address certain problems with large glass lenses, primarily the fact that a larger lens tends to collect heat in the thicker center and then often cracks.

Based on the work of Leclerc and Buffon, Fresnel developed the idea of "collapsing" the basic curved shape into a thinner profile. The curvature (and thus the magnification) remains the same, but the glass doesn't get as thick and is therefore less prone to cracking.

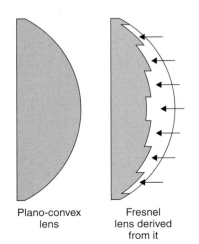

Plano-convex lens   Fresnel lens derived from it

FIGURE 2.1 The derivation of the fresnel lens.

Tungsten Fresnels

All tungsten fresnel lights are designated by their bulb size (2K, 5K, etc.) and come in two basic flavors: studio and baby. The studio light is the full-size unit, while the baby is a smaller housing and lens, which takes advantage of the smaller bulbs in use today. As a rule—the baby version is the housing of the next smaller size (for example, the 5K is similar to a studio 2K) with a box that extends farther from the bottom to house the socket in a position to keep the bulb centered on the reflector and lens. Their smaller size makes them popular for location work.

The 10K and 20K

For many years the 10K was the largest tungsten fresnel available; it is still widely used, but the larger 20K is increasingly dominant for the kinds of uses traditionally assigned to the 10K. The 10K is 110 volts (in the United States) and the 20K is 220 volts.

Still a popular unit, the 10K comes in three versions:
- The baby 10K provides high-intensity output with a fairly compact, easily transportable unit with a 14-inch fresnel lens.
- The basic 10K, known as a tenner or studio 10K, has a 20-inch fresnel.
- The big daddy of the group is the Big Eye tenner, which has a 24-inch lens.

The Big Eye is a special light with a quality all its own. The 10,000-watt DTY bulb provides a fairly small source, while the extremely large fresnel is a large radiator. The result is a sharp, hard light with real bite but with a wraparound quality that gives it a soft light quality on subjects close to the light. This is a characteristic of all big lights (the 12K HMI and the brute arc as well), which gives them a distinctive quality impossible to imitate.

Note on large lights: Never burn a 10K, 20K, or a 5K pointing straight up. The lens blocks proper ventilation and the unit will overheat. Also, the filament will not be properly supported, so it will sag and possibly touch the glass. Either condition will cause the bulb to fail, and overheating may crack the lens. The failure will cost somebody hundreds of dollars and put the light out of commission.

The 5K

Also called a senior, the baby 5K is similar in size and configuration to a studio 2K, but has an enlarged box on the bottom to allow the larger 5K bulb to sit with the filament properly positioned in front of the reflector.

(a)

(b)

(c)

FIGURE 2.2 (**a**) A Big Eye 10K. (**b**) A Mole Baby Junior (2K). (**c**) A Tweenie.

Juniors

The 2K fresnel (also known as a deuce or a junior) is the "jeep" of lights—versatile and useful in many different kinds of situations. With higher speed film emulsions and faster lenses (in film) for the the excellent low-light capabilities of many HD cameras (in video), it can often be powerful enough to be the largest source on the set. Baby deuces are the more compact 2K fresnel units; they have the body of a 1K with a larger tray on the bottom to accommodate the FEY bulb. They are also called baby juniors or BJs.

1K

The baby can use either a 750-watt bulb (EGR) or a 1000-watt bulb (EGT). The widely used name, 750, comes from the days before quartz halogen when the 750 tungsten bulb was the most common. Most are now used with the 1K quartz bulb, but are still called 750s. The baby 1K, also called a baby baby, is the small-size version. Because of its smaller lens and box, it has a wider spread than the studio 750, and this can be a useful feature when hiding small units in nooks and crannies.

650, Betweenie, and InBetweenie

The 650 is a very versatile unit, sometimes called a Tweenie. Its name comes from its position between the 1K and the inkie. With the new high-speed films, the tweenie is often just the right light for the small jobs a baby used to do. Its compact size is a tremendous asset. Mole has also added the Betweenie at 300 watts and the InBetweenie at either 100 or 200 watts. Several manufacturers make similar units.

Inkie

The inkie has long been the smallest light available. At 200 or 250 watts, it is not a powerful unit, but up close it can deliver a surprising amount of light. The inkie is great for a tiny spritz of light on the set, as an eyelight, a small fill, or for an emergency light to raise the exposure just a bit on a small area. When you finish lighting a scene, an inkie or two should always be standing by for last-minute touchups. Because they are so light, inkies can easily be mounted to a film or video camera, handheld, hung on broomsticks, hung from suspended ceilings, and rigged in all sorts of ways to accommodate strange situations.

HMI Units

12K and 18K

The 12K and the 18K HMIs are the most powerful fresnel lights available. They have tremendous output and, like all

FIGURE 2.3 A 12/18K HMI fresnel on a Lite Lift crank-up stand.

HMIs, are extremely efficient in foot-candle output per watt. Like the arc lights they are replacing in general use, they produce a very sharp, clean light, which is the result of having a very small source (the gas arc) that is focused through a very large lens.

For daytime exteriors, the big lights are among the few sources that will balance daylight and fill in the shadows sufficiently to permit shooting in the bare sun without silks or reflectors. The fact that they burn approximately daylight blue (5500K) is a tremendous advantage in these situations: no light is lost to filters.

Some ballasts have Bates connectors, but some ballasts are tied directly into the feeder cable with Camlok, pin, or other types of feeder connectors. Most larger HMI units are 220-volt lights, but some are 110-volt units, which can make load balancing difficult. As with any large light, you need to coordinate with the genny operator before firing it up or shutting it down. Be sure to clarify with the rental house what type of power connectors are used on the lights you are ordering, so that you can be confident you have the right connectors or adapters.

Many HMIs now have flicker-free ballasts that use square-wave technology to provide flickerless shooting at any frame rate. With some units you pay a penalty for flicker-free shooting at frame rates other than sync-sound speed (24 frames per second); when the high-speed flicker-free button is selected on these units, they operate at a significantly higher noise level. If the ballasts can be placed outside or shooting is without sound (MOS), as off-speed shooting usually will be, this is not a problem.

The other good news about large HMIs is the substantial reduction of the size of the ballasts owing to the change from magnetic to electronic ballasts. This is a great relief for electricians, who have had to move the old ballasts, which were the size of small refrigerators.

Header cables are the power connection from the ballast to the light head itself. Most large HMIs can take only two header cables; a third header will usually result in the light's not firing.

6K and 8K

The 6K HMI (and the newer 8K) is a real workhorse. On jobs where the budget will not permit a 12K, it performs much of the same work. Although it generally has a smaller lens, it still produces a sharp, clean beam with good spread. In most applications it performs admirably as the main light, serving as key, window light, or sun balance.

Some 6Ks are 110 volts and some are 220 volts, depending on the manufacturer and the rental house. They may

FIGURE 2.4 A 6K HMI with its ballast.

require a stage box, a twistlock connector, or a set of Siamese connectors. When ordering a 6K, it is critical to ask these questions and be sure the rental house will provide the appropriate distribution equipment. Failure to do so may result in the light's not being functional. Some makes of HMIs (such as Arriflex) provide for head balancing. This is accomplished by sliding the yoke support backward or forward on the head. This is a useful feature when adding or subtracting barndoors, frames, or other items that radically alter the balance of the light.

4K and 2.5K

The smaller HMIs—the 4K and 2.5K—are general-purpose lights, doing all of the work that used to be assigned to 5K and 10K tungsten lights. Slightly smaller than the bigger HMIs they can be easily flown and rigged and will fit in some fairly tight spots.

Smaller HMIs

The smallest units—the 1.2K, 800-, 575-, 400-, and 200-watt HMIs—are versatile units. The 1.2K and smaller units can be plugged into standard household outlets, which makes them extremely versatile. Lightweight and fairly compact, they can be used in a variety of situations. The electronic ballasts for the small units have become portable enough to be hidden on the set or flown in the grid. There are some things to watch with smaller HMI units:

- Prolonged running at a higher rated voltage may result in premature failure.
- Extended cable runs may reduce the voltage to a point that affects the output and may keep the lamp from firing.
- Excessive cooling or direct airflow on the lamp may cool the lamp below its operating temperature, which can result in a light with a high-color temperature and inferior CRI.
- All bulbs are rated for certain burning positions, which vary from plus or minus 15° to plus or minus 45°. In general, bulbs 4K and above have a 15° tolerance while smaller bulbs have a greater range.

When an HMI Fails to Fire

On every job there will be at least one HMI that will fail to function properly. Some rental houses will provide a back-up head, ballast, or both. Be sure to have a few extra header cables on hand. They are the second most common cause of malfunctions, the most common being the safety switch on the lens.

- Check that the breakers are on. Most HMIs have more than one breaker.

- After killing the power, open the lens and check the micro-switch that contacts the lens housing. Make sure it is operating properly and making contact. Wiggle it, but don't be violent—the light won't operate without it.
- If that fails, try another header cable. If you are running more than one header to a light, disconnect and try each one individually. Look for broken pins, garbage in the receptacle, etc.
- Check the power. HMIs won't fire if the voltage is low. Generally, they need at least 108 volts to fire. Some have a voltage switch (110, 120, 220); be sure it's in the right position.
- Try the head with a different ballast and vice versa.
- Let the light cool. Many lights won't do a hot restrike but some have a special hot restrike function, which sends a higher starting voltage to the head.

Care and Feeding of HMIs
- Always ground the light and the ballast with appropriate grounding equipment.
- Check the stand and ballast with a volt ohm meter (VOM) for leakage by measuring the voltage between the stand and any ground. A few volts is normal, but anything above 10 or 15 volts indicates a potential problem.
- Keep the ballast dry. On wet ground, get it up on boxes or rubber mats.
- Avoid getting dirt or finger marks on the lamps. Oil from the skin will degrade the glass and create a potential failure point. Many lamps come with a special cleaning cloth.
- Ensure a good contact between the lamp base and the holder. Contamination will increase resistance and impair proper cooling.

Xenons

Related to the HMI (they are a gas arc with a ballast) Xenons feature a polished parabolic reflector that gives them amazing throw and a near–laser beam collimation. At full spot they can project a tight beam several blocks. They are tremendously efficient with the highest lumens-per-watt output of any light (part of the secret is that there isn't much spread, of course). They currently come in four sizes, 1K, 2K, 4K, and 7K. There is also a 75-watt sungun unit. The 1K and 2K units come in 110- and 220-volt models, some of which can be wall-plugged. The advantage is obvious: you have a choice between a high-output light that can be plugged into a wall outlet or a small putt-putt generator. Be sure to check with the rental house, as some units have Camlok or other type of feeder connector. The 4K and 7K xenons are extremely powerful, and must be used with a bit of caution. At full spot they can crack a window. Just one example of their power: with ASA 320 and full spot, a 4 K delivers f/64 at forty feet from the light!

Because the current at the bulb is pulsed DC, flicker is not a problem for xenons. They can be used for high-speed filming up to 10,000 fps. There are, however, some disadvantages. All xenons are very expensive to rent and have a cooling fan that makes them very difficult to use in sound filming. Also, because of the bulb placement and reflector design, there is always a hole in the middle of the round beam, which can be minimized but never entirely eliminated.

Because of the parabolic reflectors, flagging and cutting are difficult close to the light. Flags cast bizarre symmetrical shadows. Also, the extremely high and concentrated output means that they burn through gel very quickly. Many people try to compensate by placing the gel as far as possible from the light. This is a mistake. The safest place for gel is actually right on the face of the light, which is the coolest spot.

The 75-watt Xenon sungun is excellent for flashlight effects. It is a small handheld unit that was developed for the Navy, and comes in both AC (110 volt) and DC configurations. The newer models have motorized flood-spots that can be operated during the shot. They have a narrow beam with the extremely long throw of xenons. There is, however, a hole or a hot spot in the center of the beam. Xenon bulbs do not shift in temperature as they age or as voltage shifts.

Brute Arc

The DC carbon-arc fresnel is falling into disuse since the advent of the HMI. For many years, the brute arc was the "big mama," the heaviest hitter. With many times the output of the 10K, it was the standard for fill to balance sunlight, the major workhorse for night exteriors, and sun effects through windows.

Invented by Sir Humphrey Davy in 1801, the arc was the first high-intensity electric light. It was used in theaters and then adopted by the film industry as the only source bright enough to use with the extremely slow emulsions then available. It was the only artificial alternative to the all-glass or all-skylight studios that were necessary.

The arc produces light by creating an actual arc between two carbon electrodes. As the arc burns, the negative and positive electrodes are consumed and so have to be continuously advanced to keep them in the correct position. In modern arcs this is done with feed motors. In the early days, the electrode feed mechanisms had to be turned by hand. This called for considerable experience on the part of the technician, and the term *lamp operator* was applied to the most skilled electricians. Even today the name is used on some older studio budget forms to describe set electricians.

The other reason is the gigantic power consumption of arcs (225 amps for the standard brute, which calls for a #00 cable run for each light) and the fact that it must be DC, which dictates either a studio with DC or a large DC generator. The bottom line is that, even with a very cheap daily rental, the arcs are more expensive to operate than an HMI. The arc was particularly useful in that it could be daylight- or tungsten-balanced without gels, something that no other light could do until fluorescent units with changeable bulbs came along. This is accomplished by using either white-flame carbons (daylight balance) or yellow-flame carbons (tungsten balance).

For daylight-balanced use, the white-flame carbons run high in ultraviolet, and a Y-1 filter is usually added to counteract the UV effect. MT-2 converts the white-flame carbons to tungsten color balance. All arcs have an ancillary piece of equipment called a grid or ballast. The grid serves two purposes. It is a giant resistor that limits current flow across the arc and reduces the voltage to the optimal 73 volts without reducing the amperage. For arc operation, see the Appendix.

Open-Face Lights

Lights with fresnel lenses provide a higher degree of control and refinement—smoother and more controllable with cleaner shadows. Open-face lights have no lens and are less controllable, but they make up for it by being far more efficient: an open-face light will be far more powerful than an equivalent-size fresnel light. Open-face lights are generally

FIGURE 2.5 A side-by-side comparison of a Brute Arc (on the right) and a 12K HMI PAR. Both units are mounted on Mole Litewate crank-up stands.

(a)

(b)

FIGURE 2.6 MolePARs (firestarters) (a) With a stippled bulb (Narrow Spot); (b) with a clear lens (Very Narrow Spot).

better for when just raw power is needed, such as bouncing the light or going through heavy diffusion.

Skypan

The skypan is simple in design. It consists of a reflective white pan with a heavy-duty lamp socket positioned to keep the bulb at the center of the reflector. Most have a switch on the back. The skypan is used primarily when just raw power is needed over a fairly large area, such as lighting a large backdrop. There is only one flavor of skypan but either a 5K bulb (DPY) or a 2K bulb (CYX) bulb can be used in it. When ordering, don't forget to specify bulb size and remember that this will affect your cable order and your power considerations. Only two basic accessories are available for the skypan: a skirt that does control some of the side spill (and is useful for keeping direct hits out of the lens) and a gel frame. You usually won't get them unless you specify in the order.

2K Open Face

The 2K open face is a real workhorse. Mole's version is the Mighty-Mole, Ianiro's is the Blonde, and Arriflex also has a version. Its open-faced design provides far greater output per watt than a 2K fresnel, making it the light of choice for bounce sources. If going through diffusion, it can also be a direct source. Mightys are used in book lights, frog lights, and as backlight illumination for tissued windows, tented products, etc. Most versions have a collar that clamps on the front of the light and provides the support for the barndoors, gel frames, or scrims.

1000-/600-/650-Watt Open Face

Mickey-Moles (Mole–Richardson) and the Redhead (Ianiro) and 1K Arrilite (Arriflex) are the little brothers of the 2K open face and differ only in bulb (1K) and size. They are great as small bounce sources (such as an umbrella light for portraits), small-fill bounces, and for just sprinkling a little light on background objects. Their small size (especially the Redhead, which is remarkably compact) makes them easy to hide in the set. The 650- and 600-watt baby sisters are even smaller and find use in Electronic News Gathering (ENG) and small unit video production. With a bit of diffusion they are often attached to the top of the video camera as a traveling fill light.

Lowell makes the lightweight, highly portable DP Lite that is often used in small video and ENG production. Like all Lowell lights, it has a wide variety of clever and well-designed accessories: snoots, barndoors, snap-on flags, dichroic filters, etc. Lowell's Omni Light is a smaller version of the DP and has the same range of accessories. It is an

(a)

(b)

inexpensive unit and provides basic open-faced light or can be used as a self-contained umbrella bounce.

PAR 64

PARs are raw light power in its most basic form (it is all capitals because it stands for Parabolic Aluminized Reflector). Cousins to auto headlights, they are sealed beams of light (combined bulb, reflector, and lens) available in a wide variety of sizes and beam spreads. One of the most commonly used is the PAR 64 1000 watt. Eight inches across (64/8 of an inch), they employ a highly efficient parabolic reflector that is capable of projecting the beam with very little spread.

A completely clear lens for a PAR is called a very narrow spot (VNSP), and with a light texture it is a narrow spot (NSP). This makes them useful for hitting distant background objects that cannot be reached otherwise. With a stippling effect on the lens, the light becomes a medium flood (MFL) and spreads the same amount of light over a broader beam. With a more pronounced stippling, the light is a wideflood (WFL) with an even greater beam spread. Because PARs have a long, thin filament inside the reflector, the beam of a PAR is oval rather than circular. This can be a useful feature as the beam can be oriented to "fit" the subject.

PARs are remarkable for their efficiency. A narrow spot 1K PAR, measured at the center of its beam, generates an output comparable to a 10K measured at the center of its beam. The trick, of course, is that it covers only a very small area, but it may be sufficient for many purposes such as high-speed table top or punching of light through heavy diffusion.

PARs come in two basic varieties. Film versions come in a solid rotary housing such as a MolePar, which feature barndoors and scrim holders, and in a flimsier theatrical version called a Par can—very popular in rock and roll concert lighting. Most versions allow for the bulb to be rotated freely to orient the oval beam. Many DPs refer to this unit as a "firestarter."

PAR Groups

PARs are also made in groups, such as the MaxiBrute, a heavy hitter with tremendous punch and throw. They are used in large night exteriors and in large-scale interior applications, aircraft hangers, arenas, etc. The bulbs are housed in banks that are individually oriented for some control. All the bulbs are individually switchable, which makes for very simple intensity control. All PAR group lights allow for spot, medium, and flood bulbs to be interchanged for different coverages.

Dino, Moleeno, and Wendy

The Dino is one of the largest tungsten sources available. It consists of 24 or 36 PAR 64 bulbs on a frame. Mole–Richardson makes a version called a Moleeno. A Wendy is similar, but instead of PAR 64 bulbs, it uses PAR 36 bulbs.

MaxiBrute

The MaxiBrute consists of nine 1000-watt PAR 64 globes in three racks. Each rack can be panned left/right and the entire unit can be tilted up and down. Owing to the efficiency of PAR 64 bulbs, the unit has tremendous punch, especially when used with the very narrow spot bulbs. When the budget is limited and sheer raw power is needed, this is a good choice. Mole also makes a 12-light version. They are especially useful for night exteriors. All the bulbs are individually switchable, which makes for very simple intensity control.

All PAR group lights allow for spot, medium, and flood bulbs to be interchanged for different coverages. PARs are raw light power in its most basic form. Similar to auto headlights (also PAR bulbs), they are sealed beam lights (combined bulb, reflector, and lens) available in a variety of sizes and beam spreads.

They employ a highly efficient parabolic reflector that is capable of projecting the beam with very little spread. The detachable lens is the variable that affects beam spread. A completely clear lens for a PAR is called a very narrow spot (VNSP), and with a light texture it is a narrow spot (NSP). This makes them useful for hitting distant background objects that cannot be reached otherwise.

With a stippling effect on the lens, the light becomes a medium flood (MFL) and spreads the same amount of light over a broader beam. With a more pronounced stippling, the light is a wide flood (WFL) with an even greater beam spread. Because PARs have a long thin filament inside the reflector, the beam of a PAR is oval rather than circular.

This can be a useful feature as the beam can be oriented to "fit" the subject. A narrow spot 1K PAR, measured at the center of its beam, generates an output comparable to a 10K measured at the center of its beam; however, it covers only a very small area, but it may be sufficient for many purposes such as punching of light through heavy diffusion, or a very large bounce or raking down a street for a night shoot.

FAYs

The smaller cousins of the MaxiBrute are the FAY lights, also called 5-lites, 9-lites, or 12-lites, depending on how many bulbs are incorporated. They use PAR 36 bulbs (650 watts). The FAY bulbs are dichroic daylight bulbs. Before HMIs they were widely used as daylight fill in combination with or in place of white-carbon arcs. These types of bulbs also come in tungsten versions so they can fairly easily be converted for use in either daylight or tungsten balance situations.

Most people refer to any PAR 36 dichroic bulb as a FAY, but in fact there are several types. FAY is the ANSI code for a 650-watt PAR 36 dichroic daylight bulb with ferrule contacts. If the bulb has screw terminals it is an FBE/FGK. As with the larger MaxiBrutes, the bulbs are in three adjustable banks and they generally do come with barndoors. FAY bulbs are only an approximation of daylight balance in that they do not produce light that is precisely 5600K and do tend to change color as they age.

Twelve-lites, 9-lites, and 5-lites are far more flexible than one might imagine. With heavy diffusion over the barndoors they can have a large-source soft light quality with real power. Used raw they are a quick and adaptable bounce source with individual switching control and straight on they can cover the entire side of a building for a night shot.

Ruby 7

The Ruby 7 by Luminaria is a real innovation in PAR lights. It is focusable, which is unique. Combing 7 PAR 65 bulbs in one focus frame gives a wide range of intensity and coverage.

HMI PARs

The newest addition to the PAR family is the HMI PAR, which is available as 12K, 6K, 4K, 2.5K, 1.2K, and 575. These are extremely popular as bounce units, to create shafts, and for raw power.

HMI PARs are different from tungsten units in that they have changeable lenses. The basic unit is a VNSP (very narrow spot). The auxiliary lenses can be added to make it a narrow spot, a medium flood, wide flood, and an extra wide flood. As with tungsten PARs, the beam is oval and the unit can be rotated within its housing to orient the pattern.

(a)

(b)

FIGURE 2.8 (a) MaxiBrute (large units) and (b) a Nine-Light (FAY) unit, front and back.

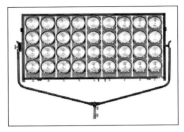

FIGURE 2.9 A Moleeno—Mole's version of the Dino Light.

(a)

(b)

FIGURE 2.10 (a) A 2K zip soft light with eggcrate. (b) A 12K HMI PAR—one of the most powerful and intense lights available. Here it is punched through a 4′ × 4′ frame with ¼ CTO to warm it up.

The 1.2K HMI PAR is one of the most useful small units around. As an HMI it has great efficiency and as a PAR it has tremendous kick for its size. The real bonus is that at only 1200 watts, it is small enough to plug into wall outlets. Since it is already 5500K (daylight color temperature), it doesn't require heavy blue gel to correct the color. This makes it ideal for use on locations that have windows (and thus lots of daylight); it is powerful enough to bounce or shoot through diffusion as a fill light for situations where your main lighting is the available daylight.

HMI PARS are available in sizes up to the 12K, which is an extraordinarily powerful light, so powerful that it is important to be very careful in what you aim it at. It can, for example, crack windows in a very short time.

Soft Lights

Soft lights have a general design of a semicircular pan with small bulbs (usually 1000-watt bulbs) that bounce into this clamshell, thus making a soft light. The size of the reflector is what determines how "soft" the light is. Larger units generally just have two or more 1000-watt bulbs. They vary from the 1K studio soft (baby soft) up to the powerful 8K studio soft, which has eight individually switchable bulbs.

All soft lights of the clamshell design have certain basic problems:

- They are relatively inefficient in light output.
- They are bulky and hard to transport.
- Like all soft lights, they are difficult to control.
- While the large reflector makes the light soft, the light is still somewhat raw.

As a result of this rawness, some people put some diffusion over the soft light for any close-up work. Big studio softs through a large frame of diffusion are probably the easiest and quickest way to create a large soft source in the studio. The main accessory of all soft lights is the eggcrate, which minimizes side spill and makes the beam a bit more controllable.

Studio Softs (8K, 4K, 2K and 1K)

Studio soft lights consist of one or more FCM 1000-watt bulbs directed into a clamshell white-painted reflector that bounces light in a diffuse pattern.

Some compact versions of the studio soft lights are called zip lights, particularly the 1K and 2K zips. They are the same width but half the height of a normal soft.

Cone Lights

A variation of the soft light is the cone light. It differs in that the reflector is a cone and it uses a single-ended bulb instead of a double-ended FCM. Because the bounced beam is more

(a)

(b)

FIGURE 2.11 (a) Ruby 7 units and 12K HMI PARS light a large day exterior. (b) The Ruby 7—a focusable multi-PAR unit. (Photos courtesy of Luminaria, Inc.)

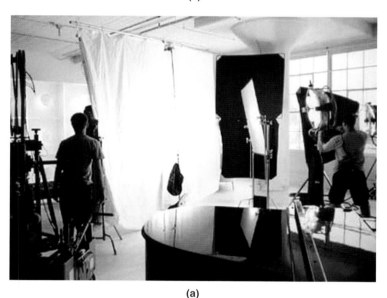

(a)

(b)

FIGURE 2.12 (a) The Ruby 7 going through a 4′ × 4′ diffusion and a large muslin on a music video. Note that the muslin is "T-boned"—meaning there is only a stand in the center and only one piece of the frame is used. (b) A DeSisti 1.2K HMI PAR.

collimated, the cone light is much smoother and prettier than a studio soft. With a showcard collar and some dense diffusion, the cone light is one of the most attractive beauty and product lights, and the smaller ones are quickly flown for a soft backlight. Cone lights come with dots that shield the bulb from the hard direct light and double shadows characteristic of open-faced lights. For extra punch when going through diffusion, the dot can be pulled.

Space Lights

The space light is almost always hung from overhead. It consists of 6 or 12 nook lights with a silk "skirt" and sometimes a bottom silk panel. It is like a huge lantern: it provides a soft overall ambient glow. A frequent use is to provide an overall ambient fill for very large stage sets.

Fluorescent Rigs

Fluorescent rigs can be used with color-correct bulbs (either daylight or tungsten balance) or as a supplemental light when shooting in a fluorescent-lit situation such as an office or factory, where the existing lighting cannot be changed. This makes for very quick shooting as they are color-balanced to the existing lighting, which is usually an overall soft ambient; with a little fill for the eyes, the lighting is often usable as is. Then it is just a matter of adding a fluorescent filter to the lens, shooting a gray card and letting the lab take the green out (in film), or by white-balancing the video camera.

Color-Correct Fluorescent Units

The leading manufacturer of fluorescent lights for film and video is Kino Flo, the inventor of this type of unit. Other companies including Mole–Richardson (the Biax); Flolight, and Lowel also make them. The Pampa light is a color-correct fluorescent unit that comes in its own travel case, which is also the outer housing of the light itself; this makes for an extraordinarily portable and efficient unit, especially for any type of travel job.

All of them employ color-correct bulbs that function at tungsten or daylight balance. Tubes are also available in green, red, and other colors for lighting chromakey. The ballasts run at high frequency, which prevents the flicker effect that are possible with ordinary fluorescents that operate at 60 Hz in the US or 50 Hz in other countries.

If the frequency of its power supply isn't compatible with the camera speed, then ordinary fluorescents will fluctuate on the filmed image (Kino Flo, Mole Biax, and Pampalights operate at a higher frequency, so this isn't a problem). Shutter angle (in film cameras) is also a factor. The best combinations of frequency, film speed, and shutter opening for film cameras are
- 50 Hz—25fps with any shutter opening
- 50 Hz—24fps with a shutter opening of 170–175 degree opening
- 60 Hz—24fps with a shutter angle of 144 or 180 degrees.

Overcranking for slow motion definitely increases the chance of getting flicker.

Kino Flo units come in a wide variety, from very large lights to illuminate broad areas down to miniature bulbs that run on either AC or DC to be tucked in small places or used to light car interiors; the fact that they run cool makes them especially useful for lighting actors in cars as there is little chance of damaging the car or burning an actor, as might happen with tungsten lights.

(b)

(a)

FIGURE 2.13 (**a**) Banks of Kino Flo units light a very large greenscreen for a stunt on *Mission Impossible*. (**b**) Several types of Kino Flo units. (Photos courtesy of Kino Flo, Inc.)

Color-Correct Bulbs

Ordinary fluorescent bulbs do not have a continuous spectrum and have a heavy spike in the green area. All tubes that are used in film and video are color-correct, meaning that they are full-spectrum and don't have the green spike. However, there is an additional issue: the CRI (Color Rendering Index) must be at least 90 or higher (on a scale that goes up to 100); otherwise, it will not render color correctly. CRI measures how accurately a source renders the actual colors of a subject. A low CRI can make color rendition very inaccurate—a condition known as metamerism.

Some "daylight" and "growlight" bulbs may be daylight balance but they are unlikely to have a CRI that is acceptable. Optima 32 and Optima 50 bulbs are color-correct and have a reasonable CRI. Kino Flo bulbs can be removed from their housing and placed in ordinary fluorescent fixtures, thus making an office or classroom ready to shoot without additional lighting. This provides no protection against flicker, however, but at 24fps this is usually not a problem.

Cycs, Strips, Nooks, and Broads

When just plain output is needed, broad lights are strictly no-frills, utilitarian lights. They are just a box with a

FIGURE 2.14 Pampa lights with daylight-balance bulbs in use on an open-shade day exterior. A four-bank unit keys them from the side, and a two-bank unit over the camera gives a soft fill. (Photos courtesy of Owen Stephens, Pampa Light.)

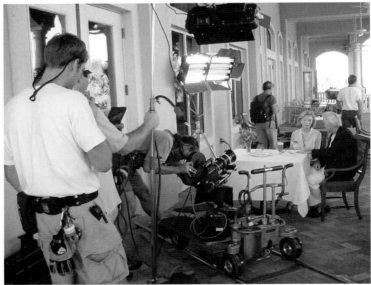

double-ended bulb. As simple as it is, the broad light has an important place in film history. In classical Hollywood hard lighting, the fill near the camera was generally a broad light with a diffuser. The distinctive feature of the broad light is its rectangular beam pattern, which makes blending them on a flat wall or cyc much easier. Imagine how difficult it would be to smoothly combine the round, spotty beams of Mightys or fresnel lights.

The smallest version of the broad is the nook, which, as its name implies, is designed for fitting into nooks and crannies. The nook light is a compact, raw-light unit, usually fitted with an FCM or FHM 1000-watt bulb. The nook is just a bulb holder with a reflector. Although barndoors are usually

(a)

(b)

(c)

(d)

FIGURE 2.15 (a) A Source Four leko by ETC. (b) A Super Wendy in use on an exterior. (Photo courtesy of Lee Lighting.) (c) A Musco light on location on an exterior. (Photo courtesy of Musco.) (d) An HMI balloon light rigged for the film *Confessions of a Dangerous Mind*. Wind is always a problem with balloon light. (Photo courtesy of Tony "Nako" Nakonechnyj.)

available, nooks aren't generally called on for much subtlety, but they are an efficient and versatile source for box light rigs, large silk overhead lights, and for large arrays to punch through frames.

A number of units are specifically designed for illuminating cycs and backdrops. For the most part they are open-faced 1K and 1.5K units in small boxes with an asymmetrical throw that puts more output at the top or bottom, depending on the orientation of the unit. The reason for this is that cyc lights must be either placed at the top or bottom of the cyc but the coverage must be even.

Strip lights are gangs of PARs or broad lights, originally used as theatrical footlights and cyc lights. They are often circuited in groups of three. With each circuit gelled a different color and on a dimmer, a wide range of colors can be obtained by mixing. This can be a quick way to alter background colors and intensities.

The Lowell Tota Lite deserves special mention. Small, cheap, and fundamental, its no-nonsense reflector design and 750-watt or 1000-watt double-ended bulb provide tremendous bang for the buck. Practically a backpocket light, the Tota can be used as an umbrella bounce, hidden in odd places, or used in groups for a frog light or cyc illumination. Two Totas can be ganged simply by inserting the male end of the stand clamp into the female side of the other Tota. Adding more lights to the stack is a problem, they are too close together to allow the doors to open fully. To make a stack of three or more, a special adaptor is available.

FIGURE 2.16 A very large softbox on an 18K for shadowless fill on a beauty shot.

Miscellaneous

Chinese Lanterns

Chinese lanterns are the ordinary paper globe lamps available at houseware stores. A socket is suspended inside that holds either a medium screw base bulb or a 1K or 2K bipost. Just about any rig is possible if the globe is large enough to keep the paper a safe distance from the hot bulb. Control is accomplished by painting the paper or taping gel or diffusion to it, but a dimmer is by far the easiest way to control the overall intensity. Dimmers are a must for any light that can't take scrims or be controlled in some other way, such as flooding or spotting.

Crane-Mounted Lights

The Musco is a very powerful wide-coverage light. It consists of 6K HMI heads permanently mounted on a crane/truck. Similar units include the BeeBee light and NightSun. It can provide workable illumination up to a half mile away and is used for moonlight effects and broad illumination of large areas. Musco lights are available only from Musco. The unit comes with its own 1000-amp generator, either an onboard or a tow rig.

The 6K heads are individually aimable by a handheld remote control that operates up to 1000 feet away from the truck. The boom allows placement of the heads up to 100 feet in the air.

Source Fours

The ellipsoidal reflector spot (leko) is a theatrical light, but is used occasionally as a small-effects light because of its precise beam control by the blades. By far the most popular model in production is the Source Four. Because the blades and gobo holder are located at the focal point of the lens, the leko can be focused sharply and patterned gobos can be inserted to give sharply detailed shadow effects. A wide variety of patterns are available: venetian blinds, trees, buildings, etc.

Not all lekos have gobo holder slots, and if you need one you must specify when ordering. In addition to the gobo holder and the shutter blades, some units incorporate a mechanical iris that can reduce the size of the beam to a tiny spot; this, too, must be specified in ordering. Also tell the equipment house that you are using it for film work—they are normally equipped with a pipe clamp, and an adaptor will be needed to put it on a normal stand. Matthews makes the TVMP adaptor that handles the job neatly.

Lekos come in a size defined by their lens size and focal length. The longer the focal length, the longer the throw of

(a)

FIGURE 2.17 (**a**) The complete Joker system including the ballast and accessories. (**b**) A Chinese lantern rigged on a C-stand.

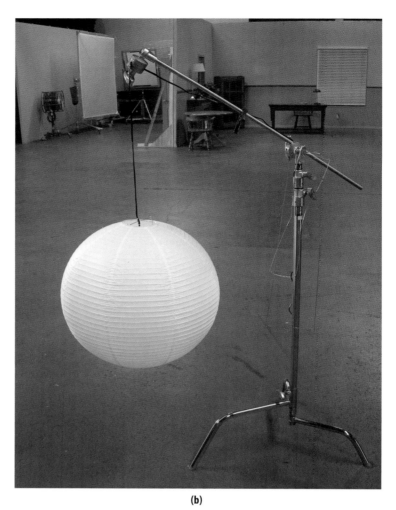

(b)

the light; that is, the narrower the beam. For example, the 4½-inch unit has a field angle of 45° while the 8 × 16 throws a beam of just 6°.

Sunguns

"Sungun" is a generic name for any handheld portable light that runs off a battery belt. Both tungsten and HMI versions are available. They can be homemade with 12-volt lamps, but commercial sunguns typically have 30-volt battery belts, which last longer. Tungsten sungun units generally go through batteries quickly; HMI units tend to last longer on a battery. They are frequently used as a bit of eyefill on walking shots or just a bit of fill for quick shots.

Softboxes

Shooting a light through a large diffusion frame is not difficult; however, it often requires flags on both sides and perhaps above and below. Softboxes, such as the ones made by

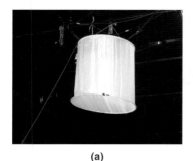

(a)

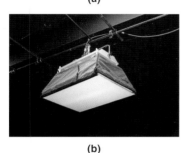

(b)

(c)

FIGURE 2.18 (a) A space light with bottom panel. (b) A chicken coop. (c) A handheld LED panel used as both a source of light and as a prop in a detective scene.

Chimera and Photoflex, are self-flagging. Already enclosed, they can convert almost any type of light into an instant soft source. Many of them also have double panels: a diffusion on the face of the light but also a second diffusion inside—in some cases, these can be changed to heavier or lighter diffusions. Always be sure to open the ventilation panels, especially the ones on the bottom and top. Also, be careful when you are using a softbox designed for hot lights (tungsten or HMI)—some softboxes are designed for still photo strobes only, which don't generate nearly as much heat.

Jokers

Jokers are a line of very efficient small HMI lights in wattages of 200, 400, and 800. Extremely portable, the smaller units can be run on either 30-volt or 14.4-volt battery belts as well as AC power. They can be used as a directional, focusable light or as a bare bulb unit for use in softboxes.

LED Panels

The newest additions to the lighting arsenal are LED lights. Extremely compact (almost flat), efficient, and cool-running, they are very popular for small spaces, car rigs, and hiding on the set—they can be hidden in spots that normal units would never fit into. Figure 2.18c shows a handheld battery-powered unit used as both a prop and a light in the scene.

Dedo Lights

Dedolights are very small units that employ two plano-convex lenses rather than a single fresnel. They have the precise control usually associated with lekos. They have very

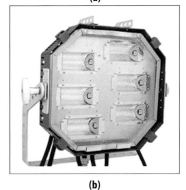

(a)

(b)

(c)

(d)

FIGURE 2.19 (**a** and **b**) The Barger Baglight, shown without the softbox with which it is normally used. (Photos courtesy of Ed Barger.) (**c** and **d**) Barger Baglights in use on a beauty commercial with DP Tom Denove. Note the computerized dimmer board in the foreground of the upper photo. (Photos courtesy of Tom Denove.)

clean, even light distribution and, like lekos, can project patterns. They have a variety of power options from 24-volt and 12-volt CD and from 100- to 255-volt AC. The low-voltage DC units can run directly from car batteries, battery belts, etc. To run the lights on AC requires a power supply. They can be dimmed without change in color temperature.

Balloon Lights

Large lights that fly in balloons are becoming very popular for night exteriors. The fact that they don't require cranes or

(b)

(a)

scaffolding (both of which are cumbersome and sometimes hard to hide) makes them very versatile. Most have HMI sources inside but some use tungsten. Figure 2.20a shows a Fisher Light Leelium balloon light in use for a night exterior; Figure 2.20b shows them in a studio. Their one drawback might be that they can't be used in a windy situation.

Barger Baglight

The compact lightweight Barger Baglight 6-lite is simple in design and highly efficient in practice. It utilizes 6 individually switched GE FCM-HIR 650-watt bulbs, each of which produces the light of a 1000-watt bulb. A combination including 750-, 500-, or 300-watt bulbs is often used to provide different levels of light adjustment. It is unique in that it fills the entire front screen of the medium or large softbox with light and the speed ring is built in. The well-designed tilt lock mechanism eliminates rogue tilting, even with the large Chimera. A 3-lite version is also available.

Scrims and Barndoors

All fresnels and most open-face lights have a few common elements used to control them. Barndoors are one of these; they come in both two-leaf and four-leaf versions. In most casese they fit into ears that are part of the front of the light.

Scrims are another form of control: they reduce the total amount of light without altering the quality of light. Many people think they are diffusion, but they aren't; however, in some cases, you can faintly see the pattern of the metal screen. Scrims are color-coded: red for a double (reduces the amount of light by half, which is a full stop) and green for a single, which reduces the light by one-half stop. A standard

(a)

FIGURE 2.21 (**a**) Typical four-leaf barndoors. (**b**) A set of scrims and their scrim bag. Shown here is a "Hollywood" scrim set, which includes two doubles in addition to a single, a half-double, and a half-single.

(b)

scrim set includes a double, a single, a half-double, and a half-single. A "Hollywood" scrim set has two doubles.

Scrims should be kept in the scrim bag or box when not in use, NOT dropped on the floor or left lying around. Scrims and barndoors should always be with the light. Bringing a light to the set without scrims and barndoors is like wearing a T-shirt that says "I'm an amateur."

Spacelights and Chicken Coops

Some lights are specifically designed to be rigged overhead, most often from a grid in a studio. Spacelights are large soft lights that create a general soft ambience over a large area. They consist of six 1000-watt bulbs pointing down into a silk "skirt." A bottom panel of silk can also be added. When more control is desired to keep the light from spilling all over, a black skirt of duvetyne (flame-retardant opaque cloth) can be added.

A chicken coop is a box with several downfacing lights. Typically they are special bulbs with silver-reflecting material that bounces the light back up into the white box to soften it; however, units are available that have PAR 64 bulbs for real downward punch.

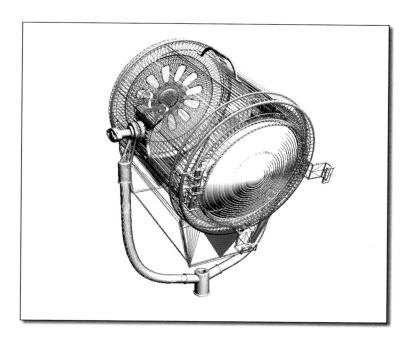

FUNDAMENTALS OF LIGHTING

I'm sure you've heard this phrase: "If you light it right…" or "With good lighting, the scene will…."

What does that mean? What is "good" lighting? Lighting has nearly infinite permutations and variations. There is certainly no one right way to light a scene. As a result there is no chance that we can just make a simple list of proper lighting techniques.

What we can do, however, is try to identify what it is we want lighting to do for us. What jobs does it perform for us? What is it we expect of good lighting? Starting this way, we have a better chance of evaluating when lighting is working for us and when it is falling short. Naturally, these are generalizations. You'll always find exceptions, as in all aspects of filmmaking—staging, use of the lens, exposure, continuity, editorial, etc.

What Do We Expect Lighting to Do for Us?

So what is it we want lighting to do for us? There are many jobs and they include creating an image that has
- Mood and tone: emotional content
- A full range of tones: gradations of tone

FIGURE 3.1 Color plays a major role in image making.

- Color control and color balance
- Depth and dimension: foreground, midground, background
- Shape and fullness in the individual subjects, making them three-dimensional
- Separation: making the subjects stand out against the background
- Texture
- Exposure

Let's look at these aspects of lighting in greater detail.

Mood and Tone

Let's talk for a moment about the word "cinematic." In conversation, it is often used to describe something that is "movie-like." For example someone might say a particular novel is cinematic if it has fast-moving action, lots of description, and very little exposition. That is not how we will use the term here. In this context, we use the term cinematic to describe all the tools, techniques, and methods we use to add layers of meaning, emotion, tone, and mood to the content.

By "content" we mean just the physical objects in front of the lens. As every good camera and lighting person knows, we can take any particular scene and make it look scary or beautiful or ominous or whatever the story calls for. In narrative fiction, this is obvious. In industrials and corporate video, just to take one example, the most frequent application is the need to make the CEO look handsome, competent, and intelligent.

In commercials, often the most difficult shot is not the actors but the product shot. It goes without saying that your goal is to make the cereal box or the dog food or the clothing or whatever the product is look as wonderful, glamorous, exciting, and desirable as possible.

The lens and set dressing, props, etc. are important here, but it is lighting that really makes the difference. Lighting is never more critical than in fashion and beauty work, where the goal is not only to make the model and clothing (or whatever the product is) look incredible, but also to do it with a real "attitude"—a look, a tone, a subtle shade that is in keeping with the concept.

(a)

(b)

FIGURE 3.2 Avoid flat lighting. (a) Flat front lighting makes the image shapeless and dull. (b) Lighting from the side brings out the shape of the subject and adds depth.

Full Range of Tones

In most cases, we want an image to have a full range of tones, from black to white (tonal range is always discussed in terms of *grayscale*, without regard to color). There are a few exceptions to this, of course; but in general, an image that has a broad range of tones, with subtle gradations all along the way, is going to be more pleasing to the eye, more realistic, and greater in impact.

Color Control and Color Balance

Color control and color balance are essential aspects of lighting. There are two sides of this issue. First (unless you are going for a specific effect) the lighting itself must be color-balanced—the two most common standards are daylight balance (5500K) and tungsten balance (3200K), but other balances are possible, using either a gray card (in film shooting) or a test chart or by white-balancing to a neutral card (video shooting)—this technique would likely be the most desirable route with lighting you can't control, such as in an office with fluorescent lighting you can't change.

Up until the eighties, it was conventional to color-balance precisely all lighting sources to very tight tolerances. Now, with improved video imagers, improved film stocks and video cameras, and (most of all), changing visual tastes, it is common to mix different color sources in a scene.

(a)

(b)

FIGURE 3.3 Adding shape, depth, and dimension to a scene.
(a) This image lacks depth; it is somewhat flat and dull.
(b) Behind-the-scenes look at the depth-lighting experiment. A 2K with a Chimera softbox is the key, a 2-bank Kino Flo is the fill, and Tweenies are used as the backlight with a venetian blind pattern through the window and the far background light. Taken together, they create a distinct foreground, midground, and background, and they separate the subject from the background.
(c) Lighting can add dimension and depth to the image. It goes a long way toward creating a foreground, midground, and background. A big part of this is separation—helping the subject stand out from the background.

(c)

Adding Shape, Depth, and Dimension to a Scene

Shape

Flat front lighting does not reveal the shape and form of the subject—it tends to flatten everything out, to make the subject almost a cartoon cutout: two-dimensional. Lighting from the side or back reveals the shape of an object—its external structure and geometric form.

This is important for the overall depth of the shot; moreover, it can reveal character, emotional values, and other clues that may have story importance. Naturally, it also makes the image more real, more palpable, more recognizable. Human vision relies on several cues to determine depth, shape, and distance: how light and shadow fall on an object is a significant part of this.

Separation

By separation, we mean making the main subjects stand out from the background. A frequently used method for doing this is a backlight. Another way to do it is to make the area behind the main subjects significantly darker or brighter than the subject. In our quest to make an image as three-dimensional as possible, we usually try to create a foreground, midground, and background in a shot; separation is an important part of this.

Depth

As image formats, what are film, video, and HD? They are basically rectangles—flat rectangles. Each is very much a two-dimensional medium. As lighting people, cinematographers, and directors a big part of our job is trying to make this flat art form as three-dimensional as possible—to give it depth and shape and perspective; to bring it alive as the real world is as much as possible. Lighting plays a huge role in this. Other methods—the use of the lens, blocking, camera movement, set design, color—play a role as well, but lighting is our key player in this endeavor.

This is a big part of why flat lighting is so frequently the enemy. Flat lighting is light that comes from very near the camera, like the flash mounted on a consumer still camera—it is on axis with the lens. As a result, it just flatly illuminates the entire subject evenly. It erases the natural three-dimensional quality of the subject.

Texture

As with shape, light from the axis of the lens (flat front lighting) tends to obscure texture. The reason is simple: we

FIGURE 3.4 Lighting is your primary tool in establishing mood and tone, which add layers of meaning to the content. This effect was achieved in a very simple way: a 2000-watt open-face light was bounced off the floor.

know texture from the shadows. Light that comes from near the camera creates no shadows. The more light comes in from the side, the more it creates shadows, which is what reveals texture.

Exposure

Lighting does many jobs for us, but none of them matters if you don't get the exposure right—incorrect exposure can ruin whatever else you have done.

In terms of lighting, just getting enough light into a scene to get an exposure is usually not difficult. What is critical is correct exposure. Certainly, it is a job for lighting (in addition to the iris, frame rate, processing (film), gain (video), and shutter angle) but don't forget to think of it as an important image making and storytelling tool. Most of the time we want nominally correct exposure—that is, exposure that fits the brightness range of the scene nicely into the exposure latitude and gamma of the film stock or camera sensors.

It is important to remember in this context that exposure is about more than just "it's too light" or "it's too dark"— exposure for mood and tone is obvious, but there are other considerations as well. For example, proper exposure and camera settings are critical to color saturation and achieving a full range of grayscale tones.

(a)

(b)

(c)

(d)

FIGURE 3.5 Effects of overexposure and underexposure. (**a**) A badly overexposed image. Exposure is always important, but in HD and SD video it is especially critical. Proper setup and monitor/viewfinder calibration are crucial. (**b**) In this image, we see that overexposure cannot be satisfactorily corrected. (**c**) A badly underexposed image. (**d**) In this image we see that underexposure can be corrected, but the image suffers from a lack of tonal range and terrible grain/noise.

Directing the Eye

We normally think of composition as a function of the frame, the lens, and the arrangement of sets and props. True enough, but if you ignore lighting as an element of composition, you are missing out on one of your most valuable tools.

What are we doing with composition? What is our goal? One of the key elements is directing the eye—guiding the viewer's eye through the frame in a meaningful manner. As you may know, the eye/brain combination does not take in an entire picture all at once. The larger the image is, the truer this becomes: we perceive a small monitor or photograph in a different way than we do a very large flat screen monitor or a theater projection screen. In all cases, however, the eye scans the picture. The more organized the composition, the more the artist or cinematographer can control how the viewer takes in the image.

There are two aspects of this: composition as an organization of the elements in the frame and a subset of that — directing the eye to particularly important elements in the frame—most often, our key actor in the scene.

The Lighting Process

When we are lighting a scene, there is more involved than making it look great. First of all, speed is important. Time on the set costs money, even on the smallest production. How fast you are can be a critical consideration in getting hired on most productions. Beyond that, you must consider getting the look you and the director have agreed upon and you must maintain editorial continuity.

The Process

All of these considerations will be facilitated if you use a logical thought process as you go about lighting the scene. All DPs have their own ways of working; you will develop *your* own way as you continue your education.

Think about these things:
1. What are the requirements?
2. What tools do you have?
3. What's the schedule?
4. What are the opportunities?

What Are the Requirements?

This one may seem too obvious to think about, but it is surprising how often it gets lost in the process. It is easy to get so caught up in making something look pretty, or in trying out some new technique, that we simply forget what we

FIGURE 3.6 Lighting can both reveal the texture of the subject and add texture of its own, as with this venetian blind pattern.

need to accomplish to tell a story visually with the lighting of the scene.

Here are the requirements you need to consider:

1. What is the look that you and the director have decided to go for on the whole project?
2. What is the dramatic intention of the scene: to shock, to make the audience laugh, to frighten them?
3. How does this particular scene fit into the overall visual flow of the project?
4. How does this scene fit into the overall flow of the day's work?

Here are some other questions you want to ask:

1. Is it interior or exterior, a combination of both? Are there large windows or other sources that can't be controlled?
2. What time of day is it (in the scene)?
3. Where does the action within the scene take place?
4. How many people in the scene? Do they move around?
5. Do we see the ceiling? Do we see the floor?
6. Are there any practical effects—such as turning on a light?
7. Is there anything that we have to balance to that can't be changed such as a TV set, neon lights, or monitors?
8. Do you need to establish lighting continuity for future scenes, cutaways, or product shots?

9. What is the ASA of the film, video, or HD camera?
10. What is the slowest lens (usually the zoom) you might use?
11. Any high-speed or macro work?

What Tools Do You Have?

What you plan to do with a scene is ultimately shaped by what tools you have available. What you can do with a 10-ton lighting truck is substantially different from what you can do with a minimal lighting kit. This is not to say that what you do with a few small lights is going to be worse than what you do with a large array of gear; it just means you have to plan things differently.

It's not just about the lights. What gels and diffusion do you have? Do you have some practical bulbs? How much grip equipment is available? What size crew do you have? What is their level of experience? How tight is the schedule? Except when you have a generator on the job, the limiting factor is often how much power is available. Lacking a generator, you are most often limited to what you can plug into the wall. In many cases, there might be only a few 20-amp household circuits you can get to. If there is already some large appliance such as a refrigerator on that line, then what you can plug in is very limited (and keep in mind that the refrigerator might not have been running when you tested the circuit).

Once you can get a genny on the job, you are not necessarily home free. Generators are expensive, and the larger they are, the more they cost. When the budget is tight, you might well be limited to a 100- or 300-amp generator (or even a 4K putt-putt). This will certainly affect the size and type of units you can run, thus affecting your overall approach to lighting scenes for the day. It's all part of what you need to think about as you develop the strategy for the day.

What's the Schedule?

How much time you have is a major consideration. It is determined by the schedule, which is made by the assistant director. Good ADs will ask the DP how much time she thinks she needs, but even on large productions, the amount of time is finite and considerations are nearly always beyond anyone's control (locations, sunsets, permits running out, etc.).

Ultimately, you will have X amount of time to accomplish your task. Also, the AD will often ask you, "How long will it take to light this scene?" This estimate is actually one of the most important things you will do during the course of a production day. It's not a casual question. A lot of things depend on it—not just scheduling the other scenes, but also deciding when to put actors "into the chairs" (makeup and hair), when to plan on breaking for lunch, and so on. Being able to provide an accurate estimate of the time involved is also a matter of your credibility as a DP. It takes practice.

When you are really on the run, it often pays to have a Plan B and a Plan C. Thus, if the clock simply runs out, you have something you know will (at the very least) work. Often there are variables you just can't plan for: a change of weather, an irate neighbor, a crying baby….

But let's move on to the physical lighting of the scene. There are dozens of ways to light any particular scene; but where do you start?

What Are the Opportunities?

Almost always, one of the first questions you will ask yourself is, "What are the opportunities?" What is there in the location, the set, or the situation that offers you some interesting ways to deal with the lighting? It might be the windows, or a desk lamp, or even a large palm you can hide something behind. It might be an existing streetlight that you can imitate by hanging something from the pole.

You may find some architectural element you can emphasize or perhaps a white rug you can bounce something off of to give the actor a nice underlight. This survey of the opportunities will most likely happen during the location scout as you walk around with the director and your gaffer. In the case of a built set, it might occur in conferences with the production designer or while looking at the drawings of set designs.

OK, so you've got a basic strategy. Having considered your resources in equipment, crew, and time, you have a basic plan. Be careful: a couple of traps are waiting to snare you at this point.

The main one is "lighting air." This happens when you don't see a proper rehearsal and you don't have stand-ins. Sometimes, on smaller projects, the director will just describe the scene to you and then go off to attend to something else. What usually happens is that you make the set look great, but there is no guarantee that you are properly lit for the action of the actors.

You must insist on seeing a proper rehearsal. It is imperative that everyone remember that rehearsals are NOT just for the actors: they are for everyone. They are for the AC, so she can set marks, they are for the DP to judge the lighting, they are for the grip to set any dolly marks, and so on.

It is not usually important that the actors go through the scene with full acting intensity. For you, the focus puller—and for the gaffer, the grip, the sound recordist, the boom operator, etc.—it is enough that you see where the actors are going to be; whether they are sitting or standing or moving and the timing of "gags" (say, switching on a TV).

Another thing inexperienced directors will do is turn this blocking rehearsal into a full-on exploration of the acting values of the scene. The blocking rehearsal is for *blocking*. The acting rehearsals come later—right before the camera rolls. *Insist* on a rehearsal!

Once you've seen a full blocking rehearsal and the actors are in the process, the set is yours. The AD will often say "DP and crew have the set." It's yours, and you should insist on having it completely. This is also the point at which the AD will usually ask, "How long will it take?"

How to Be Fast

There are dozens of secret tricks, but obviously, they are beyond the scope of this book. Most of them just come from experience and experimentation. There are, however, some things to keep in mind that will help you through the day.

1. Plan several moves ahead. Don't just light for the master; have some of the lights you will need for coverage already rigged or at least prepped and standing by. For example, many DPs insist on having an Inkie with a hand dimmer standing right by the camera in case they need a last-minute eyelight.

2. Bringing in a ladder to do overhead rigging is time-consuming. Anything that is up in the air should already be rigged and cabled, even if you won't need it until later.

3. Have a few "dead soldiers" standing by. These are just a few lights on stands and ready to go, in case you need them for a last-minute scramble or a reset. They should have power available, scrims hanging on the stand, even some precut gels and diffusion with the unit.

But in the end, what is the real hidden secret of the pros? Have a great gaffer and key grip—it makes a huge difference.

Lighting Fundamentals

Light is what we work with. Infinite and subtle in its variety, the quality of light is a life-long study. In order to shape it to our purposes, it is essential to understand the basic jobs it can do for us. Let's review the fundamental building blocks of lighting, the basic elements with which we shape a scene.

The Basic Elements

Key

The keylight is the main or predominant light on a subject. Not necessarily the brightest (the backlight is frequently hotter in intensity), it is the light that gives shape, form, and definition to the subject. If a person has only one light on him or her, that is by definition the *key*. Although we generally think of the key as coming from somewhere in the front, there are many variations: side key, side-back key, cross key, and so on.

One way of thinking of the key is that it is usually the light that creates a shadow of the subject. There may be a key for the whole scene or a key for each object in it, or any combination of these. In a moving shot, an actor may have several keys and move from one to the other.

Fill

The key, as a single defining source, may exist alone; but in most cases, the contrast between the lit areas and the shadows will be too great or the single-source look may not be appropriate for the shot. Any light that balances the keylight is referred to as the *fill*. Fill lights come in many varieties. Most glossaries will tell you that fill light is a soft light or usually placed near the camera on the opposite side from the key. Although these characterizations may apply for the most simplistic type of formula lighting, they simply are not true in all cases. The fill might be anything from an inkie with a snoot up to a 20 × 20 silk, and it might come from almost any angle.

Backlight

Backlight is any light that comes from behind the subject. When backlight comes from almost directly overhead and high enough to get over the head and onto the face and nose, it is called a *toplight*. In most cases, a backlight that is too toppy will be avoided.

Backlight is a definite stylistic choice. Since it is usually an obviously artificial light, motivated light purists seldom use it except where it occurs naturally. It is also called a hairlight.

Kickers and Rims

A kicker is often confused with a backlight. A *kicker* is a light from behind the subject, but enough to the side so that it skims along the side of the face. Kickers are sometimes called ¾ backlights. A *rim* is similar to a kicker but doesn't come around onto the side of the face so much. It is more for creating a shape-defining outline.

Eyelight

A very specialized type of fill is the eyelight. Because eye sockets are recessed in the facial structure, the combination of key and fill that works best for the overall face may not reach deeply enough to give illumination to the eyes themselves. Since it is extremely rare that we are willing to let the eyes go dark, no matter how shadowy and low the key is, it is often necessary to add some light for the eyes themselves.

(a)

(b)

(c)

(d)

(e)

FIGURE 3.7 Basic lighting for a person, sometimes called "three-point" lighting. (**a**) Key only. (**b**) Key plus background light. (**c**) A backlight added. (**d**) With a kicker. (**e**) Key, background, backlight, kicker, and fill.

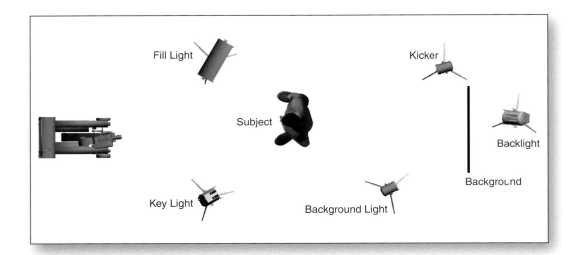

(a)

FIGURE 3.8 Diagram of a typical three-point lighting setup. The name is a misnomer as there are actually more than three lights involved, even in the simplest setups. An overhead view **(a)** and from behind the camera **(b)**.

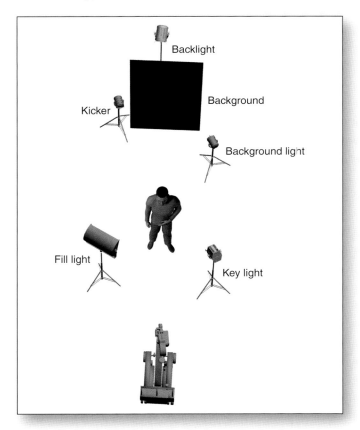

(b)

(a)

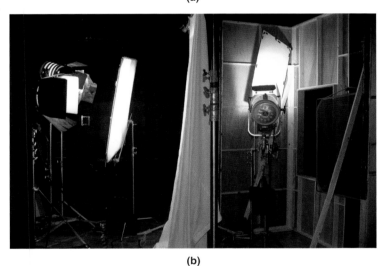

(b)

FIGURE 3.9 **(a)** This soft light window scene combines two types of softlight: diffusion and bounce. **(b)** Two 5K fresnels go through a layer of heavy diffusion and then a 12′ × 12′ muslin cloth diffusion. A 2K fresnel unit is bounced into a white beadboard above the window to simulate the light from an overcast sky.

An "Obie" light is any small lighting unit that is attached to the camera directly over the lens. Its name is derived from the beautiful actress Merle Oberon. It was discovered early in her career that this type of lighting was most complimentary to her facial structure. An Obie might be the key, the fill, or an eyelight, depending on the relative intensities of the other units.

Ambient

Ambient is just as the name implies, overall ambient. Ambient is either an overall base on which we build or a general, directionless fill. Outdoors, the ambient might be the daylight reflected from the sky and the surroundings. In a location room ambient might be an overall fill provided by bouncing a light onto a white ceiling.

FIGURE 3.10 Students rig a 4′ × 8′ foamcore bounce on a C-stand with a 2K Mighty Mole as the source. Note also the 2K zip light rigged on the wall on the right.

Quality of Light

The variations in the quality and mood of lighting are nearly endless. Just think of the many adjectives that we apply to it:

- indirect/direct
- harsh/soft
- specular/diffuse
- ambient/sourcey
- punchy/wrapping
- splashing/slamming
- contouring/frontal
- flat/chiaroscuro
- strong/gentle
- shadowy/high-key
- modulated/plain
- skimming/direct
- focused/general
- snappy/mushy

…and so on. Not all are precise and easily defined, but they all convey a sense of mood, quality, and atmosphere.

All of that leads to one conclusion—there is far more to light than can be defined by subdividing it into hard and soft, key and fill. Perform this simple experiment for yourself. For one full day, look around you; everywhere you go examine at the quality of light in the place you are in. See how it defines the space, shapes the objects, and falls on the faces of the people around you.

Every quality of light that you see can be reproduced on a set or location. Ask yourself, how would I light a scene to achieve this look? What units would I use, where would I put them, and how would I modify and shape the light to achieve this? Let's look at the major variables that we deal with. First we must realize that there are actually two factors involved in what is traditionally called hard/soft.

(a)

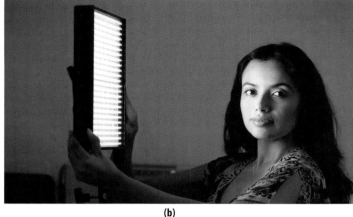

(b)

Hard/Soft

Relative Size of Source

The most important factor in the relative hardness/softness of a light is the size of the radiating source relative to the subject. The larger the radiating source in relation to the subject, the more the light tends to wrap around the contours of the subject. Where a hard light (small source) would create shadows, the large source will reach in and fill them. Hard light is characterized by the opposite effect; the transitional shadow area is relatively sharp and abrupt.

FIGURE 3.11 (**a**) Hard light, such as in this beauty shot, usually depends on the light's being in exactly the right spot relative to the model's face. (**b**) The most important thing to remember about soft light is that it is the apparent size of the source *relative to the subject* that determines how soft the light is. (Photo courtesy of Lite Panels, Inc.)

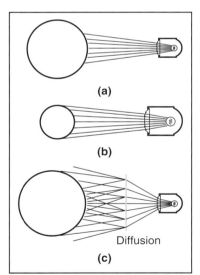

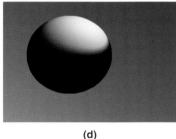

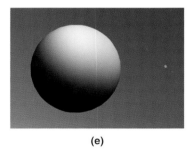

(d)　　　　　　　　(e)

FIGURE 3.12 What makes a light soft? A light is "soft" when it can "wrap" around the contours of the subject, thus making the shadows indistinct and gradual in falloff. It is a function of the relative size of the source, either from a large-bounce source or diffusion that makes the source appear larger. (**a**) A source that is small relative to the subject can't wrap around the contours. (**b**) A larger source and/or a smaller subject allows the light to wrap, thus creating softer, gentler shadows. (**c**) Diffusion makes a light softer by making the apparent source larger. How hard light and soft light light the same sphere—the soft light "wraps" (**d**), which makes the shadows much softer with gradual falloff (**e**).

FIGURE 3.13 Behind-the-scenes for the hard light vs. soft light test. A Source Four leko is used for hard light. For the soft light, a 2K with a Chimera softbox is used. A bleached muslin 4′ × 4′ was added for the softest light.

What this means is that no light is inherently hard or soft. Even a soft light unit might, under certain conditions, be a hard light, while something we would normally think of as a hard light, such as a bare-lens fresnel light, might be a soft light. The deciding factors are actual size of the source (such as the size of the lens of a fresnel light), the actual size of the subject, and the distance between them. The major determinant of this wrapping is the size of the source relative to the subject. If a very large light source is illuminating a smaller subject, the light will be able to get farther around the curves and edges. This decreases the shadow areas and tends to fill in its own shadows.

Why distance? It's simple geometry. A studio soft light is soft because the radiating source is the size of the opening. In the case of a Mole–Richardson 4K studio soft light the aperture is 36″×30″. If a subject is 1 foot high and 2 feet away from the light, it is obvious that the source is huge in relation to the subject.

Even with a large source and a small object placed far apart, only the light rays that are traveling parallel to each other reach the object. Any rays that would have the ability to wrap miss the subject; only the parallel rays illuminate it and the result is a relatively hard light.

Specular/Diffuse

The other aspect of the hard/soft character of light is whether it is specular or diffuse. *Specular light* is light in which the rays are relatively parallel. Light from the sun, a point source 93 million miles away, is specular. Specular light is highly directional and collimated. In terms of reflective surfaces, a specular reflection is one in which the outgoing light closely resembles the incoming light—in other words, a fairly mirror-like surface. In this case the angle of reflection equals the angle of incidence. A diffuse reflector is one in which the reflection does not resemble the incoming light. The diffuse surface scatters the light in many directions, and the angle of reflection is more or less random. This covers reflecting surfaces, but what about direct light? *Diffuse* is a condition where the light rays are traveling in random, disorganized directions. Light bounced off a rough white surface is diffuse. Light traveling through thick white translucent material is diffuse.

Diffusion Materials

Traditionally, diffuse light is thought of as soft and specular light is thought of as hard. As we have just seen, this isn't always true, but generally, diffuse light will tend to be softer than specular light. Diffusion material can be any semitransparent or translucent material: white plastic, silk, nylon, bleached or unbleached muslin, or shower curtain. They all serve the same purposes:

1. They reduce the specularity of the light. Relatively specular (collimated) light that falls on one side of the diffusion material emerges on the other side more diffuse (randomized); the degree of change depends on the opacity and thickness of the material.
2. They increase the size of the radiating source. The size of the source of a fresnel light is the size of its lens. If a 12-inch light illuminates a dense diffusion material 24 inches in diameter, it becomes a 24-inch radiating source; this also makes the light more diffuse and wrapping. This effect depends on the thickness and density of the material. The thicker and denser it is, the more the source becomes a pure area of diffuse radiation. If the diffusion material is very thin and light, the area of diffuse radiation increases, but also direct specular radiation still comes through.
3. Light from a radiating source is highly directional (specular). Also, the source is usually a mixture of two types of light, direct radiation from the filament or arc, and bounce-off from the reflector. The fresnel lens cannot smoothly combine these two types of light, and untreated direct light from one of these units is always just a little bit raw. Diffusers homogenize the light. Both the direct, specular light of the filament and the indirect bounce from the reflector are combined and smoothed by the diffusion.

Traditional Hollywood lighting up until the 1960s was almost entirely direct hard light without bounce light or heavy diffusion in front of the lamps. One reason for this is the slow emulsions used at the time; in order to maintain exposure, they needed everything they could get out of a light. With the high-speed films and video cameras we use today, together with the far more efficient sources we

(a)

(b)

(c)

(d)

FIGURE 3.14 Hard light/soft light. (a) Hard light is characterized by sharp, hard shadows. (b) Very soft light doesn't have hard shadows because the light "wraps" around the contours of the face. (c) Hard light with the face oriented to the light and with a fill on the shadow side almost seems like soft light. (d) The softest light of all is often window light, here a north-facing window.

(a)

(b)

(c)

(d)

(e)

FIGURE 3.15 Direction of light: (a) back light, (b) ¾ back, (c) side, (d) ¾ front, and (e) front light.

have available, it is possible to modify, diffuse, bounce, and double bounce as much as we like.

It is important to remember the loss of exposure when using diffusion material—it's just the price we pay for getting soft, beautiful light. The light is not simply lost, however. It is useful to think about where it goes. Some is bounced back to the back surface of the diffusion and wasted and some is lost as heat in the diffuser, but most of it is not lost at all; it simply spreads out to cover more area.

For example, reading a bare light at the center of the beam, you may find that you have 100 foot-candles. After placing diffusion in front of the light, you have only 50 foot-candles, but you now have exposure over a larger area.

Natural Diffusion

Environmental factors also play a role. Smoke, fog, and haze can have much the same effect as diffusion with one important distinction: the smoke or fog is on the shadow side of the subject as well; it can serve as a reflector, bouncing small amounts of light back onto the subject.

The greatest diffusion of all, of course, is an overcast day. Slight overcast essentially turns the entire sky into a huge radiating source: the ultimate soft light. It is still overhead, however, and in some cases, a bit of eyelight fill might be necessary.

Other Qualities of Light

Direction Relative to Subject

The direction from which the light hits the subject is crucial to the quality of light. It is perhaps the key determinant of how the light interacts with the shape and texture of the subject.

Light that is flat frontal will be less directional since it will be seen by the lens to cover all subjects equally. Sidelight and backlight will always be perceived as more directional, since the shadow areas it defines are far more recognizable as to origin.

Altitude

The height of the unit in relation to the subject is also critical. It is another aspect of direction. As a broad generalization, lights that are higher are going to create more shadows, and hence more shape.

As with direction, the farther away from the the axis of the lens it gets, the more likely it is to create shape, depth, and texture. Of course, as with all generalizations, this one is not quite true; we cannot say that it is always better to move a light higher or lower; however, it is fair to say this is usually the case.

(a)

(b)

(c)

High Key/Low Key (Fill Ratio)

Scenes that have an overall sense of being brightly lit are said to be high-key, which translates to lots of fill in relation to the key, not many shadows, and fairly high levels overall. The opposite of high-key is low-key lighting, which is dark, shadowy, and has little or no fill.

Historically, comedies, household, product commercials, and other light hearted material is lit high-key while mysteries, romance, and stylish upscale commercials tend to be low-key.

Specular/Ambient

Specular light is by nature directional. It originates at a source and follows a fairly straight path. When a light is placed in a scene so that we can clearly perceive its origin, we call it "sourcey," which may or may not be desirable, depending on the look we are going for. Specular hard light just outside the frame will usually be sourcey. Soft light, such as bounce light or highly diffused light, will tend not to be sourcey. Highly diffuse light that covers all of the set is called ambient light. It is undefined, directionless light.

Relative Size of Radiating Source and Lens

A more subtle factor, and one that applies only to lights with lenses, is the relative size of the radiating source and the lens. This particularly applies to large units. For example, many lighting people still miss the unique quality of the old brute arcs, which are not used much anymore. The electrical arc that generates the light is a very small, almost point source, and there is no reflector behind it. The lens of the light is quite large, creating a good deal of wrapping while the small arc creates a light that is highly specular and sharp. The wrapping gives it certain soft light characteristics while the small source keeps it clean and hard, very snappy.

Although 12K HMIs have lenses just as large as those of the brutes, their slightly larger radiating source keeps them from having the kind of bite of a brute. Some 12Ks are available with different reflectors, small and hard or slightly larger and diffuse.

(d)

(e)

(f)

FIGURE 3.16 Altitude of source: (a) light on the ground, (b) very low, (c) side, (d) high side, (e) high, and (f) top light.

FIGURE 3.17 Hard light and soft light in the same scene with actress Alexandra Fulton. (**a**) Hard light in a scene; here it is a 5K fresnel through venetian blinds. (**b**) Very soft light in the same scene. Here it was created by bouncing a 1K into a 3′ square piece of white foamcore.

(a)

(b)

Modulation/Texture

Raw light from any source, be it hard or soft, directed or reflected, can be further modified by modulation. Also known as breakup, subtle gradations can be introduced into the light pattern by cookies, celos, branches, lace, charlie bars, sheers (translucent window curtains), or other diffusion materials.

Movement

Don't forget that lights can move. There are the obvious ones: a car-headlight effect, a rising sun, and so on; but subtle movement of light can make a scene more realistic and alive. One frequently used trick is to place a branch or plant in front of a light that is coming through a window and then place a (quiet) fan so that it makes the branch or plant move very slightly. Don't overdo it, or it might end up looking like like a hurricane.

Subject/Texture

We can never consider light apart from the subject it is illuminating and the conditions under which it is working. The item being lit plays as important a role as the source

(a)

(b)

FIGURE 3.18 Light from upstage side. (**a**) One fundamental aspect of direction of light relative to the source is that it is generally better to light from the upstage side (the side away from camera). This creates shape and shadows on the camera side, adding depth and dimension. (**b**) The over-the-shoulder shot lit from the downstage side doesn't give the same sense of depth, dimension, and shape as the shot lit from the upstage side. Quite simply, the shadows aren't where we would like them to be. It is just not as complimentary to the model's features. This is a broad generalization, of course; there are many exceptions to this, but as a general principle it is a good guideline to follow. (**c**) Lighting from the upstage side (side opposite camera). (**d**) Lighting from the downstage side (same side as camera).

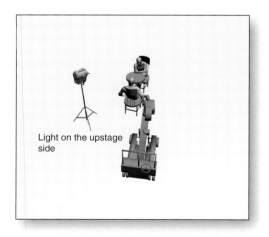

(c)   (d)

FIGURE 3.19 Carrying a lamp. This is both a specific technique and also an illustration of a general principle in lighting. It is called "carrying" a lamp. Often we want to make it look like the subject is being lit by a particular source that appears in the frame—in this case, a *practical* lamp (practical means that it actually works). Often the practical lamp (or window or neon sign or whatever the source is) can't actually light the subject in a way we would like. In that case we "carry" it—light it in a way that it looks like the source is doing the job itself. In this example a practical lamp is dimmed down so that it doesn't "burn out" and a Mole Biax fluorescent is set at an angle so that it is coming from the same direction as the lamp. Some Black Wrap is used to keep it from spilling onto the wall.

FIGURE 3.20 Adding texture to lights. Charlie bars (vertical bars, in this case made from tape on an open frame) and also some lace create texture in the scene. A Mole beam projector is the key; a 4K soft through some light blue gel ($\frac{1}{4}$ CTB or Color Temperature Blue) simulates skylight, while the beam projector recreates direct sun.

itself. There are dozens of variables, but some of the most important are

1. Reflectivity versus absorbency. There can be tremendous variation here, even between different people's skin.
2. Surface texture: diffuse versus specular.
3. Angularity versus roundness.
4. Transparency. For example, large blocks of ice not only reflect some light off of their wet surface but also transmit light internally.
5. Color. Affects not only our visual perception of color, but what colors of light will be absorbed or reflected.
6. Subject contrast. How dark or light the object is in terms of the gray scale. Also, the contrast between the subject and background or between different parts of the subject.

These are the basic building blocks we work with on the set.

(a)

(c)

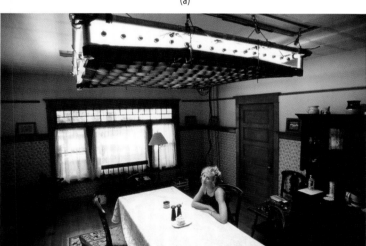

(b)

(d)

FIGURE 3.21 Making light soft. Four typical methods of making light soft: (a) A very large source such as this giant Fisher Light makes a soft light, essential for jobs such as lighting cars. (Photo courtesy of Fisher Light.) (b) A Kino Flo Blanket-Lite gives an overall soft ambience on a set. (Photo courtesy of Kino Flo, Inc.) (c) A 4' × 4' beadboard bounce and a Mighty Mole rigged on the same rolling stand, supported by a junior offset arm (along with a 2K Variac dimmer) make a highly mobile rig. (d) Two frames with muslin (a very heavy cloth diffusion)—a 12' × 12' and an 8' × 8'.

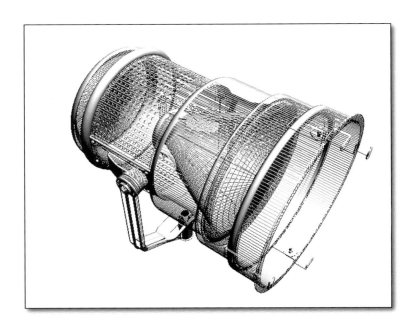

BASIC SCENE LIGHTING

We have looked at the tools of lighting, the elements of lighting, and some basic principles of light and exposure. Now let's put it all together.

A movie is made one scene at a time; a scene is made one shot at a time. The same applies, of course, to commercials, industrials, music videos, and even documentaries. In this chapter we will select several scenes from features, commercials, and classroom projects. We'll analyze their lighting schemes and talk a bit about the thought process that went into planning and executing them.

Whenever possible, a lighting scheme is planned well in advance. In nearly all cases, there are deviations from the plan; this is normal. As a general rule, the lighting of a scene is built—one light at a time. With larger scenes, there is usually a prerigging plan. On the day before, the electricians, with perhaps a rigging crew, will lay out the cable and place the larger lights in preparation for the arrival of the shoot crew.

Even in these cases, however, there are always adjustments and these are generally done one light at a time. For smaller scenes, all DPs have their own ways of working, but as a

(a)

(b)

generalization, it is possible to say that, in most instances, the lighting is built in a methodical, incremental manner. Just having electricians run around throwing up lights at random is seldom productive. The most common procedure is to set the key light and then bring in additional units one at a time to see how they fit in with the existing plan.

It is very difficult to preconceive exactly how a lighting plan will come together. It is not difficult to come up with an overall concept, but the exact details will change as you finally see the real set dressed, props in place, and actors doing the final blocking. In this chapter we will attempt to cover as broad a range of lighting situations as possible: from film school classroom experiments, to low- and medium-budget independent films, all the way up to very large studio productions.

Medieval Knights Around a Campfire

These scenes take place during the Crusades and at night, so there would have been no light other than campfires, lanterns, and torches.

The first obvious choice is to bathe the entire scene with moonlight. First it's natural, and second, without overall ambient moonlight, everything outside the circle of fire-light would fall into complete blackness. Some slightly blue moonlight will serve to outline the surrounding trees and shrubs and add a bit of fill to the scene in a naturalistic way.

Also, the blue will serve as a contrast to the warmth of the firelight (fires burn at around 2000K to 2500K). We only know a thing by its opposite. If the entire scene is lit only with warm firelight, two things might happen: first, it might get timed out at some point in post-production; second,

FIGURE 4.1 (a) Knights gather around a campfire consisting of a propane fire ring and compressed logs. They are also lit with a ¾ back flicker rig and a low-key backlight from a 9-Lite coming over the top of the trees. Another 9-Lite and an electric lantern are on the wagon in the background. (b) Firelight effect from below can be used to lend dark, mysterious moody feeling to the look of the scene.

the viewers' eyes will adapt after looking at the scene for a few minutes. This adaptation will eventually lead the viewer to see the light as basically white.

Spreading moonlight over such a large area (about two acres for all the scenes) usually calls for a large crane or, at the very least, a couple of levels of scaffolding. Either might be a problem as they may appear in the frame at some point (the trees are very low at this location) and a crane might need to be moved: a time-consuming process in a rough location like this. Scaffolding would be even more problematic.

Fortunately, the location itself offered a solution. The site chosen (with much urging from the DP) was a dry wash at the bottom of a steep hill, which was about 60 feet high. At the top of the hill was the crew parking lot—the perfect spot to park the generator.

The Plan

There are a number of ways to create fire effects, and several of them were used on this production.

First was the *real* fire—important not only as a source of illumination, but also as a major prop. Because this fire is indispensable to the frame, there is no choice: no realistic substitute for fire exists. Then the real fire was supplemented by some techniques and devices. First, flame bars were made. These are simple iron pipes with holes drilled in them. These holes allow compressed propane (highly flammable) to escape the pipes when it is fed into those pipes. Next, rubber cement (also highly flammable) was painted on the iron pipes. Given its flammability, that rubber cement makes an efficient starter when ignited.

This type of rig has several advantages. It is fairly constant, so it is good for continuity. Real logs would change from take

FIGURE 4.2 Here the moonlight dominates the scene while the fire effect adds a bit of backlight. The moonlight is two MaxiBrutes with ½ CTB. At roughly 100 yards away, the two Maxis provide about an F/1.3 at ASA 500.

FIGURE 4.3 The fire effect was provided by three fire rigs. These are a Mighty Mole, a Baby-Baby, and a Mickie Mole on a triple header with all lights run through a three-channel flickerbox. See Figure 4.4 for a closeup of the fire rig.

to take. Second, it is controllable; the operator can actually dial the flame up and down, thus regulating exposure and balance with some accuracy. Care must be taken to check exposure frequently, however, as the flame gets lower and the pressure in the propane tank decreases.

In the scene in Figure 4.1, a circular flame bar is placed in the stone ring and the gas line is buried under the dirt.

The second part of the flame is compressed fireplace logs. These burn longer and more consistently than real logs and provide a bit more of a real campfire look than the flamebar alone.

Flicker Effect

A convincing fire effect is not difficult, but it is often done wrong. First of all, it cannot be done with a single light. It cannot be done by wrinkling aluminum foil or flexing a reflector. These merely result in a hotspot that unconvincingly "waggles" across the scene.

Observe a fire sometime. One thing you will notice is that the shadows on the wall dance around. This is because, as the individual flames rise and fall, the light source itself moves around and up and down. This effect can only be duplicated with at least three sources that flicker on and off randomly.

A flickerbox is the best way to achieve this, but it can also be done with individual dimmers, a programmable dimmer board, or hand squeezers. For this production a three-channel flicker generator was used. This provided the capacity to make each light on each rig flicker at a different rate and with different high and low points. The difference between the highest point of flicker and the lowest point is important for exposure readings and also for believability.

FIGURE 4.4 The flicker rig, here in the high position. Having three different sizes of lights ensures that the effect will flicker realistically—in this case a 2K Mighty, a 1K Baby Baby, and a 1K Mickie Mole. Three lights are always necessary for a convincing effect. One half CTO on a 4′ × 4′ frame brings the temperature down to simulate fire's color. Note the position of the grip arm that supports the triple header—it is set so that it can be lowered to the ground, which is often required for a campfire effect. The flickerbox has three channels, each of which can control a light up to 2000 watts. Each channel has independent settings for high point and low point and the flicker rate is controllable in a wide range.

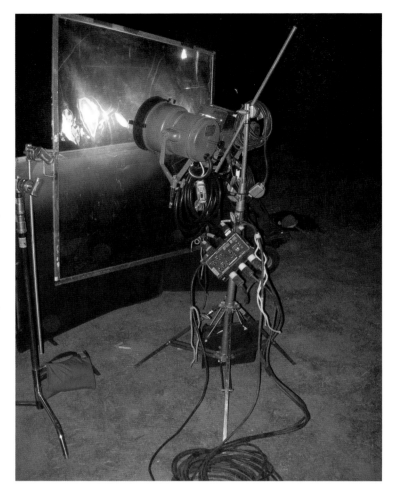

Too great a difference doesn't look real and too small a difference doesn't provide a noticeable fire effect.

For this same reason, the flicker settings should be appropriate for the situation. Candlelight, for example, barely flickers at all except when there is a gust of wind, but in order to sell the effect, we usually make it flicker a little all the time. A slight breeze created by waving something can make the candle itself flicker a bit to enhance the illusion.

For candle effects, special movie candles are available. These candles have three wicks and burn much brighter than ordinary candles.

Group Scene with Fire

Figure 4.5a: In this scene, a group of soliders listen as their leader addresses them. The wide establishing shot showed several campfires around them. Establishing the source is an important part of selling the effect. Without establishing the source by showing it, there is a danger that it might just seem like the lights are flickering. This is not a danger in a scene like this, of course.

(a)

(b)

(c)

FIGURE 4.5 Group scene with fire. (a) The scene as shot. (b) The backlight fire effect. (c) The low fire-effect from front left with the two moonlight juniors in the background.

FIGURE 4.6 Lighting diagram for the scene of knights gathering to listen to their commander (see Figure 4.5). The fire flicker rig is camera right and slightly behind them. In front at ground level is another softer, fire flicker rig with three 1K zip softs. Off to camera left and high are two 2Ks bringing in some moonlight from the side/back.

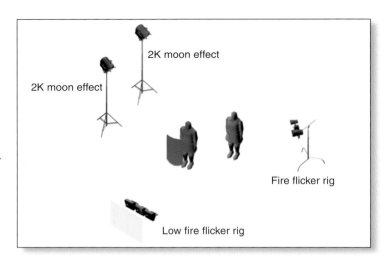

Figure 4.5b: Two flicker rigs were used on this scene. One is placed on the ground in front and camera left of the group. This simulates the campfire we saw in the wide establishing shot. The second fire rig is behind the group and camera right, its main purpose is to function as a back sidelight or kicker for some of the soldiers.

Figure 4.5c: The front fire rig needed to be as compact as possible so that it didn't stick up into the frame: Baby Zip lights were bounced into a white card rigged on a C-stand. A knight's shield was used to conceal it for the reverse angle.

The white card bounce was used, as direct light that close would have been too directional, even with soft lights. On camera left of the group we see two 2K juniors, which add a bit of moonlight fill.

Science Fiction Scene

This was a lighting experiment to try some sci fi concepts. The decision was to go all blue in order to give it mood and also disguise the fact that we had just an ordinary living room set. The units are tungsten fresnels: a 5K and two 2Ks coming over the top of the set walls with the addition of a Kino Flo Diva 4-bank on the floor. Double CTB was added to all the tungsten lights. The Kino had daylight bulbs. In addition, the HD camera had a menu setting of +99 for the blue channel in video levels. A 5K with double CTB is outside the window, coming through venetian blinds.

Film Noir Scene

The purpose of this scene was to duplicate the look of film noir (see Figure 4.8).

First of all, there were table lamps. Film noir interiors always seem to have table lamps. Here, they also provide

(a)

(b)

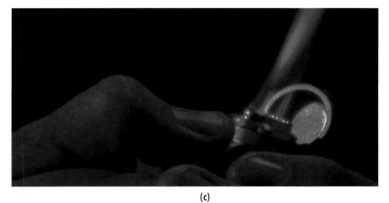

(c)

FIGURE 4.7 A science fiction scene. (a) End of scene, lit with a Kino from the floor and backlight from the 5K over the camera left wall. (b) A closeup in the scene. (c) The opening shot. The smoke and glow of the butane lighter add mood and texture to the shot. (d) Diagram of the scene.

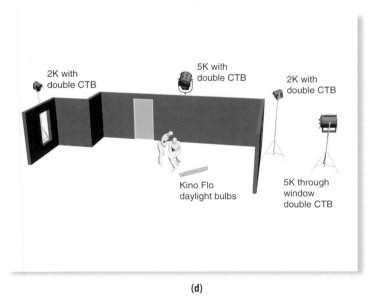

2K with double CTB

5K with double CTB

2K with double CTB

Kino Flo daylight bulbs

5K through window double CTB

(d)

(a)

FIGURE 4.8 A film noir scene. (**a**) The scene as shot. (**b**) The setup. (**c**) A diagram of the setup.

(b)

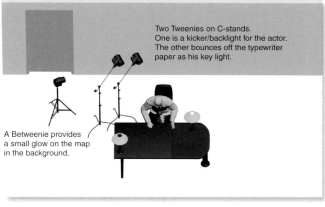

Two Tweenies on C-stands.
One is a kicker/backlight for the actor.
The other bounces off the typewriter paper as his key light.

A Betweenie provides
a small glow on the map
in the background.

(c)

some motivation for the lighting, although they play little role in lighting the actual scene (see Figure 4.8a).

Two Tweenies armed out on C-stand arms are the main units for the scene (Figure 4.8d). One of them provides a back kicker for the actor and the second is the key light: its only task is to bounce off the white typing paper to provide a subtle underlight for his face (Figure 4.8c).

An additional Betweenie gives a slight glow to the map and books on the shelf behind him (see Figure 4.8a).

Aces and Eights

This was a class lighting project and an experiment with Mole–Richardson's 2.5 K HMI beam projector. The beam projector provided a hot, sharp beam through the window. With full CTB added to the already blue HMI (and the camera set on tungsten balance), it provided an intense mood for the scene (see Figure 4.9).

A desk lamp provided some color contrast and hot spot on his head—a focal point for the image (Figure 4.9b).

A baby behind the desk adds some "kick" on the table (Figure 4.9b). A 650 Tweenie keeps the area under the desk from going totally black. Without the fog effect from a smoke machine, the shot would not have been nearly as effective.

Detective Scene

This scene (Figure 4.10a) needed to be low key to allow the handheld LED panel to be prominent in the scene.

Although the LED didn't provide much lighting on the actors in the scene, it provided the motivation for a low-bounce return (the 4′ × 4′ beadboard on the floor being hit with a 1K, Figures 4.10b and c). A 5K through each window and a 12′ × 12′ white muslin blown out behind the door (Figure 4.10c) provided the rest of the lighting plan for the scene.

Young Inventor

The challenge in this scene is the lightbulb. From top to bottom on the left: with the bulb as the only source, it burns out. Instead, the bulb is dimmed down and is carried by a MolePAR through a snootbox. Along with some light through the window and a backlight, the scene is complete (see Figure 4.10e).

Figure 4.11a: With just the actual practical light itself, the central part of the scene is burned out and the rest falls off into nothingness.

Figure 4.11b: With the practical dimmed down, the scene slides off the deep end.

Figure 4.11c: A key is added to carry the practical lamp. This means he looks like he is being lit by the practical, but it can be dimmed down to a good level.

FIGURE 4.9 (**a**) Aces and Eights. (**b**) A MoleBeam through the window provides the kind of hard directional light needed to give us defined shafts of light. A baby with some full blue fills in a part of the table not covered by the MoleBeam. (**c**) An overhead diagram of the scene.

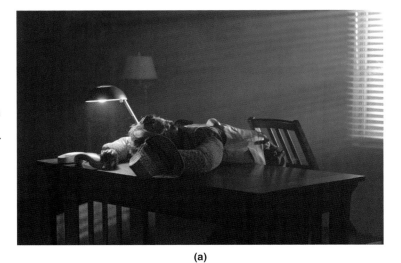

(a)

(b)

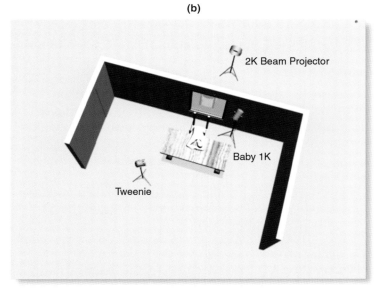

(c)

(a)

(b)

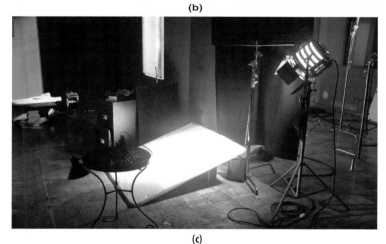

(c)

(d)

FIGURE 4.10 (a) A detective scene as lit by gaffer and DP David Chung. A handheld LED panels serves as both a prop and a practical light source. (b) A wide shot of the lighting. (c) A 1K bounced off a 4′ x 4′ foamcore serves as their key at the table. (d) A 5K through the left rear window. (e) An overhead diagram of the scene.

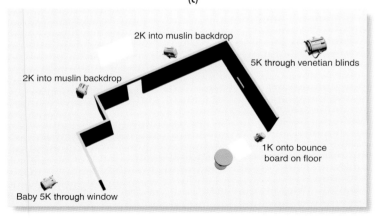

2K into muslin backdrop

5K through venetian blinds

2K into muslin backdrop

1K onto bounce board on floor

Baby 5K through window

(e)

(a)

(b)

(c)

(d)

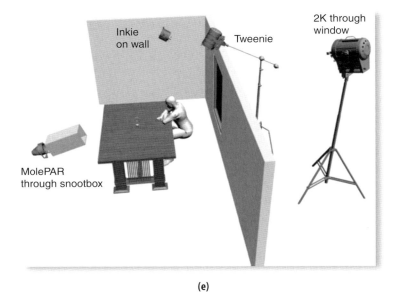

(e)

FIGURE 4.11 The young inventor. (a) With just the actual practical light itself, the central part of the scene is burned out and the rest falls off into nothingness. (b) With the practical dimmed down, the actor is underlit. (c) A key is added to "carry" the practical lamp. This means he looks like he is being lit by the practical but it can be dimmed down to a good level. (d) With a bit of backlight and an accent through the window, the scene is complete. (e) A diagram of the lighting setup.

Figure 4.11d: With a bit of backlight and an accent through the window, the scene is complete.

Miscellaneous Scenes

Potter

Figure 4.12a: This scene is from a commercial that needed a romantic but manly look. The lighting scheme was extremely simple. In front of the actor working on the pottery wheel was a window. Heavy diffusion (in this case bleached muslin) was taped to the glass.

Outside were two *firestarters* (1K MolePARS) with NSP bulbs aimed through the diffusion. The overhead lamp was dialed in on a dimmer so that it balanced the window light and was close enough to the actor to provide a very soft fill for his face.

Beauty Shot

Figure 4.12b: This shot is a simple floor bounce. A large piece of bleached muslin was placed on the floor, and a 2K open-face Mighty Mole was tilted down and aimed to bounce into it.

When using an arrangement like this, take care to avoid direct spill from the lamp—meaning that any light directly from the light must be cut off with barndoors, black wrap, or a flag, so that the subject is lit only with the bounce light from the white muslin.

Pool Room

Figure 4.12c: This barroom scene needed the harsh look of a down-and-dirty dive. The main light was a Lightwave (25 VNSP PAR bulbs) outside the window. Inside the light over the pool table, two 100-watt bulbs were hidden. Coming through the window of the back room was a 5K. The scene was shot during the day, and the small amount of existing daylight that crept in gave the scene an overall cold, gritty feel.

(a)

(b)

(c)

(d)

FIGURE 4.12 Miscellaneous scenes.

Pool Room CU

Figure 4.12d: A close-up from the barroom scene above. At the climax of the scene, the actor moves close to the windows, and we see the real intent of lighting primarily through the wooden blinds of the windows. This is a good example of how the eventual key close-up of the scene shapes the thinking about how to light the wide shot. Although there are usually some adjustments to be made when you move to the coverage, the lighting continuity must remain somewhat constant. It is important to be thinking several steps ahead as you light the master, so that it has some chance of working reasonably well for the coverage as well.

Intimate Room Scene

Lighting this scene was a bit trickier than might appear. It's an existing room, so the ceiling was low, offering no chance to hang lights from above. The blocking of the scene had them placed right next to the window. Outside was a terrace, but in most places where you might want to position a light, it would have been visible through the window.

The solution was to partially close the blinds—placing them at an angle so the lights were hidden but the light could still reach the actors (see Figure 4.13a). It turned out to be a perfect angle to give each of them an upstage key that just reached into their downstage eye, leaving nice deep shadows on the downstage side of their faces (see Figures 4.13b and c)—perfect for the dark mood of this scene. No fill was used as the chiaroscuro effect of this upstage lighting was fine with only the ambient bounce from the rest of the room. Outside the windows: one Baby Junior for each actor. With an arrangement like this, it is important to check the angle of the blinds and the lights every time the camera moves and then adjust them enough to maintain the same lighting look, but not so much as to interfere with continuity.

Here we have a typical problem. As previously discussed, interesting lighting is most often achieved by bringing it from the back—getting the lights around to the sides and behind the actors. Frequently, this placement of lights would mean the lights are visible in the frame. In this case, they have even have been visible outside the window when we went for close-ups from either side. Bringing them through the blinds gets them where we want while hiding them from the camera.

Knowing how to hide lights in the frame is an important skill. Often it's pretty easy to figure out where you want lights to come from—the tricky part is figuring out how to get them where you want, either in terms of rigging them or hiding them.

(a)

(b)

(c)

FIGURE 4.13 Intimate room scene.

FIGURE 4.14 Sitcom lighting with back cross keys.

Back Cross Keys (Sitcom Lighting)

Here we see an attempt at bad lighting or, more simply sitcom lighting. Situation comedy, indeed—all three-camera television—tends to be lit with the same basic scheme, called back cross keys. Each acting area is lit by two key lights from roughly ¾ back (upstage side, or the side away from where the cameras are) and then a soft front fill is added.

This is not actually a bad lighting scheme but it is bland, and what usually makes it so bland is that a great deal of fill is used—not that unusual for comedy in any case. The back cross keys setup gives some shape and definition and the front fill keeps it fairly suitable for television.

Reality Show Set

This short film about a futuristic reality show called for a soft TV look. The budget was low so it wasn't possible to rent spacelights, coops, or other types of overhead soft lights, so the DP had the grips build some soft boxes out of foam core and hanging bulb sockets. Each of the four soft lights held six 250-watt bulbs (ECA) (see Figure 4.16a).

The soft boxes establish an ambient base—an overall directionless light that serves as a base to build on. This is supplemented by practical lights, a couple of PAR cans streaking down the wall, a zip light, and some 2K shooting in from the corner openings through half spun. A couple of floating Tweenies are repositioned for each shot.

In or Out?

This classroom exercise aimed at a moody, low-key look. The experiment was to bounce a 1K MolePAR (commonly known as a "firestarter") into a black table. Only a single sheet of typing paper as a bounce on the table was needed

FIGURE 4.15 Black cross keys setup.

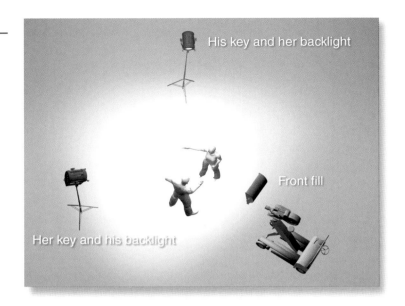

His key and her backlight

Front fill

Her key and his backlight

(a)

(b)

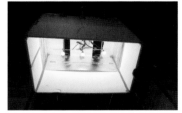

(c)

FIGURE 4.16 Reality show set (a) and the set-built softboxes (b) and (c) that provide the overall ambient light.

(a)

(b)

(c)

2K through window

MolePAR on goalpost

(e)

FIGURE 4.17 In or out?

(d)

to bring the exposure up to usable levels. A bit of blue moonlight through the window and a practical lamp were all that was added to this scene.

The 1000-watt VNSP (Very Narrow Spot) PAR 64 bulb was hung from a goalpost, which is simply a 10′ 2′ × 4′ (pipe or Speedrail is more frequently used) held by two high boy roller stands. Cardellini clamps hold the 2′ × 4′.

Day Exterior

This day exterior needed a good deal of fill for a fairly shadowless look, both to counteract the harsh midday sun and also create a bright cheerful feel. Two 12′×12′ silks on one side have two 6K HMI PARs for a key and two 12K HMI fresnels provide soft side light.

FIGURE 4.18 A day exterior.

(a)

(b)

(c)

On the opposite side, a 12′×12′ solid (black) creates some negative fill to give the scene some sense of contrast and make it a bit more gutsy—not so flat and dull.

From Under the Floor

Very large sets with confining walls can present a dilemma. The solution in this case was to light from underneath the Plexiglas floor. Dozens of Kino Flo tubes were removed from their housing and arranged underneath the elevated set to provide the primary lighting.

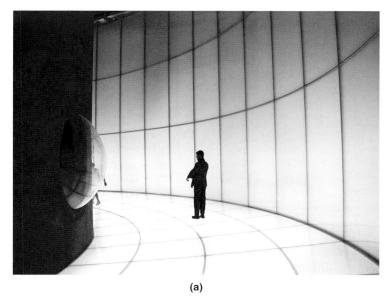

FIGURE 4.19 From under the floor. (Photos courtesy of Kino Flo, Inc.)

(a)

(b)

Ambient from Above

General lighting that is just sort of there is referred to as ambient. In some cases, the ambient just forms a base on which to build with other lights. In this case, the arctic winter

FIGURE 4.20 Ambient from above. (Photos courtesy of Kino Flo, Inc.)

(a)

(b)

(c)

setting called for a soft overall ambient as the main lighting. This was accomplished with several very large silks hung on trusses and large Kino Flo units suspended above them.

Confessions: Training Scene

The training scene from *Confessions of a Dangerous Mind*, as lit by gaffer Tony "Nako" Nakonechnyj. On one side, a series of 18K HMI fresnels through the windows are supported on cranes with half blue ($\frac{1}{2}$ CTB) added (Figure 4.21a). On the other side, 18K HMIs are bounced into grifflon to add some fill (Figure 4.21b).

(a)

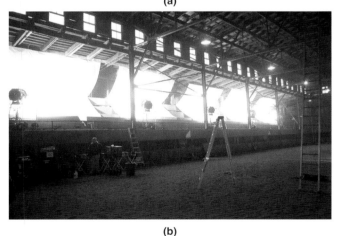

(b)

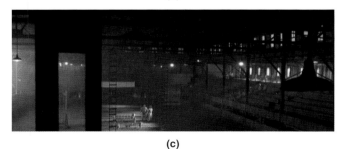

(c)

(d)

FIGURE 4.21 *Confessions*: training scene. (Photos courtesy of Tony "Nako" Nakonechnyj.) **(a)** 18K HMI fresnels on cranes outside the windows. **(b)** Another row of 18K fresnels are bounced into muslin to create some fill on the side opposite the windows. **(c)** The scene as it appeared in the film. **(d)** Focusing (aiming) the 18K units.

Figure 4.21a: the scene as it appears in the film. Notice that the practical lamps (china hats with 250-watt BBA bulbs) also play a role, but primarily as set dressing.

Confessions of a Dangerous Mind: Alley

A very simple scene but one that makes a powerfully graphic and memorable image. At first glance, one would guess that it is lit with a single large unit on a crane at the end of the alley. In actual fact, it's more complex and subtle than that. The main light is a 12K HMI PAR, which has tremendous punch, however, it didn't have the spread to give the sheen on the wall all the way down the alley. Gaffer Tony Nako added a 12K HMI fresnel, which has a wider spread.

As an additional subtlety, he created a bare bulb socket unit which held a mogul screw base sodium vapor lamp, which gave just a slight glow of yellow/orange streetlamp at the far end of the alley. This is an excellent example of the artistic subtlety, careful thinking, and preplanning that goes into a well-made lighting scheme, even on what may seem to be the simplest of shots.

FIGURE 4.23 An exterior in the studio. (Photos courtesy of Tony "Nako" Nakonechnyj.)

(a)   (b)

Creating an Exterior in the Studio

In this scene from Terry Gilliam's *The Brothers Grimm*, (Figure 4.26) a series of "Storaro" lights (multi-PAR units which use ACL aircraft landing lights instead of PAR 64 bulbs) create strong shafts of downlight for this night scene. A smoke effect is also important to this shot.

(a)

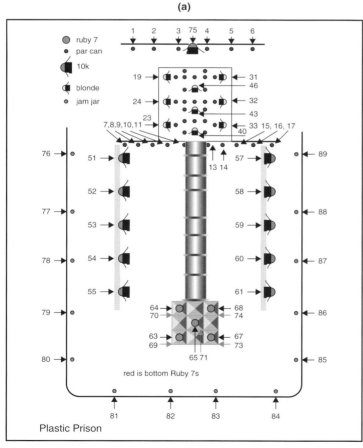

(b)

FIGURE 4.24 Tony Nako's lighting plan for a scene from *X2*. (Photo and diagram courtesy of Tony "Nako" Nakonechnyj.)

X-Men Plastic Prison

Figure 4.24 illustrates the use of large units even on a relatively small set: eleven 10Ks, nine Ruby 7s, and many PAR cans (1K PARs often used in rock and roll lighting) and Blondes (2000-watt open-face lights).

The diagram by Tony Nako (Chief Lighting Technician on the films *X-Men* and *X2*) also shows channel numbers for the dimmer system; he generally uses dimmer systems for all his lighting setups, even the largest ones. On a big studio picture, shooting is so expensive that anything that saves time in adjusting the lighting pays off in the end.

These are diagrams that Tony prints out and laminates in order to be able to give precise instructions to the dimmer board operator: essential when very large setups can have as many as 2000 lights/channels controlled separately.

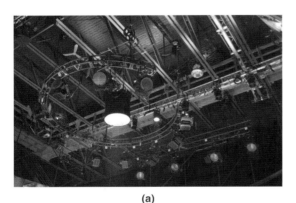

(a)

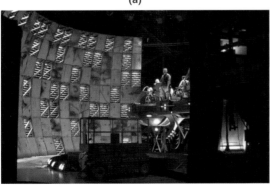

(b)

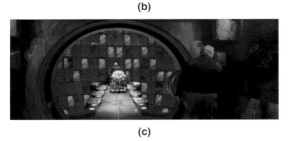

(c)

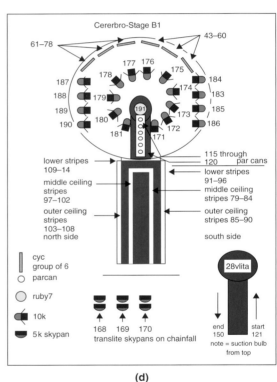

(d)

FIGURE 4.25 Stage rigging from *X-Men*. (Photos and diagram courtesy of Tony "Nako" Nakonechnyj.)

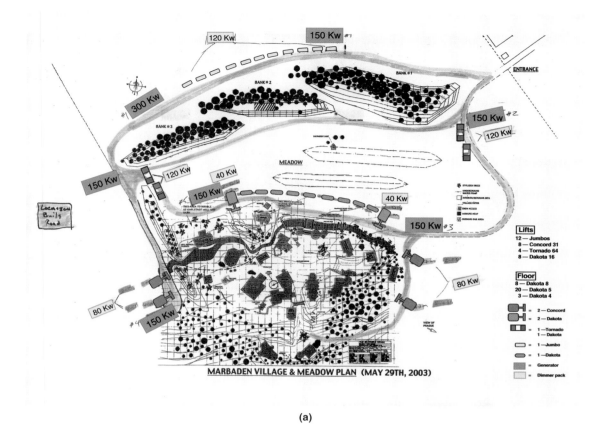

(a)

(b)

(c)

FIGURE 4.26 (a) Tony Nako lighting diagram for the night exteriors in *The Brothers Grimm*. (b) and (c) Some shots from the scene as it appeared in the film. (Diagram courtesy of Tony "Nako" Nakonechnyj.)

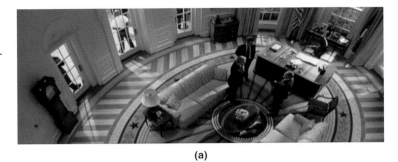

(a)

(b)

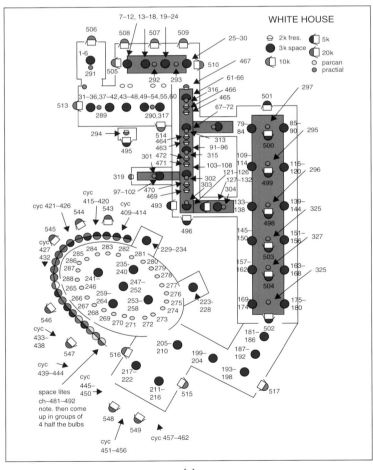

(c)

Stage Rigging

In this scene from *X-Men* (Cerebro, Figure 4.25), units are rigged from the grid. In the case of the ring of 10Ks, they are rigged on a circular truss that is suspended from the grid. A Ruby 7 with a skirt is hung directly above the actor.

Grips handle this type of rigging, with assistance from the electricians when it comes to actually hanging the units. Electricians then wire up the units (in this case to the dimmer system) and focus them.

Figure 4.27a,b: the scene as it appeared in the film.

Large Night Exterior

A lighting diagram for the night exteriors of the village in the film *The Brothers Grimm* (Figure 4.26), as done by Tony Nako, who for this film was dubbed Chief Lighting Dude by director Terry Gilliam. The large units were the Storaro series of lights, most of which use 28-volt ACL globes, which are aircraft landing lights and very punchy. Some were placed on lifts and some worked on the ground. Having so many units placed at such large distances makes it especially important to have them all on dimmers for centralized control.

In addition to lighting placement, this diagram also details power distribution and placement of dimmer packs, which are the actual dimmers controlled from a central dimmer board.

The Storaro lights were invented by cinematographer Vitorio Storaro. They are:

Jumbo = 16–28-volt ACL globes
Concorde = 31–28-volt ACL globes
Tornado = 64–28-volt 1000-watt PAR36 bulbs
Dakota = 8–PAR64 globes

Complex Stage Set

For the opening sequence of the second *X-Men* movie, a large set of the Oval Office and West Wing corridors was built in a sound stage. A big set like this naturally requires a complex lighting design and extensive control. With lots of actors and crew standing by and the enclosed nature of the set, having electricians run around dropping scrims or having the grips set nets is out of the question. The only feasible solution is to run all the lighting on dimmers. Naturally this involves considerable extra cabling—rather than just running power from the electrical source directly to the light, it is necessary to run power to the dimmer racks and then to the lights. There is extra expense involved as well, but for a large production the savings in time more than makes up for the cost and labor.

See the appendix for a sample of a lighting order for a large feature film involving dimmers.

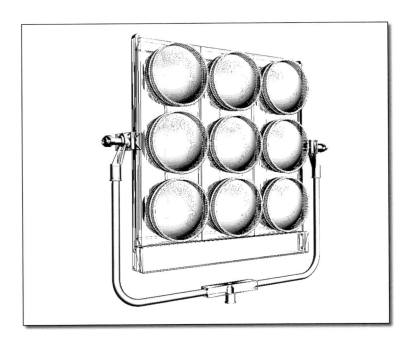

LIGHTING HD, DV, AND SD VIDEO

The differences between lighting for film and video, whether it be high def (HD), digital video (DV), or standard def (SD) are not as great as sometimes imagined. Everything we have discussed about basic lighting applies equally to film and all forms of video.

There are, however, some differences between film and video as imaging media, the most fundamental of which is the capacity to handle contrast. While film negative can handle ranges of seven to eight stops (128:1, 256:1) and even more, most video systems cannot reproduce that contrast range.

The second difference is separation in the shadows and highlights. HD video has an extraordinary response in the shadow areas, but all forms of video have trouble handling hot spots in the highlight areas.

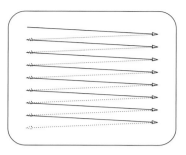

FIGURE 5.1 Scan lines in video.

If there is one key concept to remember about HD and other kinds of video, it is this: **Do not overexpose!** Video simply cannot handle overexposure; once the signal clips, it cannot be saved. (Film, on the other hand, handles overexposure reasonably well, but it doesn't do as well with underexposure.)

Many cinematographers also like to include some reference white and reference black in each scene (this is true for film shooting as well). This just means that at least one area of the shot has something that approaches pure white and another object in the frame approaches pure black. This not only prevents having the image changed for the worse in post, it also means that your scene will have a full range of tones, thereby contributing to a richer, fuller image.

Taken together these considerations lead us to four simple rules for lighting video:

- Do not overexpose the shot.
- Accommodate lighting ratio to the video limits.
- Avoid areas of extreme overexposure (hot spots).
- Include reference black and reference white in every scene.

The Video Engineer and DIT

Between the video camera and the videotape recorder, one important link stands out—the video engineer. S/he is the chief technician responsible for making sure all equipment is properly set up and operating. S/he monitors the signal and constantly checks on the quality of the recording. On larger jobs s/he will be assisted by an assistant engineer and a tape operator. The video engineer's tools include the waveform monitor, the vectorscope, and the paintbox.

On HD shoots, this position has evolved into the Digital Imaging Technician (DIT) who not only has responsibilities for the integrity of the video signal but also manages the look of the image—generally, the DP will describe the particular look he or she is going for, and the DIT will make the adjustments to accomplish that. In most cases, the DIT will also have the ability to remotely control exposure and other factors—not as a creative decision, but more to maintain consistency; this is similar to how a studio video shoot works—many camera functions are operated from the video control room.

The Waveform Monitor

While video lighting is fundamentally the same as film lighting, it is important to accommodate its limitations. The key instrument in accomplishing this goal is the waveform monitor.

The waveform monitor is the light meter of video. You must learn to use it for video as you learn to use meters in lighting

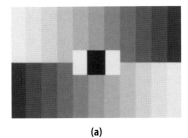

(a)

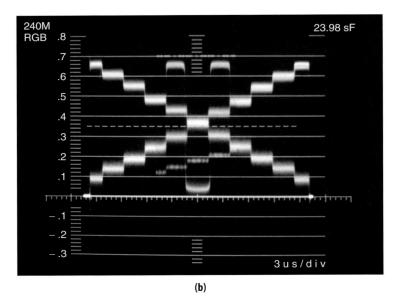

(b)

FIGURE 5.2 **(a)** The waveform monitor display of the 11-step grayscale from the Chroma du Monde test chart from DSC Laboratories. The waveform monitor **(b)** shows the brightness values of the picture: no color information is displayed.

for film. The waveform monitor is basically an oscilloscope that displays the video signal. Using the waveform monitor as a technical and creative tool depends on an understanding of the video signal.

Let's review the basics. The video picture is formed by a scanning beam of electrons. When the scanning beam reaches the edge of the screen, it goes blank (turns off) and flies back to the opposite edge, where it starts across again. This continues for $262\frac{1}{2}$ lines, followed by the longer vertical blanking interval, during which the scan returns to the top left of the screen and begins again, this time in the spaces between the scan lines it just did.

This is not a new frame, however; it is the same frame again. Each frame is painted twice, and each half is called a field. The reason for this two-field system (which is called interlaced video) is that, if a scan line painted a frame for 525 lines from top left to bottom right, the time lag between the beginning and the end would be too long. The screen would appear to be dark in the upper left while the lower right was being painted. It would be similar to a film projected at 12 frames a second—not fast enough to establish the illusion. Each of these fields is scanned in $\frac{1}{60}$ of second, making a frame $\frac{1}{30}$ of a second. In progressive video, each frame is scanned from top to bottom, and there are no interlaced fields. Twenty-four-frame-per-second progressive video has become the standard for narrative shooting as it is closer to the look of film.

On a waveform monitor, the screen is divided into 140 *IEEE* (Institute of Electrical and Electronic Engineers) units (also called *IRE* units for the Institute of Radio Engineers. This is the more common usage). A video signal ranges from 0 to 100

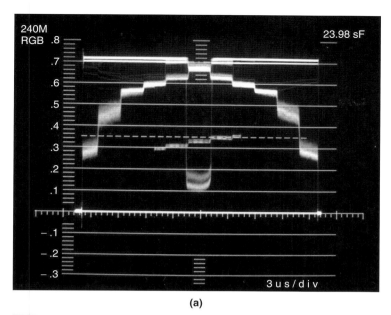

(a)

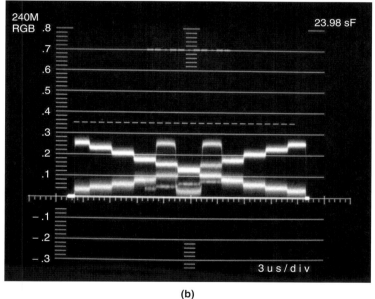

(b)

FIGURE 5.3 (**a**) This 11-step grayscale is badly overexposed. See how there are no black values at all, and the highlight values are squeezed together at the top: there will be no separation, no detail in the highlights. (**b**) This 11-step grayscale is severely underexposed: there are no highlight values at all—indeed, no tonal values above middle gray. The shadow values are crushed at the bottom; there will be no detail, no separation in the shadows; there will be nothing but a dark gray to black mush.

IRE units. The actual minimum black level is 7.5 IRE units, while maximum white is 100 units. During the blanking interval (the time when the scan line is moving back across the screen) the signal goes to 0 units, which is important in keeping it invisible as it moves back to the other side of the screen.

The sync pulse, which is a trigger that signals the beam to begin to move back across, actually dips below 0, to –40 IRE units. These blanking and sync pulses occur outside the picture area, in the so-called overscan areas.

The waveform monitor is a trace of one scan line of the picture (in actuality, most waveform monitors can display all

FIGURE 5.4 (**a**) The vectorscope display and (**b**) the color wheel. Most representations of the color wheel in this context begin with 0° at the 3:00 position. This is also the representation of color as it is manipulated in the matrix menus of HD cameras.

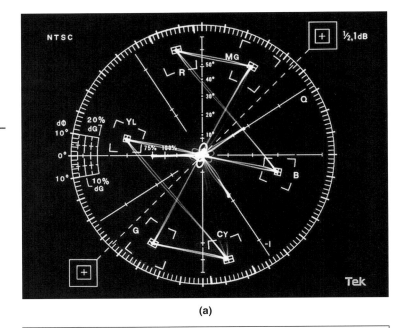

(a)

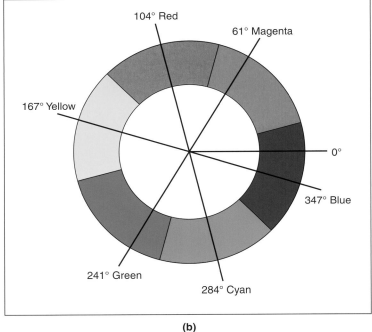

(b)

525 lines, but for clarity we will discuss single-line display). As this single trace moves across the screen, it records the relative brightness of the picture information. It is exactly the same as a series of spot meter readings across the set from left to right in a straight line. Totally black areas in the picture will show up on the monitor as 7.5 units. Bright areas will record as 90 or 100 units or more. Where the picture exceeds 100 IRE units, the video signal is overloaded. Video engineers will always try to keep the signal under 100 units. In some

cases, for artistic reasons, 100 IRE may be exceeded, but 108 IRE is seldom exceeded.

The waveform monitor is an invaluable tool in lighting a scene. It can be used to set the overall brightness level, the contrast ratios, the iris setting, and to watch for any hot spots. The pitfall is in being a slave to it. As a general rule, the lighting of the scene must accommodate the parameters of video. Don't forget that your creative instincts may sometimes conflict with these rules; in that case, you must use your judgment and the video monitor. Remember that, even in video, what you see is not always what you get.

The Vectorscope

The waveform monitor tells us little about the color content and balance of a scene—for that we need a vectorscope. The color signal of video is defined by two basic elements, hue and saturation, displayed by a vectorscope in a circular display. Hue is represented by degrees of rotation from the reference point and saturation is represented by distance from the center of the circle.

For most NTSC vectorscopes 0° is at 3 o'clock. The six basic colors are positioned as follows:

- Magenta, 61°
- Red, 104°
- Yellow, 167°
- Green, 241°
- Cyan, 284°
- Blue, 347°

Square brackets mark the position of each pure hue on the face of the vectorscope. These act as targets when calibrating to color bars.

Iris Control

Video cameras vary in sensitivity, but in general, they currently run around 100 to 320 ASA (this is an equivalent, as video cameras are not really rated in terms of ASA).

As in film, it determines the overall exposure of the scene. Because highlight areas are so much more problematic than shadow areas, the general practice in videography is to set the exposure for the highlights and deal with the shadows in another way.

As a rule, face tones are set at about 70–80% of peak brightness—depending on the complexion of the actors. If there is a bright white object in the scene (for example, a white shirt) that is registering on the waveform monitor at 120%, the video engineer would be forced to close down the iris in order to keep the shirt closer to 100%. This would also lower the level of the face 20 units, which would make it appear darker than normal. Since we are assuming that the face is important, not the shirt, this would be unacceptable. The shirt has to be dealt with somehow, and here there is no difference between film and video; the tricks are the same. We can set a net to keep light off the shirt, change the shirt to a darker one, soak the shirt in tea to tone it down, or add a little light to the face.

Electronic Pushing

Another factor that affects overall exposure is electronic pushing or gain. This is the electronic equivalent of forced development for film. It raises the sensitivity of the video sensor, allowing the camera to form an image at a lower exposure level. The boost is rated in decibels (dB) and each 6-dB boost is the equivalent of one stop. As with film, there is a penalty to pay. In this case it is increased electronic noise in the picture, not unlike the increased grain in pushed film. Most cinematographers prefer to shoot at –3 dB when the camera offers that option; this reduces noise to a minimum.

White Balance

As with film, video must be balanced to the overall color temperature of the lighting. This is achieved electronically by white balancing. A relatively quick and simple process, white balancing is necessary only at the beginning of the day or when a major change occurs in the lighting, such as going from indoors to outdoors, or using a different setup with color gel on the lights. It may also be necessary if a camera starts acting up owing to overheating or other problems.

White balancing can be accomplished either automatically by the camera itself or manually by the video engineer/DIT. In either case it consists of focusing the camera on a white or neutral gray target (such as a white showcard); then you either push the auto white balance button or manually adjust the paint controls. Many advanced cameras have the capacity to memorize more than one white balance, which can then be selected later. Most also include some preset balances such as tungsten lighting and daylight and perhaps 4300K (which is average for fluorescent lighting), which can be selected when there is no time for a white balance.

When white balancing, it is key to know what your reference is. Let's consider two situations.

1. You are shooting in a remote location that has very low voltage. The tungsten lights are burning very yellow as a result of the voltage drop. You want to be sure you get good clean color.
2. You have lit a set for late afternoon. The lights have all been gelled with $\frac{1}{2}$ 85, and the sunlight coming through the window has full 85 and No-Color Straw to simulate golden hour.

Your response would be different for each of these situations. In the case of the low voltage, you want to get rid of the yellow in the lights. In this case you would expose the white card with the yellow light from the set lighting units. White balancing would then remove the yellow, just as a filter or color timing at the lab would remove unwanted color.

In the second case, the color is an effect that you want. If you exposed the white card to the light with the CTO or no-color straw gel, the white balance would remove the color and negate the effect you are trying to build. In this case it is necessary to have a neutral light available to white balance. It should be a light without any gel added, straight 3200K or 5500K, depending on the types of lights you are using.

Transferring Film to Video

The question is often asked, "If all television programs and commercials and nearly all motion pictures end up on video anyway, why not just accept the limitations and shoot them on video to begin with?" The answer is that even if the final product is the same, how you get there is important—just as an Ansel Adams photograph of Yosemite taken with an 8×10 camera will be fundamentally different from a tourist shot of the same subject taken with a 35-mm auto focus camera. The fact that both end up as 8 × 10 enlargements does not negate the fact that the intermediate steps are key determinants of picture quality.

While it is true that the telecine and video recording of a film transfer is limited by the same 30:1 contrast ratio as video-originated material, the key factor is compression—the compression that takes place up in the toe and shoulder of the H & D curve when we take the original shot on film negative. While the live scene may have a contrast ratio that even exceeds 128:1, the highlights are not reproduced at a 1:1 equivalence when it is recorded on film. Because they fall in the shoulder of the film curve, they are compacted. There is still separation from one area of tone to the next higher area, but the difference is not as extreme as it was in real life.

No matter how bright an object is in real life, it can only reach D-max. It can't be any denser than the film emulsion maximum. All this means that while the film may still exceed the limits of the video, it is a lot closer than the live scene was. The video transfer benefits from this intermediate step.

Lighting for Multiple Cameras

Video image quality has a generally bad reputation with respect to film. Part of this is due to limited brightness range and resolution and part of it is due to historically poor

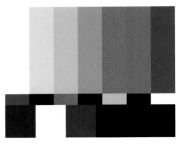

FIGURE 5.5 NTSC 75% color bars.

lighting. The bad reputation of video lighting is based on two historical factors:

1. Video is frequently the lower cost alternative. A production company that is saving money by shooting video is unlikely to splurge on the lighting crew, equipment, and time.
2. Video production is often multi-camera shooting.

Lighting for multi-camera, whether video or film, almost always involves compromises. What looks great from one viewpoint is often a disaster from another position. With some care and skill, however, it can be almost as good as single-camera lighting. There are two basic approaches.

1. Find lighting solutions that work as well as possible for all camera positions. This often involves broad sources and a more general lighting.
2. Use dimmers to alter the lighting balance as the shot shifts from camera to camera. In practice, this approach is most often applied to multi-camera film shoots for television.

For a more generalized situation, an X approach is often used. For each position, there is a front left and front right unit and a back left and back right unit. This means that no matter what the camera position and the actor's direction, there is a light that can act as a key, one that can be a fill, and one or more that can be a backlight or kicker. The dimmer operator is in control of the balances and which lights serve what purpose for each shot. It takes a good crew and a thorough rehearsal, but it can work well. Multi-camera shooting may also occur in productions shot on film, but that is much less frequent than in video.

Monitor Setup

The most important thing you can learn about video is how to set up a color monitor properly. Even with other equipment such as a waveform monitor and vectorscope on hand, the monitor is still a critical part of previewing and judging the picture. As we'll see in Chapter 7 on color theory, there is no exact correlation between the mathematical representation of color and the human perception of it.

Color bars are an artificial electronic pattern produced by a signal generator, which may be in a video camera (most professional video cameras have a bars setting) or a separate piece of equipment on the set or as a standard piece of equipment in any video post-production facility—be it telecine, editing, or duplication. Color bars are recorded at the head of every videotape to provide a consistent reference in post-production. They are also used for matching the output of two cameras in a multi-camera shoot and to set up a video monitor. On top on the left is a gray bar: it is 80 IRE units.

Monitor Setup Procedure

To set up a monitor, start with the following steps:

- Allow the monitor to warm up.
- Shield the monitor from extraneous light, but calibrate it under the conditions you will be viewing during lighting and shooting.
- Display color bars on the monitor: either from the camera or a separate generator.
- Set the contrast to its midpoint.
- Turn on the blue-only function—this makes the picture black and white. If the display doesn't have blue only, then turn the chroma (color saturation) all the way down until the color bars are shades of black and white.

The PLUGE

Notice the three narrow bars labeled 3.5, 7.5, and 11.5 in Figure 5.6a. These are the PLUGE, which stands for Picture Lineup Generating Equipment, first developed at the BBC in London.

The PLUGE was developed at the BBC. It was generated at a central location in its facility and sent by wire to each studio. This way, all of the equipment could be calibrated conveniently. This was the PLUGE alone, not combined with the color bars.

The middle black is set at 7.5 IRE black (or in the digital realm, 16,16,16). The first chip, superblack, is set at about 3.5 IRE below black, and the third chip, dark gray, is set at about 3.5 IRE above black. None of these really works to adjust a monitor to properly display 0 IRE black, so the following procedure is standard.

- Adjust the brightness control until the middle (7.5 units) PLUGE bar is not quite visible. The lightest bar on the right (11.5 units) should be barely visible. If it's not visible, turn the brightness up until it becomes visible.
- Since 7.5 units is as dark as analog video gets, you should not see any difference between the left bar (3.5 units) and the middle bar (7.5 units). There should be no dividing line between these two bars. The only division you should see is between 11.5 and 7.5. This same technique is used in setting the black-and-white viewfinder on a video camera.
- The next step is to set the contrast control for a proper white level. To do so, turn the contrast all the way up. The white (100 unit) bar will bloom and flare. Now turn the contrast down until this white bar just begins to respond. The image below shows what it should look like at this point.

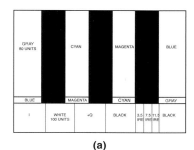

(a)

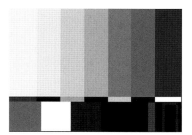

(b)

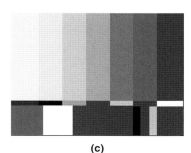

(c)

FIGURE 5.6 (**a**) Diagram of blue-only signal. (**b**) Correct monitor setup, shown here in black-and-white. (**c**) Incorrect luminance; notice how all three of the PLUGE bars in the lower right are visible.

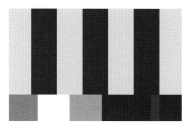

FIGURE 5.7 Blue-only color bars— notice that the bands are of equal intensity and in the upper portion the large and small bars are equally gray or black.

Adjusting Color

Color on a professional monitor is referred to as "phase." With blue only on (and thus a black-and-white picture), adjust phase until the bars are uniformly black or white. It is possible to eyeball the yellow and magenta. This is the down-and-dirty method and should be used only if other methods are not practical. The yellow should be a lemon yellow, without orange or green. And the magenta should not be red or purple. This quickie method is not recommended except in emergencies. This applies to SD monitors only. In HD, it is not possible to adjust phase. However, if you are using a downconverter on the camera with an SD monitor, this adjustment will still be necessary. A standardized test chart (Figure 5.9) can be helpful for this.

Blue-Only Adjustment

Most professional monitors have a blue-only switch. This turns off the red and green guns, leaving only the blue (Figure 5.7). If your monitor does not have a blue-only switch, you can use a piece of blue gel (full CTB) or a Kodak Wratten #47—the purest blue in the wratten series. View the monitor through the gel. If you see any of the red, green, or yellow colors, double the blue gel over to increase the blue effect.

By using the blue-only switch or a piece of blue gel, you have removed the red and green elements of the picture. Only the blue remains. If the hue is correct, you should see alternating bars of equal intensity.

- With the blue switch on (or your blue gel in front of your eye) turn the chroma or color until the gray bar at the far left and the blue bar at the far right are of equal brightness. You can also match either the gray or blue bars with their sub-bars.

FIGURE 5.8 A typical setup for the test chart. In this case, two Tweenies at a 45° angle are at exactly the same distance and angle from the Chroma du Monde chart for even lighting. Each Tweenie has a double scrim in it to reduce the light. This is for setting backfocus, which requires that the lens be as wide open as possible.

- Adjust the hue control until the cyan and magenta bars are also of equal brightness. You can also match either of them with their sub-bars. Now the four bars—gray, blue, cyan, and magenta—should be of equal intensity. The yellow, green, and red (which are black in Figure 5.6a) should be completely black.

Once you have set up your monitor, leave it alone unless the viewing conditions change—by leave it alone, I mean don't turn the brightness up just so you can see focus better, for example. Don't forget to go through the same process with your viewfinder. Most professional video viewfinders are black and white so you will only need to adjust brightness and contrast; however, it is critical that they be set properly to color bars.

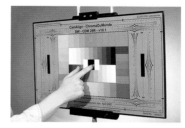

FIGURE 5.9 The Chroma du Monde test chart by DSC Laboratories. Its key features are two 11-step crossed grayscales in the middle, reference color chips, and in the center, the Cavi Black—a hole with black velvet behind it for true reference black. On each side of the Cavi Black are two 100 IRE white patches. (Photo courtesy of DSC Laboratories.)

Camera White Balance

Just as we use film stocks of different color balance and camera filtration to adjust, in video, the white balance function compensates for variations in the color range of the source lighting. White balance is accomplished by aiming the camera at a pure white surface (usually a white card) and selecting the white balance function on the camera. The internal electronics then compensate for variations in color. Naturally, it is essential that the light illuminating the white card be the same as that in the scene, just as the light on a gray reference card in film must be the same as it is on the scene.

Also, as in film, if you are using filters to alter the color, they must be removed for white balance or their effect will be erased by the white balance. The white balance function can also be used to fool the camera. If, for example, you want the overall color balance to be warm, you can put a cooling filter (blue) over the lens while doing color balance. The circuitry will then compensate, and when you remove the filter over the lens, the image will then be warm. This works for any color tone you want to add and can be accomplished by placing a filter over the light illuminating the card just as well as over the lens.

Establishing a Baseline

Video, whether it be analog SD (standard definition), DV (digital video), or HD (high definition), is heavily dependent on proper calibration of all the equipment. Unlike a film camera, which is really just a transport system for the film emulsion (the real imaging device), a video camera is itself the imaging device. A video camera records the image and then electronically processes the signal in a number of ways. There are many things that can go wrong. Proper setup is essential and not merely for the camera.

Unlike film, where most of the decisions about the image will be made with the eye and with the light meter, in video, many decisions about exposure and lighting are going to be made with the viewfinder (including zebras), the monitor, and (if available) a waveform monitor and vectorscope. Each of these must be calibrated, of course, but it is also important that the entire system be coordinated. To do this, two things are necessary: proper setup of the monitor to color bars and then calibration of the entire system using a proper test chart. A good test chart reveals many types of information about the camera, the monitor, the lighting, exposure, color balance, and much more. Some of it is more for video engineers, but the basics are invaluable to the DP, lighting director, or camera operator. A good test chart is absolutely essential to shooting on HD and SD svideo.

The Test Chart

For our examples here, we will use the Chroma du Monde, a very high-end and sophisticated test chart made by DSC Laboratories in Canada. As with any test chart, it must be evenly illuminated and all glares and flares eliminated. If there are glares on the surface, it is fine to tilt the chart down slightly. Although the Chroma du Monde is optimized for daylight balance light, if tungsten is all you have, it will do. One feature that makes this chart so useful is the Cavi Black in the middle. It is a square hole in the middle with a black velvet box behind it: this creates an area of pure black for reference.

Frame up the chart and set your optimum exposure. With the pure black of the Cavi Black in the center, you can see where pure black lies on the waveform monitor (it is also a good doublecheck on the video monitor). On the waveform, it should be at 0 IRE (or 0%). With the 11-step grayscale, you can check the overall gamma (contrast) as well as the knee and toe areas to be sure they are within spec.

Once you have adjusted the camera and monitor to a normal rendition of the image, you can use these same references to establish any particular look you are going for. The range of the grayscale, the pure black and the white areas, will allow you to see a more complete picture of what the image adjustments should be (probably more than if you were just looking at a typical scene). The primary and secondary color patches will allow you to see the effect of any color adjustments you make.

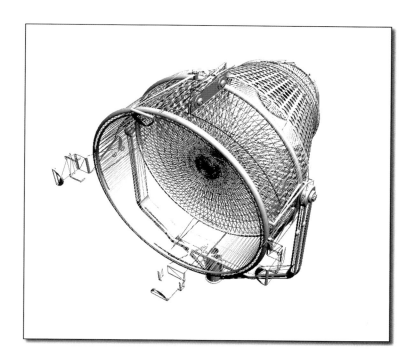

EXPOSURE THEORY

Light comes in both visible and invisible portions of the electromagnetic spectrum. Human eyes are sensitive to the small portion of that spectrum that includes the visible colors from the longest visible wavelengths of light (red) to the shortest wavelengths (blue).

Intensity of light is measured in foot-candles or in lux (in the metric system). A foot-candle (fc) equals about 10.08 lux (or, for a rough conversion, multiply foot-candles by 10 to get lux). A foot-candle is the light from a standard candle at a distance of one foot. One lux is the illumination produced by one standard candle from a distance of 1 meter. When a film is exposed for 1 second to a standard candle 1 meter distant, it receives 1 lux-sec of exposure. What's a standard candle? It's like the standard horse in horsepower. It just gives us some standard points of reference.

The Bucket

Think of exposure as a bucket. Whether it be film emulsion or the CCD receptor in a video camera, the image-making device is like a bucket. It wants to be exactly filled up—not too little and not too much—it needs to be filled exactly to the rim. This never varies, meaning that we have to provide it just the right amount of light. (We can, however, change the size of the bucket—by using a faster or slower film or in video by adding gain.)

The quantity of light in a scene varies widely: the difference between a darkly lit interior and a sunny day is enormous. This means we have to control the amount of light getting to the film or CCD. This is the job of exposure control. The task is accomplished with several means: the iris, the shutter, frame rate, and neutral density filters.

F/Stop

Most lenses have a means of controlling the amount of light they pass through to the film or video receptor; this is called the aperture. The f/stop is the mathematical relationship of overall size of the lens to the size of the aperture.

"Stop" is a short term for f/stop. A stop is a unit of light measurement. An increase in the amount of light by one stop means there is twice as much light. A decrease of one stop means there is half as much light. The f/stop is the ratio of the focal length of a lens to the diameter of the entrance pupil as shown in Figure 6.1. Thus, each stop is greater than the previous by the square root of 2.

The f/stop is derived from the simple formula

$$f/stop = focal\ length/diameter\ of\ lens\ opening$$

or

$$f = F/D$$

If the brightest point in the scene has 128 times more luminance than the darkest point (seven stops), then we say it has a seven-stop scene-brightness ratio.

Exposure, ISO, and Lighting Relationships

The units we deal with in exposure are
- f/stops
- ASA, ISO, or EI (different names for the same thing)
- Foot-candles or lux
- Output of sources as affected by distance
- Reflectance of objects in the scene
- Exposure time (frame rate and shutter angle)

It turns out that all of these can be arranged in analogous ways. They all follow the same basic mathematical pattern. Remember that f/stop numbers are fractions, the relationship of the aperture diameter to the focal length of the lens.

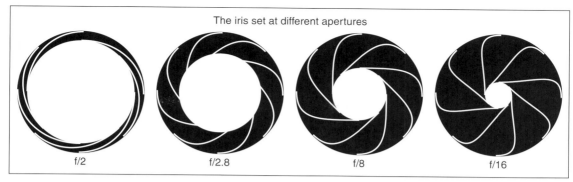

The iris set at different apertures

f/2 f/2.8 f/8 f/16

FIGURE 6.1 The aperture at various f/stops.

For example, f/8 really means ⅛; the diameter is ⅛ the focal length. And f/11 is ¹⁄₁₁, which is obviously a smaller fraction than ⅛. Each time we open the aperture one whole f/stop, we double the quantity of light reaching the film; each time we close it one stop, we halve the light reaching the film.

The f/stop scale is tiered to show that the same relationships that apply to whole f/numbers, such as f/8 and f/11, apply to intervals between them. So the difference between f/9 and f/13 is one whole stop, etc. Modern digital meters measure in one-tenths of a stop. This is helpful for calculations and comparisons, but for most practical purposes, this level of accuracy is not necessary. One-third of a stop is the practical limit of precision, given the vagaries of optics, lab chemistry, and telecine transfer. This is not to say that accurate exposure is not important—only that the degree of precision in the overall process has limits.

Lighting Source Distance

The f/stop scale applies to the inverse square law of illumination. Changes in illumination due to distance with

FIGURE 6.2 (**a**) A lens aperture closed down. (**b**) The aperture nearly wide open.

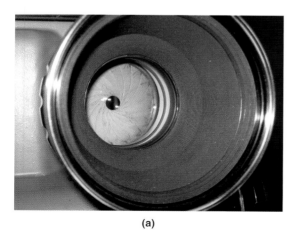

(a)

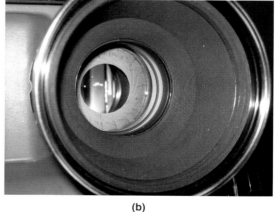

(b)

Table 6.1 ISO or ASA in One-Third Stop Increments*

6			12			25			50			100			200			400			800		
	8			16			32			64			125			250			500			1000	
		10			20			40			80			160			320			640			1250

*The same series can be interpreted as percentage of reflection or shutter speeds or quantity of light (foot-candles).

small sources follow this scale (see Table 6.1). For example, if the lamp is 11 feet from the subject, moving it to 8 feet will increase the subject illumination by 1 stop, just as opening the lens diaphragm from f/11 to f/8 would do. The inverse square law applies to point sources, strictly speaking, but spotlights follow it fairly well at the distances usually utilized.

ISO/ASA Speeds

Because one-third stop is the minimum exposure difference detectable by the unaided eye (for most negative stocks—reversal film for transparencies require greater precision), film sensitivity is rated in no finer increments than this. This scale is tiered to make the relationships between intervals more easily seen. Just as ISO 200 is 1 stop faster than ISO 100, so ISO 320 is 1 stop faster than ISO 160.

Although this is obvious memorizing this scale makes it easier to see the differences between odd intervals, such as ISO 80 to ISO 32 ($1\frac{1}{3}$ stops). The scale may be expanded in either direction by adding or subtracting digits (the intervals below 6 are 5, 4, 3, 2.5, 2, 1.6, just as the intervals below 64 are 50, 40, 32, 25, 20, and 16.

Foot-candles: The ISO scale can also be applied to foot-candles. Doubling the foot-candles doubles the exposure. The third-stop intervals give the intermediate fc values. For example, the difference between 32 fc and 160 fc is $2\frac{1}{3}$ stops.

Percentage of reflection: The ISO scale from 100 on down relates to percentage of reflection. For example, ISO 100 can represent 100%, pure white. Other reflectances, such as 64% and 20%, can then be seen to be, respectively, $\frac{2}{3}$ stop and $2\frac{1}{3}$ stops darker than pure white (Table 6.2).

Shutter speeds: Referring to the ISO scale, it can be seen that, for example, $\frac{1}{320}$ sec is $1\frac{2}{3}$ stops faster than $\frac{1}{100}$ sec. This can be helpful when unusual combinations of shutter angle and frame rate produce odd effective shutter speeds.

Table 6.2

F/Stops		$-\frac{1}{3}$	$-\frac{2}{3}$	-1	$-1\frac{1}{3}$	$-1\frac{2}{3}$	-2	$-2\frac{2}{3}$	-3	$-3\frac{1}{3}$	$-3\frac{2}{3}$	-4	$-4\frac{1}{3}$
REFLECTANCE	100%			50%			25%			12%			6%
		80%			40%			20%			10%		
			64%			32%			16%			8%	

Chemistry of Film

The energy in each photon of light causes a chemical change to the photographic detectors that are coated on the film. The process whereby electromagnetic energy causes chemical changes to matter is known as "photochemistry."

All film is coated onto a base: a transparent plastic material (celluloid) that is 4 to 7 thousandths of an inch (0.025 mm) thick. Onto the base, the emulsion adheres where the photochemistry happens. There may be 20 or more separate layers coated here, each individually less than one-thousandth of an inch in thickness. Some of the layers coated on the transparent film do not form images. They are there to filter light, or to control the chemical reactions in the processing steps. The imaging layers contain submicron-sized grains of silver halide crystals that act as the photon detectors.

These crystals are the heart of photographic film. These crystals undergo a photochemical reaction when they are exposed to various forms of electromagnetic radiation— light. In addition to visible light, the silver halide grains can be sensitized to infrared radiation. A halide is a chemical compound of a halogen (any of a group of five chemically related nonmetallic elements including fluorine, chlorine, bromine, iodine, and astatine) with a more electropositive element or group—in this case, silver. Silver halide grains are manufactured by combining silver nitrate and halide salts (chloride, bromide, and iodide) in complex ways that result in a range of crystal sizes, shapes, and compositions.

The unmodified grains are sensitive only to the blue part of the spectrum, and thus are not very useful in camera film. Spectral sensitizers are added to the surface of the grains to make them more sensitive to blue, green, and red light. (Remember, we're talking about black-and-white film here.) These molecules must attach to the grain surface and transfer the energy from a red, green, or blue photon to the silver halide crystal as a photoelectron. Other chemicals are added internally to the grain during its growth process, or on the surface of the grain. These chemicals affect the light sensitivity of the grain, also known as its speed—that is, how sensitive it is to light.

The speed of an emulsion is quantified by standards set by the ISO (International Standards Organization) or ASA (American Standards Association) rating.

ISO is the technically the correct designation, but by tradition, most people still refer to it as ASA. The higher the ASA, the lower the light level the film is capable of responding to. For color film, manufacturers list the sensitivity of film as EI, or Exposure Index. When you make film faster, the trade-off is that the increased light sensitivity comes from the use of

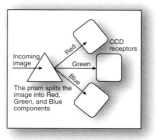

FIGURE 6.3 The image-capture section of a 3-chip video or HD camera.

larger silver halide grains. These larger grains can result in a blotchy or grainy appearance to the picture. Photographic film manufacturers are constantly making improvements that result in faster films with less grain. For Kodak, a major advance was the introduction of "T" grains in the 1970s. These tabular grains are roughly triangular, which allows them to be packed closer together, thus reducing apparent grain. Other recent improvements include the family of Vision stocks from Kodak and technical innovations from Fuji.

Film's Response to Light

There are two steps in the making of a negative:
- *Exposure.* The useful property of silver halide is that its state is altered when subjected to light, in direct proportion to the amount of light energy absorbed. This change is not visible, and if film is examined before and after exposure, little change can be seen.
- *Development.* Silver halide that has been altered by contact with light can be reduced to pure silver if placed in contact with specific chemicals referred to as developing agents. The activity of the developer and time of development will determine how much of the sensitized halide will be converted.

The Latent Image

When the shutter is open, light affects the chemistry of the emulsion and a latent image is formed. When a photon of light is absorbed by the spectral sensitizer sitting on the surface of a silver halide grain, the energy of an electron is raised into the conduction band from the valence band, where it can be transferred to the conduction band of the silver halide grain electronic structure.

This atom of silver is unstable. However, if enough photo-electrons are present at the same time in the crystal lattice, they may combine with enough positive holes to form a stable latent image site. A latent image site must contain a minimum of 2 to 4 silver atoms per grain to remain stable. A silver halide grain contains billions of silver halide molecules, and it takes only 2 to 4 atoms of uncombined silver to form the latent image site. In color film, this process happens separately for exposure to the red, green, and blue layers of the emulsion. The reason for this is simple—there is no way to sensitize a grain to color; you can only sensitize it to a specific band of the spectrum. The image that is formed is called "latent" because it remains invisible until chemically developed.

Any photon that reaches the film but does not form a latent image is lost information. Most color films generally take

20 to 60 photons per grain to produce a developable latent image. This is called the "inertia point" for the film. Below the inertia point, no image is recorded at all. Video receptors are silicon-based and, of course, are different in operation, but the basic theory is quite similar.

Chemical Processing

For the latent image to become visible, it must be amplified and stabilized to make a negative or a positive (Figure 6.4). In black-and-white film, the silver halide grains have to be sensitized to all wavelengths of visible light, so the silver halide grains are coated in just one or two layers. As a result, the development process is easier to understand.

- The film is placed in a developing chemical bath, which serves as a reducing agent. If the film is left in the solution long enough, the reducing agent converts all the silver ions into silver metal—resulting in a uniform gray fog with no discernible image. Those grains that have latent image sites will develop more rapidly. If the film is left in the developing bath for the proper amount of time, only grains with latent image information will become pure silver. The unexposed grains remain as silver halide crystals.
- The development process must be stopped at the right moment. This is done by rinsing the film with water, or by using a stop bath that brings the development process to a halt.
- After development, some of the altered halide and all of the unaltered silver halide ions remain in the emulsion. The material must be removed or the negative will darken and deteriorate over time. The removal of this undeveloped material is accomplished with fixing agents, usually sodium thiosulfate (hypo) or ammonium thiosulfate. The process is called fixing. The trick is to fix just enough and not too much, as excessive contact with fixers can begin to remove some of the desirable silver material.
- Finally, the film is washed with water to remove all the processing chemicals. Then it is dried. The washing must be extremely thorough.

When all the steps are finished, the film has a negative image of the original scene. Other types of chemistry can

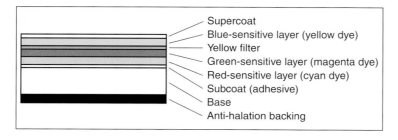

Supercoat
Blue-sensitive layer (yellow dye)
Yellow filter
Green-sensitive layer (magenta dye)
Red-sensitive layer (cyan dye)
Subcoat (adhesive)
Base
Anti-halation backing

FIGURE 6.4 The layers of color negative film.

FIGURE 6.5 A typical color negative.

result in a positive image, but this is not commonly used in motion picture applications. It is a negative in the sense that it is darkest (has the highest density of opaque silver atoms) in the area that received the most light exposure. In places that received no light, the negative is clear.

Color Negative

Color negative is basically three layers of black-and-white film, one on top of the other (Figure 6.5). The difference is that each layer is treated with a different spectral sensitizer so that it is receptive to a different band of the spectrum. These translate roughly into red, blue, and green.

- With color film, the development steps use reducing chemicals, and the exposed silver halide grains develop to pure silver. Oxidized developer is introduced into this reaction, and the oxidized developer reacts with chemicals, called couplers, in each of the image-forming layers. This reaction causes the couplers to form a color, and this color varies depending on how the silver halide grains were spectrally sensitized. A different color-forming coupler is used in the red-, green-, and blue-sensitive layers. The latent image in the different layers forms a different colored dye when the film is developed.
- The development process is stopped either by washing or with a stop bath.
- The unexposed silver halide grains are removed using a fixing solution.
- The silver that was developed in the first step is removed by bleaching chemicals. (Note: it is possible to skip this step or reduce it so that some of the silver remains in the negative. This is the basis of "skip bleach" or ENR processing, which is discussed elsewhere.)
- The negative image is then washed to remove as much of the reagents and reaction products as possible. The film strips are then dried.

Unlike a black-and-white negative, a color negative contains no silver with the exception of those treated by the special processes referred to above and known as "bleach bypass."

The end result is a color negative in the sense that the more red exposure, the more cyan dye is formed. Cyan is a mix of blue and green (or white minus red). The green-sensitive image layers contain magenta dye, and the blue-sensitive image layers contain yellow dye.

The colors formed in the color negative film are based on the subtractive-color formation system. The subtractive system uses one color (cyan, magenta, or yellow) to control each primary color. The additive color system uses a combination of red, green, and blue to produce a color. Video is based on an additive system. The overall orange hue of a color negative is the result of masking dyes that help to correct imperfections in the color reproduction process.

Additive vs. Subtractive Color

In a photograph, the colors are layered on top of one another, so a subtractive-color reproduction system is used. In subtractive color, each primary is affected by its opposite on the color wheel.

- Red-sensitive layers form a cyan-colored dye.
- Green-sensitive layers form a magenta-colored dye.
- Blue-sensitive layers form a yellow-colored dye.

The H&D Curve

To understand film response we must look at its curve. This classical approach to densitometry (the scientific analysis of exposure) was devised by Hurter and Driffield in 1890; hence it is called the H&D curve or sometimes the D log E curve. It plots the amount of exposure E in logarithmic units along the horizontal axis and the amount of density change in the negative D along the vertical axis. This is sometimes shortened to log E curve (Figure 6.6).

In theory, it makes sense that we would want the film to change in density in exact proportion to change in the amount of light reflected by different parts of the scene. After all, we are trying to make an image that accurately portrays the real scene, right?

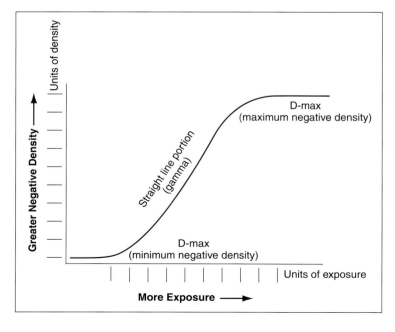

FIGURE 6.6 The Hurter and Driffield D log E curve for negative density.

FIGURE 6.7 A theoretical ideal film—one that exactly reproduces the exposure changes of the subject in a one-to-one ratio with negative density.

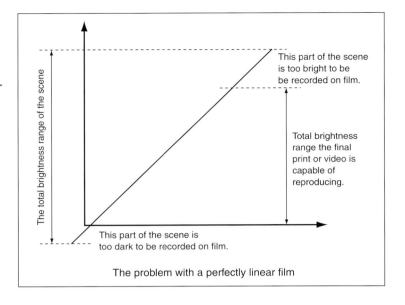

The total brightness range of the scene

This part of the scene is too bright to be be recorded on film.

Total brightness range the final print or video is capable of reproducing.

This part of the scene is too dark to be recorded on film.

The problem with a perfectly linear film

Let's look at a theoretical linear film (Figure 6.7). For every additional unit of exposure, the density of the negative changes exactly one unit. That is, the correspondence between the amount of light in the scene and the change in the density of the negative is exact. Sounds perfect, doesn't it? The slope of the line for this film would be precisely 45 degrees.

The slope of this line is a measure of the "contrastiness" of the film. In a film where large changes in exposure only change the negative density a little (low-contrast reproduction), the slope is very shallow. Where a film is very contrasty, the slope is very high; in other words, small changes in the amount of light cause the film density to change drastically. The extreme is something called "litho" film, which is used in the printing industry. Everything to litho film is either black or white—there are no shades of gray. That is, if the light is above a certain level, the image is completely white. If it is below a certain level, it is completely black. This is as contrasty as a film can get. The slope for litho film would be a vertical line.

No film acts in the perfectly linear manner of this first example (i.e., the changes in the film exactly correspond to the change in the amount of light). In this diagram, we see a film that only changes $\frac{1}{2}$ unit of density for each additional unit of light. This is a low-contrast film.

Figure 6.8 shows the difference between a high-contrast and a low-contrast emulsion. In the high-contrast example, for each additional unit of exposure, it changes 2 units of negative density. Looking at the brightness range of the exposure against the brightness range of the negative

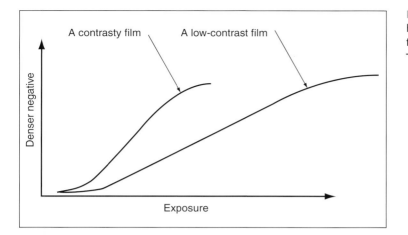

FIGURE 6.8 Differences between a high-contrast and a low-contrast film.

density, we see that it will show more contrast in the negative than actually exists in the scene. The slope of this line is called the "gamma" of the film: it is a measure of its contrastiness.

Contrast refers to the separation of lightness and darkness (called "tones") in a film or print and is broadly represented by the slope of the characteristic curve. Adjectives such as flat or soft and contrasty or hard are often used to describe contrast. In general, the steeper the slope of the characteristic curve, the higher the contrast. The terms "gamma" and "average gradient" refer to numerical means for indicating the contrast of the photographic image.

Gamma is measured in several different ways, as defined by both scientific organizations and manufacturers. They are all basically a way of calculating the slope of the straight-line portion of the curve more or less by ignoring the shoulder and the toe portions of the curve. Gamma is the slope of the straight-line portion of the characteristic curve, or the

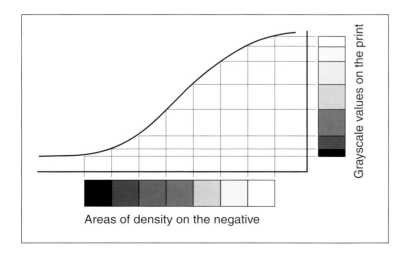

FIGURE 6.9 Grayscale compression in the toe and shoulder.

tangent of the angle *a* formed by the straight line with the horizontal. The tangent of the angle *a* is obtained by dividing the density increase by the log exposure change. Gamma does not describe contrast characteristics of the toe or the shoulder, only the straight-line portion.

But there's another wrinkle. In the lowest range of exposure, as well as in the highest range, the emulsion's response changes. In the lowest range, the film does not respond at all as it sees the first few units of light. There is no change in the photochemistry at all until it reaches the inertia point, where the amount of light first begins to create a photochemical change in film or an electrical change on a video tube. After reaching the inertia point, it begins to respond sluggishly: negative density changes only slightly for each additional unit of light. This region is the toe of the curve. In this area, the changes in light value are compressed (Figure 6.10).

At the upper end of the film's sensitivity range is the shoulder. Here also, the reproduction is compressed. The emulsion is becoming overloaded; its response to each additional unit of light is less and less. The end result is that film does not record changes in light value in the scene in a linear and proportional way. Both the shadows and the highlights are somewhat crushed together. This is, in fact, a big part of what gives film the film look that video has not yet been able to achieve (High Def comes a lot closer than previous systems, but still has trouble with the highlights). It is a way of compressing very contrasty scenes so that they fit onto the film.

The Log E Axis

Let's think about the log E axis (horizontal) for a moment. It is not just an abstract scale of exposure units. Remember that it represents the various luminances of the scene. All

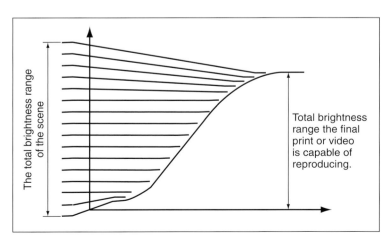

FIGURE 6.10 Compression of the real-world brightness values so that they fit onto the film. This is what makes it possible to make usable images, even from scenes with high-contrast ranges. The same principle applies to video, whether analog or digital.

The total brightness range of the scene

Total brightness range the final print or video is capable of reproducing.

scenes are different, and thus all scenes have different luminance ratios. What we are really plotting on the horizontal axis is the range of luminances in the scene, from the darkest to the lightest.

In 1890, the German physiologist E. H. Weber discovered that changes in any physical sensation (sound, brightness, pain, heat) become less noticeable as the stimulus increases. The change in level of stimulus that will produce a noticeable difference is proportional to the overall level: if three units of light create a perception of brightness that is just noticeably brighter than two units, then the smallest perceptible increase from 20 units of light will require 30 units. To produce a scale of steps that appear to be uniform, it is necessary to multiply each step by a constant factor. In fact, the perception of brightness is logarithmic.

What Is a Log?

Logarithms are a simple way of expressing large changes in any numbering system. If, for example, we wanted to make a chart of something that increases by multiplying by 10—1, 10, 100, 1000, 10,000, 100,000, etc.—we very quickly reach numbers that become unwieldy because they are so large. It would be extremely difficult to make a graph that could handle both ends of such a range.

In log base 10, the most common system, the log of a number represents the number of times 1 must be multiplied by 10 to produce the number. You must multiply 1 by 10 once to make 10, so the log of 10 is 1. To arrive at 100, you multiply 1 by 10 twice, so the log of 100 is 2. The log of a number is the exponent of 10; i.e., $10^2 = 100$, so the log of 100 is 2. Ten to the 4th power (10^4) 10^4 is 10,000, so the log of 10,000 is 4 (Table 6.3). This means that we can chart very large changes in quantity with a fairly small range of numbers. Logs are used throughout lighting, photography, and video.

Brightness Perception

Our perception of brightness is logarithmic, and we'll see that this has far-ranging consequences in all aspects of lighting for film and video. If we chart the human perception of brightness in steps that appear smooth to the eye, we can follow its logarithmic nature. It is apparent that each step up in a seemingly even scale of gray tones is, in terms of its measured reflectance, spaced logarithmically. As we'll see later, this chart is in fact fundamental to the entire process of lighting and image reproduction.

Remember that these are not fixed values (the darkest point on the log E axis is not a certain number of foot-candles/sq-ft,

Table 6.3 Logs and Reflectance of Surfaces

Number	Log
1	0.0
2	0.3
4	0.6
8	0.9
10	1.0
16	1.2
32	1.5
64	1.8
100	2.0

Perception	% Reflectance
White	100%
	70%
	50%
	35%
	25%
Middle gray	17.5%
	12.5%
	9%
	6%
	4.5%
Black	3.5%

for example), because we open or close the aperture of the camera to adjust how much light reaches the film, and we use faster or slower film and so on. What really counts is the *ratio* between the darkest and lightest, and that is what we are plotting on the log E axis. This is called the brightness range of the film, sometimes abbreviated as BR. Each unit on the log E axis represents one stop more light.

Contrast

The word "contrast" has different meanings, depending on whether you are talking about the contrast of the subject you are photographing or the negative you will use to make the print. In general, *contrast* refers to the relative difference between dark and light areas of the subject or negative. *Subject contrast* refers to the difference between the amounts of light being reflected by the darker, or shadow, areas of the scene and the lighter, or highlight, areas (for example, a dark door as opposed to a white wall).

Negative contrast refers to the relative difference between the more transparent areas of the negative and those that are more opaque. The negative is described in terms of density. These densities can be measured with an instrument called a densitometer, which measures how much light passes through the negative and how much is held back. The contrast of photographic subjects can vary a great deal from one picture to another. On clear, sunny days the contrast of an exterior scene can be great, while on cloudy days it can be relatively low in contrast. The contrast of a given scene depends on how light or dark the objects in the picture are when compared to each other and how much light is falling on them. Let's get back to our theoretically ideal film. This film would change the density of the negative exactly one unit for each one unit of change in the brightness of the subject.

No reproduction medium now known is capable of reproducing anything near the brightness range exhibited in most real-world situations. Nearly all film emulsions are nonlinear. This linearity fails for two reasons.

- It takes a certain amount of light energy to initiate the activation of the photosensitive elements in the emulsion (the inertia point). Thus the density rises gradually at first in this area (called the toe), finally accelerating into the straight-line portion of the curve.
- With increasing exposure to light, more silver halide is converted, until it has no more sensitive material to activate. At that point, increasing the exposure does not increase the ultimate density of the developed negative. This saturation occurs gradually and produces what is known as a shoulder.

The toe of the film is a result of the fact that film reacts slowly to small amounts of light. It is only when greater amounts of light reach the emulsion that the change becomes linear. This is the straight-line portion of the film. The film base itself always has some density, however slight. On top of this, there is always a slight amount of fog engendered by light scattering in the camera, the lens, the emulsion, and also chemical fog in the processing. The cumulative effect of all of these is called "base-plus-fog." Density measurements are usually described as x density above base-plus-fog.

This toe and shoulder behavior results in a compression of the actual scene. If the contrast gradient of the film is correct and exposure is correct, this compression behavior will allow the full brightness range of the scene to be represented on the final print. In effect, it is the failure of film emulsion and video receptors to represent accurately the real world that allows us to produce photographs and video that are usable. Each film emulsion reacts to light in a special way. Some react more quickly to low light than others, creating a rather abrupt initial rise in density, or short toe. Others react more gradually to increases in light and have a long toe. Films with similar sensitivities and ranges can have quite different response curves requiring dissimilar exposure and development.

Another important factor is the range of subject luminance, which can be usefully recorded. Low-contrast films can continue to build density over a long luminance range, whereas contrasty films saturate rather quickly and tend to block at either end. This is how we can match the type of film used to the type of scene being photographed. Cinematographer David Watkin used a low-contrast film stock for the movie *Out of Africa*, where he dealt with many very contrasty situations in the harsh African sun. The results were outstanding. Both Fuji and Kodak now make emulsions that are more moderate in contrast than normal film stocks.

Determining the precise film speed, coupled with precise exposure, is critical when the range of light in the scene is greater than the scale of the film. In Figure 6.11, we see three exposures of the same scene represented by the bars at the bottom of the diagram. Not enough exposure places much of the information completely off the low end of the curve, while too much exposure places it off the high end—in either case, once you are off the curve, further changes in exposure register no change in the negative; the film doesn't see them. The ideal exposure places all of the information where it makes some change on the negative.

If there is too much exposure, two things happen. First, even the darkest parts of the scene are in the middle range

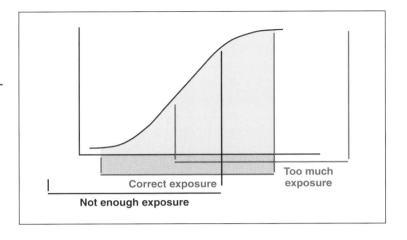

of the curve: even the darkest shadows will reproduce as middle gray tones. Graphically, overexposure appears as a shift of the subject brightness range (log E) to the right. (In effect we are making the scene values brighter by opening up the aperture.) Here we see that this overexposure places the scene values too much in the shoulder. Some information is lost in the flat part of the shoulder: lost, because the differences of scene brightness values result in a lack of change in the density of the negative.

Furthermore, because everything is shifted to the right, none of the scene values falls in the toe of the curve: there will be no deep black values at all in the final print, even though they existed in the original scene. Underexposure is shown as a shift of the log E values to the left. Here every subtle nuance of the high tones will be recorded because they fall in the straight-line portion of the curve. But at the dark end of the scale—trouble. The dark values of the scene are mushed together in the toe. There is little differentiation among the medium gray values, the dark gray values, and the black shadows: in the final print, they will all be an undifferentiated black hole. The shadows will reveal no detail.

"Correct" Exposure

"Correct" exposure, then, is essentially the aperture setting that will best suit the scene brightness range (the horizontalaxis: log E) to the characteristic curve of the imaging medium. What is needed is to slip the scene values comfortably between the toe and the shoulder. A typical scene with a seven-stop range of light values fits nicely on the curve if we place the exposure exactly in the middle. It is important to remember, however, that correct exposure is a purely technical thing; there are occasions when you will

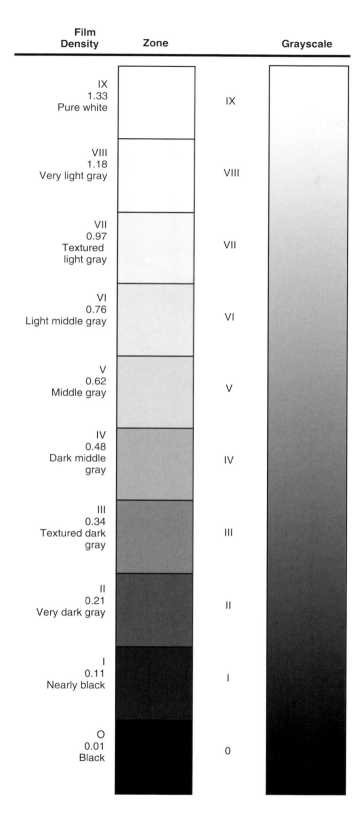

Film Density	Zone	Grayscale
IX 1.33 Pure white	IX	
VIII 1.18 Very light gray	VIII	
VII 0.97 Textured light gray	VII	
VI 0.76 Light middle gray	VI	
V 0.62 Middle gray	V	
IV 0.48 Dark middle gray	IV	
III 0.34 Textured dark gray	III	
II 0.21 Very dark gray	II	
I 0.11 Nearly black	I	
O 0.01 Black	0	

FIGURE 6.12 Zones 0 through IX, a stepped grayscale and a continuous grayscale. By convention, zones are represented in Roman numerals.

want to deviate from ideal exposure for pictorial or technical reasons. The relationship of the gamma (the angle of the straight-line portion of the film) to the toe and the shoulder is what determines a film's latitude. It can be viewed as two characteristics: the emulsion's room for error in exposure or the capacity of the film to accept a certain brightness range.

Brightness Range in a Scene

The problem is exacerbated if we consider a scene that has more than seven stops of brightness (seven stops is just an average; it all depends on the particular film stock). Here there is no aperture setting that will place all of the values on the useful part of the curve. If we expose for the shadows (open up the aperture), we get good rendition of the dark gray areas, but the light values are hopelessly off the scale. If we expose for highlights (by closing down to a smaller f/stop), we record all the variations of the light tones, but the dark values are pushed completely off the bottom edge.

How do we deal with this situation? Later we'll discuss some rather abstruse solutions to the problem (flashing, Varicon, Panaflasher, etc.), but there is one solution that is really what we're all about: we change the brightness range of the scene so it will fit the curve of the film. In other words, we alter the illumination of the scene. This is done by lighting or by modifying the existing lighting. This, then, is one of the most essential jobs of lighting and grip work: to render the scene in a scale of brightness values that can be accommodated by the optics and emulsion of a film camera or by the optics and electronics of video. It's why we get the big bucks. It is also critical in the choice of locations, camera angles, and time of day to shoot.

Modern films have consistently improved in latitude even as they have increased in speed and reduced grain. The new high-speed emulsions, in particular, are amazing in their ability to record subtleties even in heavily overexposed highlights and in very dark shadows. Although there has been some improvement, the ability to handle brightness ratios is still one of the most crucial differences between film and video.

Determining Exposure

So we have two basic tasks:
- To manipulate the brightness ratio of the scene so that it can be properly reproduced on film or video.
- To set the aperture so that the scene values fall on the appropriate part of the curve.

In practice these often turn out to be two sides of the same coin. The first task is essentially the work of lighting and lighting control; the second task involves measuring the

Table 6.4 Percentage of Reflectance for Zones

Zone X	100%
Zone IX	70%
Zone VIII	50%
Zone VII	35%
Zone VI	25%
Zone V	17.5%
Zone IV	12.5%
Zone III	9%
Zone II	6%
Zone I	4.5%
Zone 0	3.5%

Table 6.5 Zones, Negative Density, and Description

Zone	Density	Description
0	0.02	Dmax (Black)
I	0.11	First perceptible value lighter than black
II	0.21	Very, very dark gray
III	0.34	Fully textured dark gray
IV	0.48	Dark middle gray
V	0.62	Middle gray—18% reflectance
VI	0.76	Light middle gray
VII	0.97	Fully textured light gray
VIII	1.18	Very light gray
IX	1.33	First perceptible gray darker than pure white
X	1.44	Pure white

scene and making a judgment about the best setting for the lens.

Figure 6.15 shows how film speed is determined by the manufacturer. Strictly speaking, this method applies only to black-and-white film. The speed of color film is determined by testing and is expressed as either EI (exposure index) or ISO (International Standards Organization) number for black-and-white film and as EI for color film. Although they are not as commonly used as they once were, you will still hear reference to "lighting ratio." The lighting ratio is the relationship of the key light to the fill light. If we consider the average face, it is the difference between the lighter side and the darker side.

The Tools

The two most basic tools of the cameraman's trade are the incident meter and the spot meter. There is a third type of meter, the wide-angle reflectance meter (what still photographers would simply call a "light meter"), but it has extremely limited use in film.

The Incident Meter

The incident meter measures scene illumination only. In other words: the amount of light falling on the scene. To accomplish this purpose, most incident meters use a hemispherical white plastic dome which covers the actual sensing cell.

The diffusing dome accomplishes several purposes. It diffuses and hence averages the light that is falling on it. It also approximates the geometry of a typical three-dimensional subject. Unshielded, the dome will read all of the front lights and even some of the side-back and back-light that might be falling on the subject. Left to itself, the hemisphere would provide a reasonable average of all the

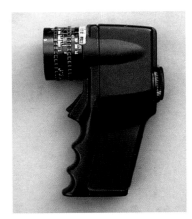

FIGURE 6.13 A spot meter—a specialized form of reflectance meter.

FIGURE 6.14 An incident meter.

sources falling on the subject. In practice, many people use their hand to shield the backlight off the reading and use a combination of hand shielding and turning the meter to read the backlight and sometimes the key, fill, side lights, and backlights separately.

The classical practice, however, is to point the hemisphere directly at the lens, eliminate only the backlights, and then take a reading exactly at the subject position. Reading key, fill, and backlight separately is, in fact, only a way of determining the ratios and looking for out-of-balance sources. The actual reading, which will determine the aperture setting, is the averaging one. Later we will look at applications which go beyond the simple classical approach and are useful in dealing with unusual situations. Most meters that are used with the diffusing dome also come with a flat diffusing plate, which has a much smaller acceptance angle (about 45° to 55°) and has a cosine response rather than an averaging one. This means that the angle of the light falling on the plate has an effect on the reading, just as it does in illuminating a subject.

The flat plate makes taking readings for individual lights simpler and is also useful for measuring illumination on flat surfaces, as in art copy work, animation plates, etc. Incident meters are generally also supplied with a lenticular glass plate which converts them to wide acceptance-reflectance meters. These see little use on most sets as they have very wide acceptance angles and it is difficult to exclude extraneous sources from the reading.

For the most part, incident meters are set for the film speed and shutter speed being used (either electronically or by using slide-in plates) and then read out directly in f/numbers. Some meters have an alternative mode which reads foot-candles directly; the user is then able to calculate exposure separately. This is useful if there is no slide for the EI being used.

The Reflectance Meter

Reflectance meters read the actual luminance of the subject, which is itself an integration of two factors: the light level falling on the scene and the reflectivity of the subject (Figure 6.14).

On the face of it, this would seem to be the most logical method of reading the scene, but there is a catch. Simply put, a spot meter will tell us how much light a subject is reflecting but this leaves one very big unanswered question: how much light do you want it to reflect? In other words: incident meters provide absolute readouts (f/stops) while spot meters provide relative readouts which require interpretation. While most spot meters were formerly calibrated in exposure value (EV) units, some of the new electronic spot meters provide direct readout in f/stops, but it would probably be better if they didn't, as they are a source of much confusion.

Think of it this way: you are using such a meter and photographing a very fair-skinned girl holding a box of detergent in front of a sunset. You read the girl's face: f/5.6, the box reads f/4, the sky is f/22. So where are you? Not only do we not know where to set the aperture, we don't even know if the situation is good or bad. Let's step back a moment and think about what it is that light meters are telling us. To do this we have to understand the cycle of tone reproduction and lay down a basic system of thinking about it.

The Zone System

We must remember that the exposure values of a scene are not represented by one simple number: most scenes contain a wide range of light values and reflectances. In evaluating exposure we must look at a subject in terms of its light and dark values: the subject range of brightness. For purposes of simplicity, we will ignore its color values for the moment and analyze the subject in terms of its monochromatic values.

Let's visualize a continuous scale of gray values from completely black to completely white (Figure 6.12). Each point on the grayscale represents a certain value that is equivalent to a tonal value in the scene. In everyday language we have only vague adjectives with which to describe the tones: "dark gray," "medium gray," "blinding white," and so on. We need more precise descriptions. Using Ansel Adams's classic terminology, we will call the most completely black section Zone 0 and each tone that is one f/stop lighter is one zone higher. For example, a subject area that reflects three stops more light than the darkest area in the scene would be designated Zone IV. It is crucial to remember that these are all relative. Zone 0 is not some predetermined number of footcandles—it is the darkest area in this scene.

Still photographers might be accustomed to thinking of ten zones in all, but if there is a great contrast range in the scene, there might well be zones XII, XIII, or more. (Zone system purists will no doubt object to such an extreme simplification of the method, but it is sufficient for the present discussion since few cinematographers do their own darkroom work.) What we are measuring is subject brightness (luminance), which can vary in two ways: its inherent reflectance and the amount of light that falls on it. Reflectance is a property of the material itself. Black velvet reflects about 2% of the light that falls on it. A very shiny surface can reflect up to 98% of the light that falls on it. This is a brightness ratio (BR) of 1:48.

However, this is the reflectance ratio if the same amount of light falls on both objects. In reality, different amounts of light fall on different areas in the same frame (indeed, we earn our living making sure they do). In natural light situations the reflectance ratio can be as much as 3200:1. Picture the most extreme example possible: a piece of deeply absorbent velvet in dark shadow in the same scene with a mirror reflecting the sun.

The brightness range of a typical outdoor subject is about 1000:1. This is 15 stops, but here's the rub: imaging systems cannot reproduce this range of subject brightness, just as the human eye cannot accommodate such a range. Recall that the human eye reacts in two different ways. First, the iris (the aperture of the eye) expands or contracts to allow more or less light to pass. Second, the eye shifts its imaging from the cones to the rods. This is like switching to a higher speed film.

Zones in a Scene

Examine a typical scene with the spot meter—see Figure 6.13. If you assign the darkest value to Zone 0, you can then find areas that are 1, 2, 3, 4, 5, 6, 7, and perhaps 8 stops brighter than the darkest area. These are Zones I through IX. This is an important exercise and is vital to understanding exposure control. Ignoring the effect of color contrast can be cumbersome. It can be helped by viewing the scene through a viewing glass, which is a neutral density filter.

Now picture each of these tonal values arranged in ascending order. What you have is a grayscale, and fortunately it is a commonly available item. Most grayscales are made to reasonably rigorous densitometric standards and are useful calibration tools. Let's take a look at what it really is.

The Grayscale

There are a great many grayscales, but they all have one thing in common: they vary from black to white. Most are divided into 6 to 10 steps, but they certainly don't have to be: many are 20 steps or more. How white the white is and how black the black is vary somewhat, depending on the printing quality and the materials involved. Some scales include a piece of black velvet since black paper can never be truly black. For our purposes, we will consider only gray scales in which each step represents one full stop increment over the previous—that is, where each step is $\sqrt{2}$ times the reflectance of the previous one.

Why 18%?

Zone V is the middle zone of a 10-zone scale, and we would therefore assume it to be 50% reflectance. It isn't—it is 18% reflectance. The reason for this is that the eye perceives changes in tone logarithmically rather than arithmetically,

FIGURE 6.15 The Zone System as applied to a black-and-white photo.

as we saw above. If each zone were, for example, 10% more reflective than the previous one, the eye would not read it as a smooth spectrum.

Discussion of the zone system is always in terms of grays, but any color can be interpreted in terms of its grayscale value. The importance of value cannot be stressed too much. The value relationships between colors carry about 90% of the information in any picture. In a black-and-white photograph the gradients of light and shadow on surfaces contains the information about form, clearly defining all the objects. The black-and-white photo also contains the information about the amount and direction of light in the scene. Color contributes a small amount of information, but a great deal of the beauty and interest of the picture.

Each step is greater than the previous by $\sqrt{2}$; a familiar number, no? The square root of 2 is also the derivation of the f/stop series. What appears middle gray (Zone V) to the eye is actually 17.5% reflectance, which is universally rounded off to 18%. There's more: it turns out that if you take dozens of spot readings of typical scenes, most will turn out to have an average reflectance of about 18%. Simply put: 18% is the average reflectance of the normal world. Clearly it is not the average reflectance in a coal mine or in the Sahara at midday, but in most of the rest of the world it is a reasonable working average. This gives us a solid ground on which to build. In fact, it is the standard on which incident meters are built. As you recall, in the introduction to incident meters we noted that most incident meters, when set for film speed and shutter speed, read out directly in f/stops.

How do they do this? How can they know if we are photographing diamonds on a white background or a chimney-sweep in the basement? They don't know; they just assume that we are photographing a scene of average reflectances, that the diffusing dome averages the light, and that the meter calculates the f/stop needed to photograph the scene for good exposure based on these assumptions. More simply: if we are photographing a card that is exactly 18% reflectance (a photographic gray card) and we read the light with an incident meter and set the aperture to the stop the meter indicates, the print will, in fact, come out to be Zone V.

Try this experiment. Set a photographic gray card in even, uniform light. Read it with a spot meter and note the f/stop the meter indicates. Then read the light with an incident meter. The readings should be exactly the same. If they're not, have your meters checked. Now try a reverse experiment. Read a uniformly lit scene with an incident meter and notice the indicated stop. Now take the spot meter and read various parts of the scene until you find something that the spot meter indicates as the same f/stop. You have just found a Zone V subject brightness.

Now photograph the scene with a black-and-white Polaroid or with black-and-white film. Compare the Zone V subject with the gray card: they should be roughly the same. This is the simple key that unlocks the world of exposure control:
- an incident reading,
- an average 18% reflectance,
- a spot meter reading of a gray card, and
- Zone V

are all the same thing looked at from a different perspective.

As a result, you have many different ways to read the exposure of a scene and arrive at the same result.
- You can read it with an incident meter.
- You can place a gray card in the scene and read it with a spot meter.
- You can find something in the scene that is Zone V and read it with the spot meter.

Let's think about that last one, because it really points us in a whole new direction. It depends on your making a certain judgment. You have to look at a scene in the real world of color and decide that it is about Zone V or middle gray. (It takes some practice to do this, but it is an incredibly important exercise; I urge you to do it often.) What about the next logical step? What if there isn't anything in the scene that is middle gray? What do we do then? Let's remember that each step on the grayscale is one stop different from its neighbor (remember, this is a simplified version of the Zone system). So if Zone V equals f/4 (given a particular film and shutter speed), then Zone VI must be f/5.6 and Zone IV must be f/2.8, right?

So if there's nothing in the scene that equals Zone V, but there is something in the scene that equals Zone VI, we're still in business. If it equals f/5.6, then we know that Zone V would be f/4. We also know that Zone V (f/4 in this example) is the same as an incident or average reading and is therefore the correct f/stop to set on the lens.

So what is there that we can count on to be roughly Zone VI under most conditions? Easy one: Caucasian skintone. Average Caucasian skin is around Zone VI; it is in fact one of the few constants we can count on. Get out your light meter and check it out. If you are ever stuck without an incident meter, or worse, without a spot meter, you can always use the old "palm trick." Use your spot meter or any reflecting meter to read the palm of your hand. This equals Zone VI. Then open up one stop to get Zone V and you have your reading. There is a greater variation in non-Caucasian skin, so there is no one standard; however, many DPs take Zone V as a starting point for African-Americans.

I think you can see where this is leading us. We don't have to confine ourselves to just reading things that equal Zone V and Zone VI: in fact, we can do it with any zone. It all depends on your judgment of what gray tone a subject brightness should have. In real life, it takes years of practice and mental discipline to accurately determine subject brightnesses in terms of grayscale values, but in the long run it is a useful skill. If you can previsualize what grayscale value you want a particular subject to be in the final print, you then have the power to place it where you want it in the exposure range. This turns out to be a powerful analytical and design tool.

Place and Fall

What do we mean by "placement"? We just saw it in its simplest form. We placed the skin-tone value of the hand on Zone VI. We can, if we want, place any value in the scene. Say we have a gray background in the scene that the director wants to be light gray. We decide that by light gray, she means Zone VII (two stops above middle gray). We then read the background with a spot meter and it indicates f/4. We then count down two stops and get f/2. If we set the lens at f/2, that gray background will photograph as light gray or Zone VII.

Let's try the reverse as a thought experiment. Say we had the same background under exactly the same lighting conditions, but the director decided she wanted it to be dark gray, which we take to mean Zone III. We read it with the spot meter and of course nothing has changed; the spot meter still indicates f/4, only now we want the gray background to appear much darker, so we place it on Zone III, counting up two stops to get f/8. Common sense tells us that if we photograph the scene at f/8 instead of f/2, it is going to come out much darker in the final print: the gray background will not be Zone III (dark gray) but Zone VII (light gray) instead.

Nothing has changed in the actual set; we have changed the value of the final print by placing the value of the background differently. But what's the fly in this ointment? There is more in the scene than just a gray background, and whatever else is there is going to be photographing lighter or darker at the same time. This brings us to the second half of the process: fall.

If you place a certain value in a scene on a certain zone, other values in that scene are going to fall on the grayscale according to how much different they are in illumination and reflectance. For our example, let's assume we are using a Pentax Spotmeter which has a zone dial attached to it. The Pentax reads in EVs. Typical white skin tone is a Zone VI; you read an actor's face and find that it reads EV 10. Turn the dial so that 10 aligns with Zone VI. Now read the exposure indicated opposite Zone V: this is the exposure to set the lens aperture, adding adjustments for filter factors, etc.

Let's try an example. We are lighting a set with a window. We set a 10K to simulate sunlight streaming in through the window. We then read the curtains and the spot meter indicates f/11. We have decided that we want the curtains to be very hot, but not burned out. On the film stock we are using today, we know that white burns out at about three stops hotter than Zone V. So we want to place the curtains on Zone VIII (three stops hotter than the average exposure). By placing the curtains on Zone VIII, we have determined the f/stop of the camera: it will be f/4, right?

We then take an incident reading in the room where the people will be standing. The incident reading is f/2.8. This means that people standing in that position will photograph one zone too dark. Maybe for this scene that's OK, but let's assume we want to actors to have normal exposure, which will result in normal skin tone values. In other words Zone VI falls at f/4 (one stop above the incident reading, which equals Zone V). Their skin tones will come out as Zone V instead of Zone VI.

To correct the situation, we have to change the balance. If we just open up the lens, we shift the placement of the curtains, causing them to burn out. We must change the ratio of the illumination, not just shift the aperture of the camera. We can either tone down the 10K hitting the window with a double scrim (reducing it one stop) or we can raise the exposure of the subject area by increasing the light level there one stop. Either way, are manipulating the subject values of the foreground to fall where we want them, based on our placement of the curtains on Zone VIII. We could just as easily have approached it from another direction, of course. We could place the foreground values where we want them and then see where the curtains fall. It's the same thing. By reading the scene in different ways, you can place the values of the negative where you want them to fall.

Placement is important in determining subject brightness ranges and contrast ratios and in reading subjects you can't get to for an incident reading. In order to expose by placement you must previsualize which zone you want a subject value to reproduce as. For Ansel Adams, the godfather of exposure, previsualization was what it was all about—and remember, he dealt mostly with landscapes over whose lighting he had no control.

Reading Exposure with Ultraviolet

Ultraviolet lights present a special problem. Several companies make ultraviolet light sources, including Wildfire and Nocturn. When combined with props or clothing painted with UV-sensitive fluorescent paints or dyes or with objects that naturally fluoresce (such as your old Jimi Hendrix poster), an incident reading is meaningless. The only valid means of assessing exposure is a reflected reading. A wide-angle reflectance meter will work (if you have one), or you can get an adapter for your incident meter. If neither is available, a spot reading will work. Here, it is important to consider the zone values and then use your own good judgment and calculate the exposure accordingly.

The Shutter

Nearly all film cameras have rotating reflex shutters, which control exposure by alternately rotating closed and open sections past the film plane: while the closed section is in front of the film gate, the film moves; while the open section is in front of the gate, the film is exposed. Some video cameras also have variable exposure times; this is not done mechanically such as in a film camera. In video changing the shutter speed is done electronically on most cameras.

The exposure time of the camera is determined by two factors: the speed at which the shutter is operating and the size of the open section. The speed is determined by the frame rate at which the camera is operating. The open section of the rotating shutter assembly is known as the "shutter angle" and is measured in degrees. Sensibly, most shutters are half-open and half-closed, which makes the shutter angle 180°. Some shutters are 165°, and many are adjustable (Table 6.6).

With the camera operating at 24 fps and a 180° shutter, the exposure time is $^1/_{48}$ of a second ($^1/_{50}$ at European 25 fps).

Table 6.6

180° Shutter	Exposure (in stops)	165° Shutter	120° Shutter
180	No change	165	120
140	$-^1/_3$	130	100
110	$^2/_3$	100	80
90	1	80	60
70	$1^1/_3$	65	50
55	$1^2/_3$	50	40
45	2	40	30
35	$2^1/_3$	30	
30	$2^2/_3$	25	
22	3	20	
18	$3^1/_3$	15	

Table 6.7

FPS	8	12	16	24	25	32	48	96	120	240					
	$^1/_{16}$	$^1/_{24}$	$^1/_{32}$	$^1/_{50}$	$^1/_{50}$	$^1/_{60}$	$^1/_{100}$	$^1/_{200}$	$^1/_{250}$	$^1/_{500}$					

FPS	24	25	30	32	38	48	60	76	96	120	150	190	2 40	300	380	480
Stops	Normal	$^1/_3$	$^1/_2$	$^2/_3$	1	$1^1/_3$	$1^2/_3$	2	$2^1/_3$	$2^2/_3$	3	$3^1/_3$	$3^1/_3$	4	$4^1/_3$	

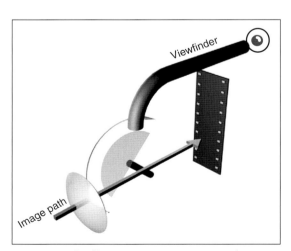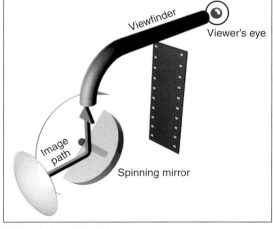

FIGURE 6.16 The film camera spinning mirror shutter open (left) and closed (right).

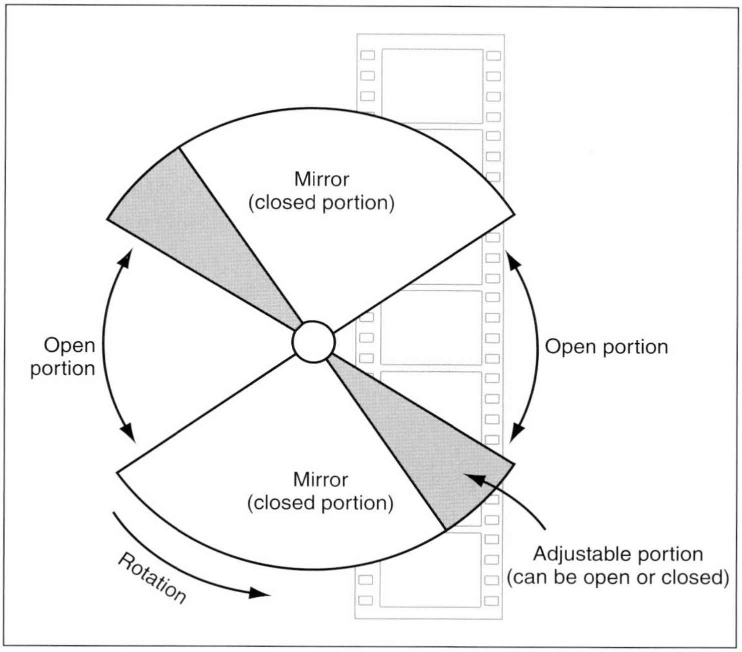

FIGURE 6.17 The spinning mirror shutter (butterfly type).

This is commonly rounded off to $^1\!/_{50}$ of a second and is considered the standard motion picture exposure time.

For light meters that use different slides for various ASAs, just assume $^1\!/_{50}$ of a second exposure. Exposure time can then vary in two ways: by changing the frame rate (which is common) and by varying the shutter angle (which is less common). Exposure is determined by this formula:

Shutter speed for 180° shutter $= ^1\!/_2 \times$ fps
Exposure in seconds $=$ shutter opening (degrees)$/360$
$\times$ frames per second

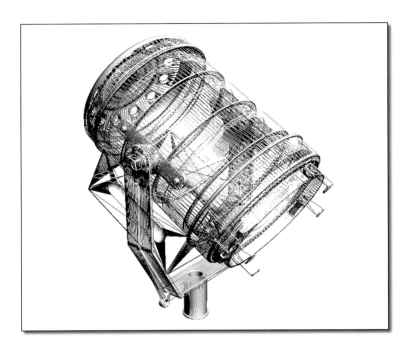

THEORY AND CONTROL

OF COLOR

The Nature of Light

Light is composed of photons, which have the properties of both matter and light. Even Newton recognized that individual photons don't have color, but they do have different properties of energy that cause them to interact in different ways with physical matter. When reflected, light is perceived by the eye/brain combination as color.

Visible light is a small part of the continuous spectrum of electromagnetic radiation, most of which is not directly observable, and, indeed, was unknown until the 19th century. The visible spectrum extends from red to violet—the colors of the rainbow. They were originally classified as

Red, Orange, Yellow, Green, Blue, Indigo, and Violet. (R-O-Y-G-B-I-V). Below the visible spectrum is infrared radiation and above violet are ultraviolet, x-rays, and gamma rays. Indigo is no longer recognized as a color of the spectrum so the I is no longer used. Whereas once students memorized it as Roy G. Biv, Roy has lost the vowel in his last name and we are now stuck with Roy G. Bv.

For our purposes, it is conventional to consider visible light a wave, as it exhibits all the properties of a wave and follows the same rules as all electromagnetic waves.

Color Perception

The perception of color is a complex phenomenon that involves the physics of light, the nature of physical matter, the physiology of the eye, its interaction with the brain. Sometimes, even social and cultural factors play a role in the perception of light. We can break it down to five aspects:

- Abstract relationships: purely abstract manipulation of color for its own sake.
- Representation: for example, a sky is blue, an apple is red.
- Material concerns: texture—chalky, shiny, reflective, dull, etc.
- Connotation and symbolism: associative meanings, memory, cultural significance, and so on.
- Emotional expression: the fiery red of passion, the cold blue of night, etc.

Most people can tell you that the three primary colors in light are red, green, and blue, but few can say why these, of all colors, are the primaries. The reason is in our eyes.

The Tristimulus Theory

The human retina is filled with two kinds of light receptors, called rods and cones (Figure 7.3). The rods are primarily responsible for the perception of light and dark: value or grayscale.

The cones primarily perceive color. The retina has three kinds of cones. The response of each type of cone as a function of the wavelength of the incident light is in Figure 7.4. The peaks for each curve are at 440 nm (blue), 545 nm (green), and 580 nm (red).

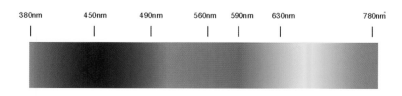

FIGURE 7.1 The naturally occurring color spectrum and respective wavelengths in nanometers.

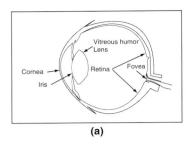

(a)

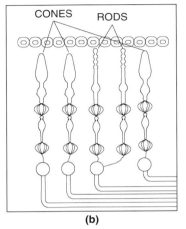

(b)

FIGURE 7.3 (**a**) Physiology of the eye. (**b**) Rods and cones in the retina.

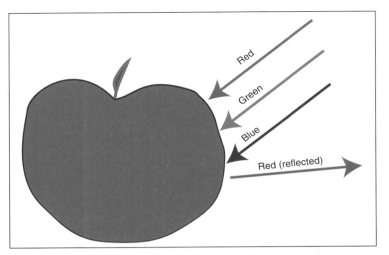

FIGURE 7.2 The color of an object is determined by what parts of the spectrum it reflects.

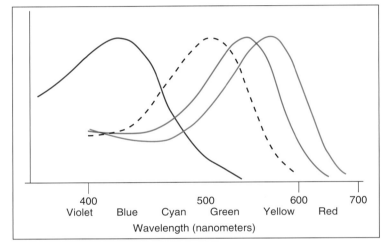

FIGURE 7.4 Color response of the red, green, and blue cones in the eye. The dashed line represents the response of the rods.

There are about seven million cones in each eye. Located primarily in the central portion of the retina called the fovea, they are highly sensitive to color. People can resolve fine details with these cones largely because each one is connected to its own nerve end. Muscles controlling the eye always rotate the eyeball until the image of the object of our interest falls on the fovea. Cone vision is known as photopic or daytime vision.

Other light receptors, called rods, are also present in the eye, but they are not involved in color vision. Rods serve to give a general, overall picture of the field of view, and are receptive only to the quantity of light waves entering the eye. Several rods are connected to a single nerve end; thus, they cannot resolve fine detail. Rods are sensitive to low levels of illumination and enable the eye to see at night or under extremely low lighting conditions. Therefore, objects that appear brightly colored in daylight, when seen by the color-sensitive cones, appear only as colorless forms by moonlight because only the rods are stimulated. This is known as scotopic vision.

The Purkinje Effect and Movie Moonlight

As the adjacent spectral sensitivity curves show, the eye is not equally sensitive to all wavelengths. In dim light, particularly, there is a definite shift in the apparent brightness of different colors. This was discovered by Johannes von Purkinje. While walking at dawn one day, von Purkinje observed that blue flowers appeared brighter than red, while in full daylight the red flowers were brighter than the blue. This is now called the Purkinje effect and is particularly important in photometry—the measurement of light. The Purkinje effect fools the brain into perceiving moonlight as slightly blue, even though, as reflected sunlight, it is the same color as daylight. This is the reason it is a convention to light night scenes blue.

Light and Color

Color is light, but the color of objects is a combination of the color of the light and the nature of the material it is falling on and being reflected by. Essentially, the color of an object is the wavelengths of light it does *not* absorb. Sunlight appears white—it contains all colors. Light is an additive system of color. Red, Green, and Blue are the primaries. When mixed in pairs, they produce Magenta, Cyan, and Yellow (a hot red, a blue/green, a bright yellow). The mixture of all colors in light creates white. The human eye has receptors (cones), Red/Green, Blue/Yellow, which translate light waves of differing length to the optic nerve. The eye is not equally sensitive to all colors. This has far-ranging implications in color theory, exposure, and even light meters.

Additive and Subtractive Color

The additive color system involves light emitted directly from a source before an object reflects the light. The additive reproduction process mixes various amounts of red, green, and blue light to produce other colors. Combining one of these additive primary colors with another produces the additive secondary colors cyan, magenta, yellow. Combining all three primary colors produces white.

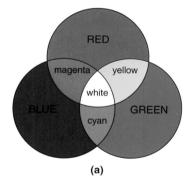

(a)

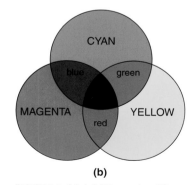

(b)

FIGURE 7.5 (**a**) Additive color. (**b**) Subtractive color.

Paint is a subtractive system of color. The primaries are Red, Blue, and Yellow. The mixing of paint removes (subtracts) light. All colors mixed would produce a muddy gray brown, or theoretically black.

Qualities of Light

Color has four basic qualities: hue, value, chroma, and temperature. The first three are physical properties and are often called the dimensions of color. The last is a psychological aspect of a color.

Hue

A hue is a wavelength of light. It is that quality by which we give names to color (red, yellow, blue, etc.). The average person can distinguish around 150 distinct hues. The hue of a color is simply a definition of its wavelength: its place on the natural color spectrum. In video it is called "phase" and is measured around a circle from 0° to 360° (see Chapter 5, Lighting HD, DV, SD, and Video).

Hue, chroma (saturation), and value (lightness/darkness) make up the three distinct attributes of color (in addition to the fourth—temperature). The terms "red" and "blue" are primarily for describing hue—hue is related to wavelength for spectral colors.

Value

Value is relative lightness or darkness of color. Every pure hue has its own value before mixing. No color is as dark as black or as light as white, but pure violet is darker than pure orange, yellow is lighter than green, etc. The average person can distinguish about 200 distinct value changes.

Chroma

Chroma is the strength of the color or relative purity of a color—its brilliance or dullness (grayness). Any hue is brightest in its pure state, when no black or white has been added to it. Adding black or white or both (gray), or adding the color's complement (the color opposite it on the color wheel) lowers the intensity, making a color duller. A color at its lowest possible intensity is said to be neutral. The average person can see only about 20 levels of chroma change.

Color Temperature

Another aspect of a color is temperature. The temperature is the relative warmth or coolness of a hue. This derives from the psychological reaction to color—red or red/orange being the warmest and blue or blue/green, the coolest. It has been proved that people coming in from the cold to a room painted in cool colors take longer to feel warm than those

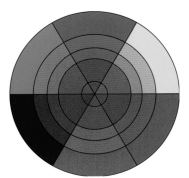

FIGURE 7.6 Value on the color wheel. Value is basically "lightness" in color.

coming into a room painted in warm colors. Even body temperature has been found to differ by a few degrees in rooms painted warm to those painted cool. Color temperature is derived from physical temperature—a neutral body when heated will first glow red, then orange, and eventually white.

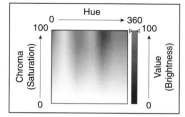

FIGURE 7.7 Hue, chroma, and value.

The Color Wheel

Artists have found it helpful to bend the linear spectrum around in a circle called the color wheel. The British scientist Sir Isaac Newton, who discovered the spectrum in the seventeenth century, also turned it into a color wheel.

On the color wheel, instead of being at opposite extremes, red and violet lie next to each other. A circular spectrum better describes our perception of the continuous flow of hues, and it establishes opposites across the diameters. The color wheel is created by wrapping the visible spectrum into a circle and joining the far red end (long wavelengths) to the far violet end (short wavelengths).

Primary colors are hues that cannot be mixed and from which all other colors can be mixed. In light they are red, green, and blue. Secondary colors are hues made by mixing two primaries

RED + BLUE = Magenta

BLUE + GREEN = Cyan

RED + GREEN = Yellow

Tertiary colors are combinations of the secondary colors. The primary, secondary, and tertiary colors together make up the twelve colors of the basic color wheel.

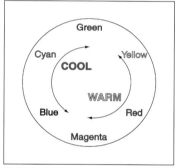

FIGURE 7.8 Warm and cool colors.

Color Mixing

Complementarity

Hues directly opposite each other on the color wheel are called complements. They are called complements because they contain or complete the triad of primary colors—for example, the primary red is opposite the secondary green, which contains the primaries yellow and blue.

Advancing and Retreating Color

Another psychological response: the hottest colors move forward aggressively as do black, brown, dark blue, and dark green. Pale cool tones retreat, pale green and blue the furthest. Yellow, though light, advances when intense.

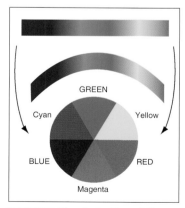

FIGURE 7.9 The derivation of the color wheel from the spectrum—as devised by Newton.

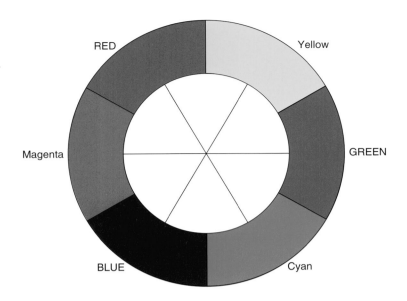

RED

Yellow

Magenta

GREEN

BLUE

Cyan

Weight and Balance

The way we see color depends not only on the color itself but also on the size of each color area, on the shapes that contain the color, and on the interaction between neighboring colors. Darker hues, like darker values, tend to be heavier looking than lighter ones, yet warm intense colors like yellow and orange can overpower a darker color.

Transparency and Reflection

Both transparency and reflection tend to lighten color. Transparency is the ability to see through the color to another under it. Reflection on a form as well as transparency will lighten it. In paint the transparency and reflective quality of the paint will affect the value and intensity of the color as well; this principle is used in set painting, prop, and wardrobe—and can affect lighting choices.

Film and Video Colorspace

The medium, whether it is paint, television, film, fabric, or printed matter, also affects the possible range of colors, i.e., the combination of all the possible variations in hue, value, and chroma that can be achieved in a medium, is referred to as its color gamut. In monitors and video systems, it is often referred to as colorspace.

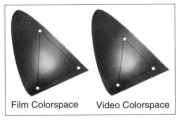

Film Colorspace   Video Colorspace

FIGURE 7.11 Relative colorspace of film and video.

Color Harmonies and Interaction of Color

Like music, color can be strongly emotive and expressive. Certain combinations of color, as of sound, seem to have a special beauty or be intrinsically pleasing in ways most people recognize intuitively. The notions of balance and resolution are implied in color harmony. Harmony refers to clear relationships based on divisions of the color wheel. Some examples of color harmony follow:

- *Monochrome color harmony*—This refers to a harmony of tones of all the same hue but at different values and intensity (e.g., tints and shades of blue).
- *Analogous color harmony*—This is a harmony of hues close to or touching one another on the color wheel, although of different values and intensities (i.e., yellow-green; green and blue-green; or yellow, green, and blue).
- *Triadic harmonies*—These harmonies are based on groups of three colors more or less equidistant from one another on the color wheel. The three primary or the three secondary colors form triadic harmonies, but any group of three will serve, if they are evenly spaced around the color wheel.
- *Complementary harmonies*—These harmonies involve the pairing of any two colors that sit opposite each other on the color wheel (e.g., red with green, yellow with violet).
- *Split complementary harmonies*—These harmonies group a color not with its complement, but with the pair of colors adjacent to its complement (e.g., yellow with red-violet and blue-violet, blue with yellow-orange and red-orange, red with yellow-green and blue-green).
- *Discord and discordant colors*—Colors can be mismatched or out of harmony, often referred to as clashing colors. This happens when a grouping of harmonious colors is placed next to a color outside the harmony.

Interaction of Color and Visual Phenomena

All perception of color is based on an interaction of color. One color cannot be seen unless it has others around it. Scientists have put individuals in a room painted in one color. The subjects could not distinguish what color the room was; instead, they saw white. Only when another color was introduced to the environment were they able to see color. More important is the understanding of how color changes when surrounded by or touching other colors. The effect of simultaneous contrast is greatest at the edges between colors or on patterns of small scale.

Degradation of colors is one color adjacent to another color, giving a tinge of its complement to the other color. Therefore, two adjacent complementary colors brighten each other. Therefore, noncomplementary colors will have the opposite effect. A yellow next to a green will give the

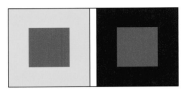

FIGURE 7.12 Simultaneous contrast in practice.

green a violet tinge, making the latter appear muddy. This is known as the degradation of color.

The Laws of Simultaneous Contrast

Devised by the French chemist Michel-Eugene Chevreul, the law of simultaneous contrast was first described in his book *The Law of Simultaneous Contrast* written in 1839. When one object is next to another, it is useful if any color difference between them is emphasized. Think of a man in a brown jacket standing in front of a brick wall. He is easier to distinguish if the eye/brain combination emphasizes whatever color difference exists between the jacket and the wall. To do this, the visual system modifies our perception of the red in both the jacket and the wall, but the adjustment is larger in the jacket since it is smaller and surrounded by the wall. The result of this adjustment is called simultaneous contrast. Put more simply: our perception of a color is changed by a color that surrounds and touches it. Both colors are actually changed by being next to each other. When two different colors come into direct contact, the contrast intensifies the difference between them (Figure 7.12).

A light color next to a dark color will appear lighter and the dark will appear darker. The same is true for hue (e.g., yellower/greener), temperature (hotter/cooler), and chroma (brighter/duller).

- Colors are modified in appearance by their proximity to other colors.
- All light colors seem most striking against black.
- Dark colors seem most striking against white.
- Dark colors upon light colors look darker than on dark colors.
- Light colors upon dark colors look lighter than light colors.
- Colors are influenced in hue by adjacent colors, each tinting its neighbors with its own complement.
- If two complementary colors lie side by side, each seems more intense than by itself.
- Dark hues on a dark ground which is not complementary will appear weaker than on a complementary ground.
- Light colors on a light ground which is not complementary will seem weaker than on a complementary ground.
- A bright color against a dull color of the same hue will further deaden the color.
- When a bright color is used against a dull color, the contrast will be strongest when the latter is complementary.
- Light colors on light grounds (not complementary) can be greatly strengthened if bounded by narrow bands of black or complementary colors.

- Dark colors on dark grounds (not complementary) can be strengthened if similarly bounded by white or light colors.

Metamerism

All this is closely related to metamerism. Two colors that match under one light source but do not match under a different light source are called metamers. They are said to be a metameric match. Metamerism occurs because the appearance of a color depends on the wavelengths it reflects which, in turn, depend on the wavelengths of the light source.

This can have an important influence on the selection of colors for sets or props, especially in the case of green screen or blue screen work. Always take the light source into consideration when previewing paint chips, wardrobe, makeup, etc. Obviously, this is the reason that the makeup room and wardrobe trailer should have a light source that approximates what will be used on the set.

The CIE Color System

The CIE color models are highly influential systems for measuring color and distinguishing between colors. The CIE color system was devised by the CIE (*Commission International de l'Eclairage*—the International Commission on Illumination) in 1931 and has since become an international standard for measuring, designating, and matching colors (Figure 7.14). In the CIE system, the relative percentages of each of the theoretical primary colors (red, green, blue) of a color to be identified are mathematically derived and then plotted on a chromaticity diagram as one chromaticity point, whereupon the dominant wavelength and purity can be determined. All possible colors may be designated on the chromaticity diagram, whether they are emitted, transmitted, or reflected. Thus, the CIE system may be coordinated with all other color designation systems. Any color on the CIE chromaticity diagram can be considered to be a mixture of the three CIE primaries, X, Y, and Z. That mixture may be specified by three numbers X, Y, and Z, called "tristimulus values."

The light from a colored object is measured to obtain its spectral power density (SPD) and the value for the SPD at each wavelength is multiplied times the three color-matching functions and summed to obtain X, Y, and Z. These values are then used to calculate the CIE chromaticity coordinates.

Standard Light Sources in CIE

The following CIE standard sources were defined in 1931:
- Source A—A tungsten-filament lamp with a color temperature of 2854K

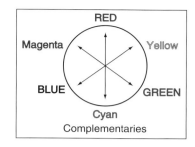

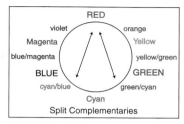

FIGURE 7.13 (**a**) Complementaries are two colors directly across from each other on the color wheel. (**b**) Split complementaries are the two colors on either side of the complementary.

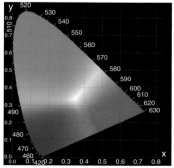

FIGURE 7.14 A diagram of the CIE color system.

- Source B—A model of noon sunlight with a temperature of 4800K
- Source C—A model of average daylight with a temperature of 6500K.

This is slightly different from the standard 5500 K daylight as defined by the U.S. government. The 5500 K standard is still widely used for lighting instruments, globes, and correction gels.

Digital and Electronic Color

Electronic color is displayed on television and computer screens through the use of a cathode-ray tube (CRT). A CRT works by moving back and forth behind the screen to illuminate or activate the phosphor dots on the inside of the glass tube. Color monitors use three different types of phosphors that appear red, green, and blue when activated. These phosphors are placed close together and, when combined in differing intensities, can produce many different colors. The primaries of electronic color are therefore red, green, and blue, and other colors can be made by combining different intensities of these three colors. There are differences in the measurement system of analog and digital video. The intensity of each color is measured on a scale from 0 to 255 (in the digital system), and a color is specified by telling the monitor the RGB values. For instance, yellow is specified by telling the computer to add 255 red, 255 green, and 0 blue.

FIGURE 7.15 Typical sources as defined in degrees Kelvin.

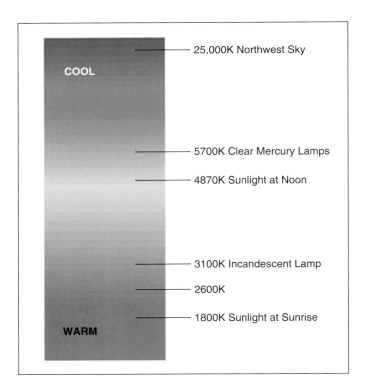

COOL

25,000K Northwest Sky

5700K Clear Mercury Lamps

4870K Sunlight at Noon

3100K Incandescent Lamp

2600K

1800K Sunlight at Sunrise

WARM

Control of Color

What Is White?

The eye will accept a wide range of light as white, depending on external clues and adaptation. The phenomenon is both psychological (adaptation) and environmental. The color meter (and color film, which is very objective about these things) will tell us that there are enormous differences in the color of light in a room lit with tungsten light, one lit with ordinary fluorescents, and one flooded with noon daylight. Our perception tells us that all three are white light, mostly because we are psychologically conditioned to think of them as white and physiologically, the eye adapts. Without a side-by-side comparison, the eye is an unreliable indicator of what is neutral light. Unfortunately, color film emulsions and video CCDs are extremely sensitive and unforgiving. An absolute color reference is essential.

Color Temperature

In film and video production, the most common system used in describing the color of light is color temperature. This scale is derived from the color of a theoretical black body (a metal object having no inherent color of its own, technically known as a Planckian radiator). When heated to incandescence, the black body glows at varying colors depending on the temperature. Color temperature is a quantification of the terms "red hot," "white hot," etc.

Developed by Lord Kelvin, the 19th-century British scientific pioneer, color temperature is expressed in Kelvin in his honor. On the Celsius scale, the freezing point of water equals 0°. The Kelvin scale takes absolute zero as the zero point. Absolute zero is −273° Celsius on the Kelvin scale; thus 5500 Kelvin is actually 5227° Celsius. Kelvin is abbreviated K and the degree symbol is omitted. Because a tungsten filament heated to incandescence is very similar to a Planckian radiator, the color temperature equivalence is very close for tungsten halogen lamps, but not for HMIs, CIDs, and fluorescents. A graphic representation of the various wavelengths is called an SED (spectral energy distribution) or SPD (spectral power distribution).

When a metal object (such as the tungsten filament of a lightbulb) is heated to incandescence, its SED is quite similar to that of a Planckian radiator and is fairly smooth across all wavelengths, even if some are stronger than others. This is not necessarily true for all light sources. Fluorescent lights, for example, have very spiky outputs, which tend to be heavy in green.

Table 7.1 Strategies for Dealing with Off-Color Sources

Existing Source	Your Lights	Strategy	Comments
Any fluorescents	None or fluorescents	Shoot fluorescent balance	Use fluorescents only (adding fluorescent fill if necessary) and let the lab time the green out of the print
Any fluorescents	Tungsten or HMI	Replace the lamps	Remove existing fluorescent lamps and replace with "full spectrum" fluorescent bulbs, which provide photographic daylight or tungsten balance
Cool white fluorescents	HMIs	Gel the fluorescents (daylight balance)	Add minusgreen gel to the existing fluorescents, which removes the green. With cool white fluorescents, this will result in daylight balance. Tungsten lights can be blued or HMIs used.
Warm white fluorescents	Tungsten	Gel the fluorescents (tungsten balance)	Add minusgreen gel. With warm white fluorescents, this will result in a tungsten balance. Tungsten lights may be used or HMIs with 85.
Cool white fluorescents	HMIs	Gel the HMIs	Add plusgreen to the HMIs, which matches them to the heavy green output of the fluorescents. Then use a camera filter to remove the green or have the lab time it out.

Table 7.2 Typical Camera Filtration for Common Industrial Sources*

Film Type	Existing Source	Camera Filters
Tungsten	High-Pressure Sodium	808 + CC 30M
	Metal Halide	85 + CC50M
	Mercury Vapor	85 + CC50M
Daylight	High-Pressure Sodium	808 + CC508
	Metal Halide	81A + CC30M
	Mercury Vapor	81A + CC 50M

*Always confirm with film testing, a Polaroid or digital photo.

Color temperatures can be very misleading; for many sources (especially those exhibiting discontinuous SEDs), it is only an approximation and is referred to as "correlated color temperature." Color temperature tells us a great deal about the blue/orange component of light and very little about the magenta/green component, which can produce extremely unpleasant casts in the film even if the meter indicates a correct reading for the color temperature.

An approximate measure of how close a source is to a pure black body radiator is the color rendering index (CRI), a

Cool White Fluorescent   Tungsten 3200K

Plusgreen 50

Warm White Fluorescent   Tungsten 3200K

Minusgreen ¼ CTO

Cool White Fluorescent   Daylight 5500K

Cool White Fluorescent   Tungsten 3200K

Fluorofilter

Cool White Fluorescent   Daylight 5500K

Warm White Fluorescent   Tungsten 3200K

Minusgreen ¼ CTO

Optima 32   Tungsten 3200K

Cool White Fluorescent   Daylight 5500K

Minusgreen

Cool White Fluorescent   Tungsten 3200K

Plusgreen 50

Cool White Fluorescent   Daylight 5500K

Minusgreen

Optima 32   Tungsten 3200K

Cool White Fluorescent   Tungsten 3200K

Fluorofilter

FIGURE 7.16 Various combinations of daylight, tungsten, and fluorescent sources as corrected by various combinations of Rosco gels.

FIGURE 7.17 The Gossen Color Pro color meter. (Photo courtesy of Gossen Foto- und Lichtmesstechnik GmbH).

scale of 1 to 100 which gives some indication of the ability of a source to render color accurately. For photographic purposes, only sources with a CRI of 90 or above are generally considered acceptable.

Color Meters

We measure light in two ways: blue/orange and green/magenta. Think of it as a separate axis for two different aspects of color. They are completely independent. A light can be green or magenta regardless of how blue or orange it is. Color meters measure these two axes separately.

Most light sources are not a narrow band of the spectrum; hence they are not a pure hue. Most colored light is a combination of various wavelengths; there is no one number that can describe the color accurately. Rather, it is defined on two scales: red/blue and magenta/green. As a result, most meters give two readouts (they are called three-color meters, since they measure red, blue, and green), one for the warm/cool scale and one for the magenta/green scale. In the case of the Gossen color meter, the magenta/green readout is not in absolute numbers, but directly in amount of filtration needed to correct the color to normal on the magenta/green scale; this is the CC index or color correction index. It describes the green/magenta aspects of the color source. It is most relevant when shooting with fluorescents, sodium vapor, mercury vapor, or other types of discharge sources that usually have a large green component.

Another problem with color temperature is that equal changes in color temperature are not necessarily perceived as equal changes in color. A change of 50K from 2000K to 2050K will be a noticeable difference in color. For an equivalent change in color perception at 5500K, the color temperature would need to shift 150K, and about 500K at 10,000K.

For this reason, the mired system has been devised. Mired stands for microreciprocal degrees. Mireds are derived by dividing 1,000,000 by the Kelvin value. For example, 3200K equals 1,000,000/3200 = 312 mireds. To compute how much color correction is required, you use the mired values of the source and the final desired color. If you have source at 5500K and wish to convert it to 3200K, subtract the mired value of the desired color from that of the source. 5000K = 200 mireds. 3200K = 312 mireds and then 312 − 200 = 112 mireds. 85 orange has a mired value of +112. On the mired scale, a plus shift value means the filter is yellowish; a minus value means the filter will give a blue shift. When combining filters, add the mired values.

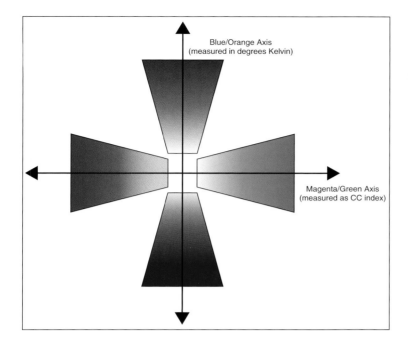

FIGURE 7.18 Color of light is measured along two independent axes—one for red/blue and another for green/magenta.

Color Balance of Film

No color film can accurately render color under all lighting conditions. In manufacture, the film is adjusted to render color accurately under a particular condition, the two most common being average daylight (type D film), which is set for 5500K, and average tungsten illumination (type B film) designed for 3200K. There is a third, which is based on the now disused "photo" bulbs, which were 3400K (type A film), rather than 3200K; these are rare now.

Given the fact that providing tungsten light is costly and electricity-intensive, while sunlight is usually far more abundant, most motion picture films are type B, balanced for tungsten. The idea is that we put a correcting filter on when we can most afford to lose light to a filter factor—in the sunlight. Kodak and Fuji now have several daylight balance films available.

Color Balance with Camera Filters

There are three basic reasons to change the color of lights:
- To correct the color of the lights to match the film type (instead of using a camera filter)
- To match various lighting sources
- For effect or mood

To shoot with type B film under blue light (in the 5500° area), an 85 orange filter is used. The 80A or 80B blue filters for shooting daylight film with tungsten light are rarely used as they absorb so much light and are very inefficient. There is some light loss when using a correction filter and the filter

Table 7.3 Conversion Values and Light Loss

	Typical Conversion	Mired Value	Stop Loss
CTO filters			
85	5500K >3200K	+131	¾ stop
Full CTO	5500K > 2900K, 6500K > 3125K	+167	⅔ stop
½ CTO	5500K > 3800K, 4400K > 3200K	+81	½
¼ CTO	5500K > 4500K, 3800K > 3200K	+42	⅓
⅛ CTO	5500K > 4900K, 3400K > 3200K	+20	⅓
CTB filters			
CTB, Full Blue	3200K > 5500K	−131	1½
½ CTB, Half Blue	3200K > 4100K	−68	1
⅓ CTB, ⅓ Blue	3200K > 3800K	−49	⅔
¼ CTB, ¼ Blue	3200K > 3500K	−30	½
⅛ CTB, ⅛ Blue	3200K > 3300K	−12	⅓

factor must be used to adjust the T/stop. For convenience, most manufacturers list an adjusted EI (exposure index) which allows for the filter loss.

When using this adjusted EI, do not also use the filter factor. EI is not technically the same as ASA (American Standards Association), which is the scale used to rate film for still photography, but in practice they are the same. This is because the speed of color film is not measured in the same way as black-and-white emulsion (see Chapter 6).

You will also notice two different EIs on cans of black-and-white film as well. This is not related to correction filters, since none is needed. It has to do with the fact that black-and-white films vary in their sensitivity to colors. In most cases the EI for tungsten light will be ⅓ stop lower. Most black-and-white films available today are panchromatic, meaning they are relatively sensitive to most of the visible spectrum. Early black-and-white films were orthochromatic; they were not sensitive to blue light at all. This meant that actors with blue eyes appeared to have white eyes. Smaller color mismatches can also be corrected with color filters as well. If the scene lighting is 2800K, for example (too warm), then an 82C filter will correct the light reaching the film to 3200K.

There are three basic filter families used in film and video production: conversion, light-balancing, and color-compensating. This applies to both lighting gels and camera filters.

Conversion Filters

Conversion filters work in the blue-orange axis and deal with fundamental color balance in relation to the color sensitivity of the emulsion. Conversion filters affect all parts of the SED for smooth color rendition. Although there used to be more, currently there are only two types of color

Table 7.4 The Basic Filter Families and Their Designations

85:	Conversion	Daylight to tungsten.
80:	Conversion	Tungsten to daylight.
82:	Light balancing	Cooling filters.
81:	Light balancing	Warming filters.
CC's	Color Compensating	Primary and secondary colors.

emulsions: daylight and tungsten. The basic filter families are shown in Table 7.6. The conversion filters we use in film and video are called CTO and CTB (see below).

Light-Balancing Filters

Light-balancing filters are warming and cooling filters; they work on the entire SED as with the conversion filters, but they are used to make smaller shifts in the blue-orange axis.

Correcting Light Balance

Daylight sources include

- Daylight itself (daylight is a combination of direct sun and open sky)
- HMIs
- Cool-white or daylight-type fluorescents
- Color-correct fluorescents
- Dichroic sources such as FAYs
- Arcs with white-flame carbons

In general, daylight sources are in the range of 5400–6500K, although they can range much higher. Near sunrise and sunset, they are much warmer as the sun is traveling through a much thicker layer of atmosphere and more of the blue wavelengths are filtered out. The quantity of dust and the amount of humidity in the air are also factors, accounting for the different colorings of light prevalent in different locales. Perhaps most famous is the translucent blue light of Venice made famous by the painter Canaletto.

Correction is achieved with either 85 or CTO, both of which are orange filters. The Rosco product is Roscosun 85 (85 refers to the Wratten number equivalent); it has a mired shift value of 131 which will convert 5500K to 3200K. (Technically, this is equivalent to a Wratten 85B; Wratten 85 has a mired shift value of 112, which converts 5500 to 3400, slightly cool for tungsten balance.)

CTO

CTO is the initialism for color temperature orange. CTO is warmer than 85 and has a higher mired shift value: 159. This means that it will convert 6500K to 3200K, which is excellent when correcting cooler sources such as HMIs, which are running blue or heavily skylit situations. It is also useful when going for a warmer look, as it will convert 5500K to 2940K. (5500K = mired 181, shift value of 159. Warmer equals positive. 181 + 159 = 340 mired. Divide 1,000,000 by 340 = 2940K.) The difference is basically American vs. European, probably owing to the fact that European skylight is generally bluer than American skylight.

An important variation of 85 is the combination of color correction and neutral density. The purpose of this is to

Table 7.5 Combination 85s

Name	Conversion	Loss
85N3	Daylight to tungsten	$1\frac{2}{3}$
85N6	Daylight to tungsten	$2\frac{2}{3}$
85N9	Daylight to tungsten	$3\frac{2}{3}$

Table 7.6 Gels for Correcting Green Sources

	Nominal CC Equivalent	For Use When CC Index Is Approx
To Reduce Green		
Minusgreen	30	−12
$\frac{1}{2}$ Minusgreen	15	−5
$\frac{1}{4}$ Minusgreen	075	−2
To Add Green		
Plusgreen	30	+13
$\frac{1}{2}$ Plusgreen	15	−5
$\frac{1}{4}$ Plusgreen	075	−3

avoid having to put two separate gels on a window, which might increase the possibility for gel noise and reflections, not to mention the additional cost (which is substantial). Unfortunately, no one makes a $\frac{1}{2}$ 85 plus ND filter, which would be useful to preserve a natural blueness in the windows.

Tungsten to Daylight

Filters for converting warm tungsten sources to nominal daylight are called full blue, tough blue, or CTB (color temperature blue).

The problem with blueing the lights is that CTB has a transmission of 36% while 85 has a transmission of 58%. This means that while you lose almost a stop and a half with CTB, you lose only about $\frac{2}{3}$ of a stop with CTO. CTB is very inefficient; its most common use is to balance tungsten lights inside a room with the daylight blue window light that is coming in. This is a losing situation from the start: the window light is liable to be far more powerful than the tungsten lights to begin with. If we then lose 2 stops off the tungsten by adding CTB, we are really in trouble (not to mention the fact that we also have to put an 80B filter on the lens with tungsten-balance film and we lose heavily there too). In practice most people try to avoid this solution; the alternatives are

- Put 85 on the windows and shoot at tungsten balance. By doing this, we avoid killing the tungsten lights, we don't have to use an 80B on the camera, and we lose $\frac{2}{3}$ of a stop off the windows, which may keep them more in balance with the inside exposure.
- Put $\frac{1}{2}$ 85 on the windows and $\frac{1}{2}$ blue on the lights.
- Put $\frac{1}{2}$ CTB on the lights and let the windows go slightly blue. This is actually a more realistic color effect and is much preferred these days.
- Use daylight balance lights (FAYs, HMIs, or Kinos) inside.

Fluorescent Lighting

One of the most common color problems we face today is shooting in locations where the dominant source is fluorescent. The problem with fluorescents is that they are not a continuous spectrum source: in most cases they are very heavy in green. Another problem is that even if they may appear to be approximately correct in color, their discontinuous spectra may cause them to render color very poorly. This is measured as the color rendering index (CRI). A CRI of 90 or better is considered necessary for film and video work. As a result, fluorescents cannot be corrected only by changing the color with a gel on the lighting unit or filter on the camera lens.

Also because of their discontinuous spectra, discharge sources (of which fluorescents are one example) can't be considered to have a true color temperature. The black body color temperature that they approximate is called the correlated color temperature (CCT). On practical locations it is not always possible to turn off the fluorescents and replace them with our own lights. The many options and combinations can get to be a bit confusing sometimes. Although there are many types of fluorescent tubes, they generally fall into cool white and warm white varieties. Additional tips on shooting with fluorescents include:

- In the field, it may be necessary to use a combination of these techniques. Whatever you do, SHOOT A GRAY CARD to give the lab a starting point for correction. In video shooting, you can white-balance the camera to remove the excess green.
- Shooting with ordinary fluorescents alone and letting the lab remove the green results in a very flat color rendition. Adding some lights (such as tungsten with plusgreen) gives a much fuller color feeling to the image.
- Several high-output units are available that use color-corrected (full-spectrum) fluorescents and can be used in conjunction with HMI or tungsten lighting (with either daylight or 3200K fluorescent tubes) and provide perfect color. They are very efficient in power usage and give a soft even light.
- Full minusgreen is equivalent to CC30M (30 magenta). In an emergency, it is possible to use a piece of CC30M.
- Don't forget that most backlighted advertising signs (such as those in bus shelters) have fluorescent tubes.
- If you are shooting a large area such as a supermarket, factory, or office, it is far more efficient to add green to your lights than to have the crew spend hours on ladders gelling or changing bulbs.
- When you add plusgreen or fluorofilter to lights they give a very strongly colored light which to the eye looks very wrong and doesn't appear to visually match either HMI or tungsten light; it looks odd. Try taking a digital photo with a professional SLR digital camera. Many people find that full correction (full plusgreen, for example) is too much.

Correcting Off-Color Lights

Arcs

Carbon arcs give off heavy ultraviolet: Rosco Y-1 or Lee LCT. Yellow reduces the uv output. Correction of white-flame carbon arcs to tungsten balance: use Rosco MT2 (together with Y-1) or Lee 232. Rosco MTY is a combination of MT2 and Y-1.

HMI

HMIs generally run a little too blue and are voltage-dependent. Unlike tungsten, their color temperature goes up as voltage decreases. It is important to check each lamp with a color temperature meter or color Polaroid and write the actual color temp on a piece of tape attached to the side. For slight correction Y-1 or Rosco MT 54 can be used. For more correction, use $\frac{1}{8}$ or $\frac{1}{4}$ CTO. Many HMIs run a little green. Have $\frac{1}{8}$ and $\frac{1}{4}$ minusgreen available.

Industrial Lamps

Various types of high-efficiency lamps are found in industrial and public space situations. They fall into three general categories: sodium vapor, metal halide, and mercury vapor. All of these lights have discontinuous spectra and are dominant in one color. They all have very low CRIs. It is possible to shoot with them if some corrections are made. High-pressure sodium lamps are very orange and contain a great deal of green. Low-pressure sodium is a monochromatic light: they are impossible to correct.

Stylistic Choices in Color Control

As with everything in film and video production, stylistic choices affect the technical choices and vice versa. This is especially true with color correction. Until a few years ago, considerable time and money were spent on correcting every single source on the set and every light or fixture that appeared in the frame to precisely 3200K (for tungsten) or 5500K (for daylight or HMIs) with no green. As a result of the influence of commercials and music videos, there is more of a tendency to let them go green and even let many different mixed sources appear in the frame. This is a much more naturalistic look and has become a style all its own. It has been said that green is the new orange. Some commercials and features even go out of their way to establish the green fluorescent look.

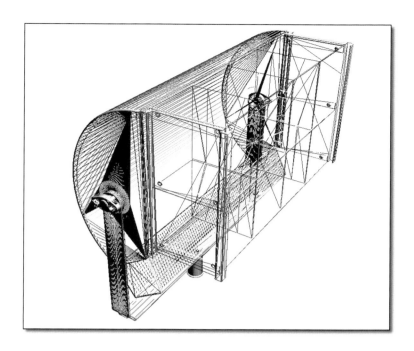

ELECTRICITY

The set electrician need have only a rudimentary knowledge of electricity, but must have a firm grasp of the fundamentals. For our purposes, we must start with an understanding of the four basic measurements of electricity: volts, amps, watts, and ohms. From there, we will look at the issues that confront a set electrician and briefly review standard set operating procedure for the electrical crew.

Electrical current occurs when a positively charged pole is connected to a negatively charged pole. In direct current (DC) it flows from negative to positive. Direct current is what you would get from a battery, for example, but there are other sources of DC, such as generators and power supplies.

The electricity available in most homes and buildings is AC (alternating current). It flows in one direction and then reverses. In the United States, it does this reversal 60 times a second. In Europe and other countries, it reverses 50 times a second. This cycle is measured in hertz (Hz); thus, U.S. main power (the electricity available on the main power grid of the country) is 60 hertz. DC is simple: only two wires are

(a)

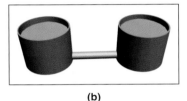

(b)

FIGURE 8.1 (**a**) Two water tanks and a pipe are an analogy for voltage or electrical potential. (**b**) Two water tanks equally full and at the same height have no electrical potential—no water will flow.

needed. A hot wire and a ground. Electrons, like ET, want to go home. Their home is the earth. Sounds silly, but it's true. Connect any electrical power source to a metal rod stuck in the ground, and current will flow. This is called "grounding" (or an earth ground.)

Measurement of Electricity

For our very basic uses on the set, we only need be concerned with the four fundamental measurements of electrical power: volts, watts, amps, and ampacity.

Potential

Electricity is measured in terms of potential. That is, how much power (or work) it is capable of doing. Potential can be thought of as pressure. Electricity flows from a source of high potential to low potential. Electrical potential is measured in volts or voltage (named for Alessandro Volta, inventor of the chemical battery).

A water analogy works well for electricity. Imagine a big water tank with a pipe leading out of it to a lower tank (see Figure 8.1). The amount of water in the upper tank determines the pressure. If there's a lot of water, there's high pressure in the pipe; when the water level goes down the pressure goes down, too. The water pressure is like voltage. Clearly, the size of the pipe influences how fast the water flows and how much of it can flow through in a certain time.

The size of the pipe is resistance. In electricity, it is measured in ohms. The flow of water is the same as current in electricity. Current is how much total flow of electrons there is. Current is measured in amperes or amps.

The pipe might be very large, but if there is not potential in the circuit (if the upper tank is dry), then there will be no current. The size of the pipe is how much can flow if there is potential. The maximum capacity the pipe can safely carry is the same as ampacity. All electrical cables and connectors are rated for their ampacity. Too much water flowing (too much pressure) might make a pipe burst. Too much amperage flowing on a wire or connector (exceeding ampacity) will make it overheat and melt or start a fire.

For example, an ordinary household wall outlet is rated for 20 amps. That is how much current it can carry without overheating and melting or causing a fire. The wire that goes to the wall plug is usually #12 wire—which has an ampacity of 20 amps. Europe (and most of the world) operates with 220-volt electrical supply. The United States uses 110-volt power supply for most residences and offices. Higher voltage is used for industrial sites and for transmitting power over long distances. The high-voltage transmission towers you see out in the country are usually about 13,000 volts, for example.

Higher voltage is easier to transmit long distances with minimal loss. Voltage is rarely constant. It can vary throughout the day according to the load on the system. This is why voltage often drops a bit in the summer when we all have our air conditioning on.

The total amount of work done is measured in watts or wattage. For example, with lightbulbs, a 200-watt bulb delivers a lot more light than a 40-watt bulb.

So here are our basic terms:

> Volts or voltage = electrical potential
> Amps or amperage = the amount of current flowing
> Ampacity = amount of current a device can handle
> Watt = a measure of the work done or capacity of a bulb

The simplest calculations are all we need on the set. The basic formulas are

> Watt = amps × volts
> Amps = watts/volts

U.S. electrical mains vary in voltage, but generally they run from 110 to 120 volts.

> A 1000-watt lamp at 120 volts = 8.3 amps
> A 1K (1000-watt) lamp requires 8.3 amps, a 2K draws 16.6 amps, a 10K takes 83 amps, etc.

Paper Amps

To be safe, we always round up. This allows for loose connectors, damaged cable, and other unseen extra factors. For practical calculations, we say that a 1K draws 10 amps, even though it actually draws 8.3 amps (at 120 volts). These are called paper amps. By this rule, a 10K (which actually draws 83 amps) pulls 100 paper amps and so on. It also makes mental calculations vastly easier—useful when it's 3 AM and you're in your 16th hour of shooting.

Electrical Supply Systems

Three-Phase

Countries using 120 volts as a residential standard have two basic kinds of supply: three-phase and single-phase. There are many others, of course, but these are the most common.

A basic electrical system is a hot wire and a ground, but this is not the most efficient way to deliver it to a house or office. Three-phase consists of three hot wires and a neutral. The power comes in on the hot wires (or legs) and goes out on the neutral (this is an oversimplification, of course). The hot legs are the ones that are energized—in other words,

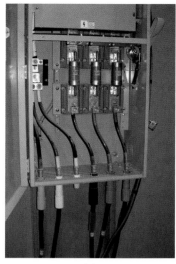

(a)

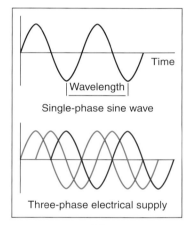

(b)

FIGURE 8.2 (a) A 600-amp disconnect (power supply box—sometimes called a bullswitch or "the cans"). It is three-phase (black, red, and blue). Each leg (phase) has a 200-amp fuse. Note the double neutral. This is because it is on a stage that has a dimmer system. With dimmers it is possible to have a very out of balance load: this puts a greater strain on the neutral. (b) The timing of three-phase and single-phase power supplies typical in the United States.

FIGURE 8.3 Two sizes of AC generators, both of them "tow-away," meaning they are towed.

grab one and you'll get a shock. For this reason, switches and fuses are always connected on the hot legs.

The three hot legs are out of phase—this means that as they turn on and off 60 times a second, they are not doing it at the same time: they are 120° out of phase. This is because the three hot legs are each supplied from a different coil on the generator. As each coil passes the electromagnet, it is energized. Each does this 60 times a second, but in sequence.

Remember that, with AC current, it is not a simple matter of the electricity's coming in one side and going out the other. In fact it is sort of vibrating back and forth. The electrons flow one direction, and then reverse.

As a consequence, if the load on each of the three legs is exactly equal (that is, each has an equal number of watts taking power from it), then the current flow on the neutral will be zero. Think of it this way: the neutral in a three-phase AC system only carries the excess left over from an imbalanced load. This is important because the neutral wire is usually the same size (same ampacity) as the three hot legs. Thus, a severely out-of-balance load could potentially put more amperage on the neutral than it can handle. It is the best boy electric's job to balance the load as closely as possible. Failure to do so can also harm the generator or cause street transformers to fail.

According to the National Electrical Code (NEC), the three legs are designated red, black, and blue. This is a problem because we often color-code the legs with electrical tape. Black tape on a black cable would be indistinguishable. For this reason, the convention on film sets is to designate them red, yellow, blue.

Single-Phase

Single-phase is a variant on three-phase. Instead of three hot legs, there are two hot wires and a neutral. This is the most common system in residential houses. Both single-phase and three-phase systems have an additional wire: the ground. Although it is essentially the same as the neutral, it is an extra safety. If the neutral is lost or there is some other sort of malfunction, the ground (always color-coded green) is a backup ground that carries the current away.

Power Sources

Power for film and video production usually comes from one of three sources: stage service, generators, and tie-ins.

Stage Service

Most studios and sound stages provide electrical service. Older stages will sometimes have DC (left over from the days of carbon arcs) and extreme caution must be used not to plug any AC-only equipment into DC, which would severely damage drills and compressors. Smaller studios generally have at least 300 amps available, but be sure to ask. The most common situation is for a stage to have several hard-wired distribution points with fuse boxes and disconnect switches that terminate in pin plug, Tweco, Camlok, or similar connectors. You can then easily plug in an appropriate amount of feeder cable and set a distribution box wherever you need it.

The only difficulty with a setup like this is that while it is easy to check the load balance at each box, there is usually no simple way to check the overall balance. It is generally sufficient to just try to distribute the load as evenly as possible. If you sense danger, check with the house manager; she may be able to take an electrician down to the main service for a balance and load check.

FIGURE 8.4 Small portable sources are known as "putt-putt" generators, usually about 5500 watts. Those that are adapted for film usually have crystal sync, thus making them suitable for use with HMI lights.

Generators

On location, generators provide the simplest and safest power source. Generators are available in all sizes: from portable 30-amp putt-putts up to tractor-trailer rigs capable of providing several thousand amps of service.

Four issues are paramount when ordering a generator:
1. Capacity. Be sure to allow an extra margin of safety in calculating the total load. It is in most cases unhealthy for a generator to run at full load.
2. AC/DC. Gennies are available in AC, DC, or mixed AC and DC. It is vital to think about your needs and specify the correct service. If you are running Brute arcs, you will need 225 amps of DC for each arc. If you are running HMIs or video, you must have AC.
3. Crystal sync. If you are using HMIs, you must order a generator that has constant speed governed by a synchronizing crystal. Don't assume that all gennies are crystal. Specially modified portable gennies are available that are crystal. Always request a frequency meter. This will allow you to monitor the frequency of the AC output to ensure that it is within acceptable limits. Under normal conditions with HMIs anything greater than a quarter of a cycle variation from 60 hertz (from 59.75 to 60.25) is cause for concern.
4. Soundproofing. Some gennies are soundproofed to allow sync sound to be recorded. If you can park the genny far enough away or it's a situation with high ambient noise, a soundproofed genny may not be necessary.

Other things to remember:
1. Physical size. Consider where the genny will be driven and parked. Be sure it will fit and that your feeder cable can reach it.

FIGURE 8.5 The output panel on a generator.

2. Portability. There are five types of gennies: portable handcarry units, portable putt-putts that roll, towed units that can be hitched to a truck, piggyback units that sit behind the cab of an equipment truck, and independent units from van size to full tractor-trailer size. Consider which will be appropriate for your needs.
3. Distance of runs. On very large exteriors, it may make more sense to rent two or three smaller gennies instead of doing monstrously long cable runs to a single large genny.
4. Fuel. Don't assume that the genny rental operation will provide fuel and lubricants. Usually they do, but always ask.

Generator Operation

If a generator operator is not provided, it will be the best boy's responsibility to ensure the safe and efficient operation of the unit. Every genny is different, so be sure to ask the rental house if the genny has any particular needs or bad habits. Some general principles are

1. Set the generator as close to level as possible.
2. Check to make sure that the exhaust vents are open and clear before starting.
3. Check the oil, fuel, and antifreeze levels before starting.
4. Always warm a generator up for at least ten minutes before applying a load.
5. Make all connections before engaging the generator.
6. Always run a generator for ten minutes *after* the load is shut off before turning the engine off.

Always run a ground wire from the generator chassis to a rod stuck in the earth, a water pipe, or similar ground. Generator efficiency is reduced by high altitude and high temperature. The reduction is roughly 3.5% for every 1000 feet over 500 feet above sea level. The reduction for high temperature is roughly 2% for every 10°F above 85°.

If you are working with foreign equipment, remember that a 50-Hz genny is 20% more efficient when run at 60 Hz.

Some generators can run concurrently: producing both AC and DC at the same time. However, on most units, running concurrent means losing the three-phase capability.

Tie-ins

The third common power source is the tie-in: tapping into the power supply of a building. Tie-ins are cheap, convenient, and provide reliable power, but in some areas they are strictly illegal, and the electrician and production company can be subject to civil and criminal penalties. It is your responsibility to know the local laws and act appropriately. Even if a production company pressures you to save them money with a tie-in, keep in mind that you are taking responsibility for people's lives and the safety of valuable property. Any time you deal with electricity, it is not to be taken lightly.

Under no circumstances should anyone perform a tie-in until he or she has been *trained* and *checked out* by a senior film electrician. You can be killed while doing a tie-in. Don't take chances. Also, always tie in after the electric meter; otherwise you will be guilty of stealing electricity. Many localities require that tie-ins be performed only by licensed electricians; some require that a fire marshal be present.

Tie-in Safety

Everyone should know the basic safety rules of tie-ins:

1. Two people should be present at a tie-in. There is a very real risk of electrocution in any tie-in. The second person must know CPR techniques, electrical rescue techniques, and be a level-headed type who won't panic. If at all possible, the second person should be another film electrician.
2. Only one hand in the box at any time. The most dangerous situation is for current to run across the chest and heart from one hand to another.
3. Stand on a rubber mat or low wooden box (half or quarter apple box; a full apple box might make you a little wobbly). Wear rubber sole shoes.
4. Wear safety glasses.
5. Have a fire extinguisher nearby.
6. Never stick anything metal in the box. Metal screwdrivers should be wrapped with electrical tape down the shank.
7. If the fuse box is behind a door, lock, sandbag, or have a guard on it so that no one can swing the door open and slam you face first into the live connectors.
8. Always tie in on the load side after the fuses or main circuit breakers.
9. Always meter the voltage of all legs and meter the case to determine that it is not hot. Check to see if it is AC or DC.
10. Use sash cord to tie the feeder cable up in a strain relief. Make sure there is no pressure on the tie-in clips that might pull them loose. Put the strain relief on before you make the connections. Ensure that the metal ends are not free to swing into the box or get in your way.
11. Use pieces of rubber mat or cardboard to card off the hot lugs and provide insulation anywhere that the tie-in clips might contact a hot lug and the case and arc.
12. Always clamp onto the neutral (white) first and then the hot legs. Always disconnect the neutral last when breaking the tie-in. If you have a case ground (green), connect it first and then the neutral.

13. Always use a bullswitch (disconnect and fuses) between your tie-in and the load.
14. Never leave a tie-in up overnight.
15. Always tape all neutrals so they can't come loose.
16. Color-code all connections and lines.
17. Be sure you are using the appropriately sized connectors.
18. Tape or brace the door of the fuse box so it can't swing closed on the connectors.
19. Put a rubber mat or show card over the open box so that no one can accidently touch it. If necessary cordon off the area.
20. Pray someone will invent some safe and easy-to-use tie-in connectors so we can stop using clumsy, dangerous, and unreliable Tricos, Anderson clamps, and alligator clips.
21. If you do so many tie-ins that you find yourself looking at the box and thinking it looks like some perfectly innocent metal parts, stop for a moment and remind yourself, "This is live electricity; it wants to kill me." Go slow and easy.
22. If you are not a trained, tested, and certified electrician, or if there is any doubt in your mind about your ability to perform the tie-in safely, DON'T DO IT. If you feel the tie-in would not be safe or legal, DON'T DO IT. The gaffer is the absolute and final authority concerning electrical safety on the set. If he or she says no tie-in, there will be no tie-in.

Determining KVA

In many industrial and commercial situations, the service is high-voltage and a portion is stepped down by transformers for the 120-volt service. In these situations, it is not enough to look at the wire feeding the 120-volt box; you must also consider the capacity of the transformer, which is often only designed to run a few houselights and wall sockets. Transformers are rated in KVA, which means kilovolt amps. When we realize that a *volt amp* is really a watt (remember that volts times amps equals watts), the process becomes clear. Let's take a simple single-phase example: a transformer is rated at 77 KVA. This is 77,000 watts.

$$\text{Amps} = \frac{\text{KVA} \times 1000}{\text{volts}}$$

We divide by the voltage and get 640 amps. Thus we cannot exceed 640 amps per leg even if the feed wire and the fuses are rated higher.

$$\frac{77 \times 1000}{120} = 640$$

With two-phase, four-wire service, there is an additional factor:

$$\text{Amps} = \frac{\text{KVA} \times 1000}{\text{volts} \times 2}$$

In three-phase, given KVA and voltage, amperage is found by this formula:

$$\text{Amps} = \frac{\text{KVA} \times 1000}{\text{volts} \times 1.73}$$

In order to understand these relationships, we must recall the following:

- Two-phase current = $2 \times$ single-phase current.
- Three-phase current = $1.73 \times$ single-phase current.
- The current in the neutral of a two-phase, three-wire service is 141% greater than either of the other two conductors of that circuit.

Before transformers burn out, they issue a very distinct and unmistakable burning odor. Learn to recognize that smell and add it to your mental list of things to check periodically when running a heavy load through a house transformer. If you detect it, reduce the load immediately, but don't panic. It usually isn't necessary to shut down the bullswitch and throw everybody into a tizzy. Just switch off as many lights as you can until you can rebalance.

Wall Plugging

For very small setups where only a small amount of light is needed (such as documentary and small-unit video) it is possible to plug small units into the walls. In most areas, wall convenience outlets are usually 15-amp and occasionally 20-amp circuits. The standard two- or three-prong Edison plug duplex outlet that we are all familiar with is by convention rated at 20 amps. If there is nothing else on the circuit, they will usually hold a 2K light (16.6 amps). Some things to remember:

1. Check to see what's on the circuit. Switch off anything that isn't needed. The simplest technique is to station people throughout the house while someone switches each breaker on and off and labels it. It takes a few minutes, but it's worth doing.
2. Have some spare fuses handy or if it's circuit breakers, be sure the fuse box is not behind a locked door.
3. Never plug into a circuit that serves computers, delicate electronics, any type of medical life support equipment, or security systems.
4. Switch the lights off whenever you can.
5. Don't assume that each room has its own circuit. It is general practice in laying out household electrical

to have circuits serve different areas to distribute the load. The same circuit might serve an outlet in the hallway and in an upstairs bathroom, while an outlet a few feet away is served by an entirely different circuit. If possible, try to get the architectural plans of the building to see the electrical layout.

6. Never bypass the fuses.
7. Let the lights burn for a few minutes after plugging. Better that the fuses blow now than when you are shooting.

Batteries

Battery rigs, consisting of ten 12-volt car batteries (for a total of 120 volts) can run a few film lights for an hour or less. Even large light such as 10Ks and Brutes can be run off high-amperage battery rigs, but only for very short periods of time. They can be concealed in a car trunk, on a running rig, or other places where you can't get power.

One of the most useful applications of battery rigs is to power work lights for night wraps when the tie-in is taken down or the producer wants to get the generator off the clock.

Battery Capacity

The capacity of a battery is usually expressed in amp-hours (1 Ah = 3600 coulombs). If a battery can provide 1 ampere (1 A) of current (flow) for 1 hour, it has a capacity of 1 Ah (amp-hour). If it can provide 1 A for 100 hours, its capacity is 100 Ah.

Battery manufacturers use a standard method to determine how to rate their batteries. The battery is discharged at a constant rate of current over a fixed period of time, such as 10 or 20 hours, down to a set terminal voltage per cell. So a 100-amp hour battery is rated to provide 5 A for 20 hours at room temperature. The efficiency of a battery is different at different discharge rates. Batteries fall into three basic categories: lead acid, heavy antimony, and nicad.

Lead Acid

Lead acid batteries include ordinary automobile batteries. Typically, they take an 8- to 10-hour charge. Batteries are rated in amp-hours. For example, a 100 amp-hour battery will deliver 5 amps for 20 hours. Anything less than 60 amp-hours is generally unacceptable; 80 amp-hours is better for film use. If possible, order a battery with renewable cells and always request a hydrometer to test the state of charge.

Heavy Antimony

Heavy antimony batteries are designed for heavy, continuous use, such as powering forklifts. They are generally available in 6-volt configurations, and so you may have to hook up a series circuit. The disadvantage is that they tend to be extremely heavy.

Nicads

Batteries composed of nickel and cadmium are called "nicads"; they are the most commonly used power unit in film and video. The advantage of nicads is that they hold a charge much longer than other types of batteries and their output strength remains constant until they fail. Unfortunately, they give very little warning when they fail. It is difficult to ascertain the charge state of a nicad battery, since most of them are sealed units. When using nicads to power video, film cameras, or sunguns, it is important to maintain a charge sheet to know when each battery gets charged and used.

Nicads require particular caution to preserve their full lifespan. Like all batteries they are happiest when being used; sitting on a shelf is detrimental to most batteries. Never store a nicad in a discharged state. Also never let it go to deep discharge, when it is drained to the last volt.

On the other hand, it is not wise to partially discharge repeatedly, then recharge a nicad battery. The reason for this is the memory effect, which will cause a nicad battery to fail to provide full output if it is repeatedly discharged partway. To avoid this, it is important to periodically discharge a nicad fully and then recharge it to full capacity. When doing this, don't forget to avoid deep discharge. Dischargers are available that will drain nicads safely and efficiently. If a nicad develops memory problems, discharge and recharge it four or five times.

Nicads must be treated with respect. Punctures, sharp blows, and other shocks can cause internal shorts, which can then be fatal to the battery. As with all batteries, they lose capacity when cooled and should be kept off the floor if it is cold.

Li-Ion and NiMh

Two new types of batteries are lithium ion (Li-ion) and nickle metal hydride (Ni-MH). They are especially popular for camera batteries but have other uses as well. Ni-Mh batteries are much less affected by the memory problems of nicads. Li-ion batteries do not suffer significantly from memory effects. They also contain less hazardous materials.

Load Calculations and Paper Amps

Lighting units are rated in terms of their wattage. A resistance unit (such as a tungsten filament) draws amperage based on its size (amps equals watts divided by volts); the larger the filament, the greater the draw. At 1000 watts or more, the term kilo (thousand) watts is used; hence their common names, 10K, 5K, etc.

For broad calculations we round off to 10 amps per thousand watts—this is called "paper amps." It gives us a margin of safety and simplifies the arithmetic.

In planning and executing a power distribution system, we have two jobs: to determine the amount of electricity needed and to order cable and connectors of the correct size to carry the load and get the power where we need it.

And don't forget the inevitable iron for the stylist, the hot curlers for the hairdresser, and the most critical power need on the set—the coffeepot. These items draw surprisingly high amperages.

Determining the load is a simple matter. We merely add up the total wattage of the units we plan to use.

Ampacity

Cable and distribution equipment is rated in terms of their ability to carry electrical loads without overheating. This is called "ampacity". The larger a cable or connector (and hence the lower its resistance), the greater the amount of current flow it can carry without overheating. If we push more amperage through a cable than it is rated for, it will overheat, and then melt and possibly burn.

We must then select the cable that will safely carry that load. To do so, we must look at an ampacity table. See Table 8.1.

Ampacities are not absolute; they vary according to situation, temperature, type of wire, type of usage, and courage. The conditions are generally related to heat buildup. For example, two individual cables lying next to each other on a cold concrete floor can handle a greater load than two cables run side by side in an enclosed metal conduit in a boiler room.

Wire size is designated by a number; the lower the number, the larger the wire. Most household wiring is done with #12 wire. The power cords on a typical piece of home electronics might be #14 or #16. Speaker wire is usually #20. The largest cable we commonly use in film production is #0000 (pronounced *four ought*). Cable larger than #0000 is rated in MCM (mean circular mils), and is a measurement of the cross-sectional area of the conductor. A *mil* is $\frac{1}{1000}$th of a inch.

For example: we are burning one 10K, two 5Ks, four 2Ks, and two 1Ks. This is a total of 30K watts. Multiplying by 9 (1 + 2 + 4 + 2) gives us 270 amps. Of course, we always allow more for unexpected additional units and to run the equipment at something less than its full rated load—usually a wise idea. This gives us 300 amps. If we are dealing with three-phase four-wire service, we will assume that we will distribute the load as evenly as possible over the three legs. This gives us 100 amps per leg.

Color Coding

All service equipment must be color-coded. In the United States the standard colors for 110- and 220-volt circuits are

- Neutral: white
- Ground: green
- Hot legs: red, blue, and yellow or black. Electricians should carry color-coding tape with them and check that all circuits are correctly color-coded.

The international colors are

- Neutral: blue
- Hot leg: red
- Ground: yellow/green

The Neutral

The neutral is a very important part of the system. If the neutral is mistakenly plugged into a hot leg, creating 220 volts, serious equipment damage and injury could result. To prevent this, many rental houses make plugging a neutral into a hot leg difficult to do. Two strategies are common:

1. The neutral has a different size connector.
2. Reversed neutral. In bundled cable, the neutral is run backward so the males and females are at opposite ends from the hot legs.

Losing the neutral can also be very dangerous. Under certain conditions, losing the neutral can allow the voltage to wander and rise to dangerous levels. The neutral should *never* be fused. To prevent loss of neutral connections, the neutral lines must be taped with gaffer's tape to make sure they don't pull apart. Always connect the neutral first and disconnect it last. If there is a short or an arc, you want the current to have a better place to go than through you.

Distribution Equipment

Tie-ins

There are six main varieties of tie-in connectors: Tricos, Anderson clamps, Mueller or alligator clips, busbar lugs, and bare wires. They come in 60-amp, 100-amp, and 200-amp sizes, referred to as #1, #2, and #3.

Anderson clamps are generally for larger jobs, are unwieldy and difficult to tighten, and won't fit in any tight space. They are all exposed metal, which makes them more dangerous. Alligator clamps are only for extremely small jobs. They don't tighten down with sufficient pressure and are not recommended for this reason.

(a)

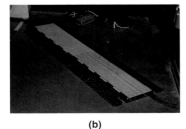

(b)

FIGURE 8.6 (**a**) Banded cable (four wire #2) is "figure-eighted" whenever there is extra cable. This prevents a power factor effect (resistance), which is hard on a generator and the distribution. (**b**) A cable crossing protects the feeder (and prevents tripping hazards) when it lays across a traffic zone.

Busbar Lugs

Busbar lugs are for connecting the feeder cable directly to a busbar. They can be used for tie-ins and are used in spider boxes, which are busbar distribution boxes. Some large generators use busbars and lugs for the primary connection. With the new five-wire grounded systems, the lugs are required to be keyed so that the neutral and ground lugs will fit only into the proper sections of the busbar.

Bare wires are simply a piece of feeder cable that has the insulation stripped off at one end and terminate in a connector (Tweco, Camlok, pin plug, twistlock) at the other end. They are designed for use where there are large empty lugs available or for difficult situations where it is impossible to get clamps in.

Connectors

Connectors can be a nightmare, especially if the equipment comes from several different rental houses and adaptors are needed.

The simplest are *pin plugs*, copper cylinders that are split down the middle. They are also used to connect the head cables of many large tungsten lights (5K and above). They need frequent maintenance to ensure a solid connection. If the contact is loose, push a screwdriver into the split to spread the connector and create better copper-to-copper contact.

*Camlok*s are more positive in their locking and seldom freeze together. They also form a watertight and completely enclosed connection that is much safer. *Union connectors* are more common in the theater and video studios. They are high-tech versions of three-pins and have a secure locking device.

Ordinary plugs such as you will find around the house (two parallel flat blades and a round ground pin) are referred to as *Edison* plugs, Hubble, U-ground, and household plugs. The adaptors that convert a 3-blade grounded Edison to a 2-blade ungrounded is called a *3-to-2*.

Twist locks have the pins arranged in a circle. One or more of the pins has a nib on the end that creates a positive lock when given a final twist. Twist locks are safe and easy to use and come in an enormous variety of arrangements.

As the name implies, *stage plugs* are old theater equipment. They are a fiber block with two copper plates on the sides. One copper plate is spring-loaded. They fit into square plug holes that have copper plates at the top and bottom. Stage plugs come in full and half sizes. Two half stage plugs will fit into one plug hole. They are not legal in most areas.

Bullswitches

A bullswitch is a portable disconnect switch with fuses for each hot leg. They come in 60-, 100-, and 300-amp sizes, most often with bladed cartridge fuses. A bullswitch should be put in every distribution system, usually right after the tie-in or generator. In some cases you may want it near the set where it can be used as a master switch to shut everything down.

Feeder Cable

Feeder cable runs from the power source to the distribution boxes. The real workhorse of the business is #2 welding cable. Rated at 115 amps, it is compatible with the most common fuse boxes and distribution boxes (generally 100 amps per leg). It is flexible and easy to work with. On the East Coast it most often terminates in Tweco or Camlok connectors; on the West Coast pin plugs are common. For larger service #0 (one ought) and #00 are frequently used. For the really big jobs, such as a 225-amp Brute arc, #0000 is the largest size most rental houses carry. These cables all come as individual wires, in 25-, 50-, and 100-foot lengths. Picking up a 100-foot length of #0000 is not a one-person job.

Wire Types

A typical wire coding is as follows: $^{12}/_3$ SJ 600V (UL). This indicates that the wire has 3 conductors of #12 wire. It is type SJ (see chart below), is rated for service up to 600 volts, and is certified by Underwriter's Laboratory.

(a)

(b)

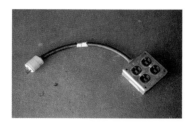

(c)

FIGURE 8.7 (a) A lunch box. (b) A gang box. (c) A four-way.

Code	Type
A	Asbestos. Dry use only.
T	Dry only, operate at less than 140° under full current load.
F	Fixture wire. CF is cotton insulation. AF has asbestos insulation, SF is silicone insulation.
R	Rubber or neoprene.
S	Appliance cord, stranded conductors, cotton between wire and insulation, rubber outer jacket. S is rough service, SJ is more flexible and is for lighter service, SV is for light service.
SP	Lamp cord.
SPT	Lamp cord, plastic insulation.
X	Very tough, heat- and moisture-resistant.
…H	Higher load current temperatures, up to 167°F.
…HH	Up to 194°F load current temperature.
…N	Jacket is nylon. Gas- and oil-resistant.
…O	Neoprene jacket.
…W	Wet use.
UF	Underground feeder. Moisture-resistant.
USE	Underground service entrance cable. Moisture- and heat-resistant.

(a)

FIGURE 8.8 (**a**) A suicide pin— often needed for a distro system that has a reverse ground but not all equipment matches that system. (**b**) A 600-amp distro box with three Camlok splitters and a ground squid attached.

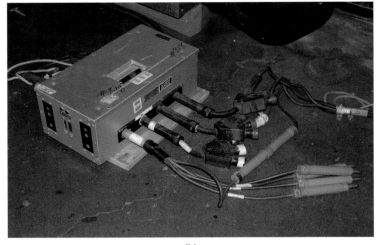

(b)

E   Entertainment cable. The new code requirement for film and video use. Double-jacketed and heavier.

S & SJ   Commonly used as cable in film and video; wire types such as THHN, THN, and THWN are prevalent as household wiring.

Distribution Boxes

Distribution or "distro" boxes (sometimes called "D-boxes") accept feeder cable inputs (in the United States, most commonly Camlok) and have output connectors for sub-feeder such as 100-amp or 60-amp Bates or similar. Most distro boxes are "pass-through," which means that there are also outputs for the same size feeder as the inputs, thus allowing other distro boxes on the same line.

Outputs for the Bates connectors must also be fused. As a rule, any line must be fused for the smallest load it can handle. In this case, since each output goes to 100 amp Bates, that output must also be fused for 100 amps, regardless of the size of the input cable.

FIGURE 8.9 A connector box such as this makes the use of "threefers" or "tees" unnecessary and thus simpler.

Lunch Boxes, Snake Bites, Gangboxes, and Four-Ways

At the end of a Bates cable, it is usually necessary to have some Edison connectors. To do this, the most convenient solution is a "lunch box," which consists of a 100-amp Bates input and 100-amp Bates pass-through. The output is five Edison circuits, duplex connectors. Snake bites go directly from Camlok or pin plug to Bates outputs, usually 100 amp. A gangbox is 100-amp or 60-amp input with four or five Edison connectors. A four-way is a 20-amp Edison input with four Edison outputs.

Extensions

Lines that terminate in Bates, Camlok, or pin plug can be connected directly into the distro box. Large lights (5K and above) usually have one of these types of connectors and go right into the box. Smaller units are Edison and go into a Bates connector, Camlok, or pin.

If the head cable of the light doesn't reach to the box, there are several options. To extend out to a light that has a Bates, Camlok, pin plug, or other type of connect, we need sub-distribution. Bates cables are the most commonly used for this. For lighter loads (up to 20 amps) we can use single extensions. A sturdier cousin of the household extension cord, it consists of a length of $^{12}/_3$ (three conductors of #12) with Edison plugs at both ends. It is also called a "single," a "stinger," or a "$^{12}/_3$."

A variant of the single is the four-way or plugging box, terminating in a box with four or five female Edison plugs.

Planning a Distribution System

The primary challenge of planning is to get the power where you need it. The basic trick is to get enough stage boxes (or whatever distribution boxes you are using) so that your final cabling to the lights is reasonable.

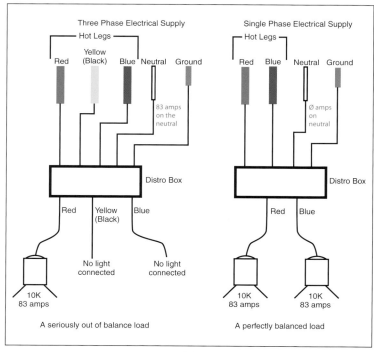

FIGURE 8.10 (a) Balanced and unbalanced loads. One is single-phase and the other three-phase for purposes of illustration only: the same principles apply to both systems. (b) Distribution plan for a studio shoot.

(a)

(b)

FIGURE 8.11 This is the distribution diagram for a medieval knights film (shown in the Chapter 4) that was used during preproduction. Enough information has been given so that the gaffer can make the final calculations on generator size, ampacity of distro cable, number of distro boxes, connectors, and adaptors. This multi-day shoot would have scenes shot in different parts of the larger area—cabling for future scenes was a time-saver.

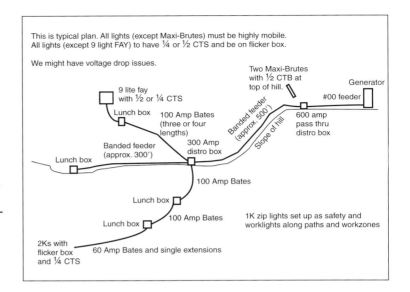

The most common ways in which people get into trouble with distribution are

1. Not enough distribution boxes, so that complex webs of extensions, stingers, and gang boxes cross and recross the set.
2. Not enough secondary distribution (Bates extensions or porcelains).
3. Enough power but not enough breakouts: gangboxes, lunch boxes or Bates outlets, depending on which system you are using.

As much as any other part of lighting, planning a distribution system requires thinking ahead, anticipating variations, and allowing slack for the unexpected.

Balancing the Load

Once the power is up, one major responsibility remains—balancing the load. Simply put, keeping a balanced load means keeping a roughly equal amount of current flowing on all legs, whether it be a three-wire or a four-wire system.

If a system is rated at 100 amps per leg and the load is 100 amps, what's wrong with having everything on the same leg? After all, the fuses aren't going to blow—are they? There are several problems. First, we have to remember that electricity travels in two directions. Remember Fudd's First Law, "What goes in, must come out." To put it more mathematically, the current on the neutral is equal to the sum of the difference between the load on the hot legs. In other words, on a three-phase system, if each leg has 100 amps, the current on the neutral will be zero, and the phases cancel each other out. On the other hand, if the same system has 100 amps on one leg and nothing on the other legs, the current on the neutral will be 100 amps.

Table 8.1 Typical Ampacities for Copper Cable

Rated at 90°C	Rated at 90°C	Rated at 75°C	at 60°a
Type W, SC, SCE, E			
#0000	400	360	300
#000	350	310	260
#00	300	265	225
#0	260	230	195
#2	190	170	140
#4	140	125	105
#6	100	95	80
#8	80	70	60
Types, S, SJ, SJO, SPT, ET, etc.			
#2	95		
#4	70		
#6	55		
#8	40		
#10	30		
#12	25		
#14	18		
#16	13		
#18	10		

aIf the type of cable is not known, use these ampacities.

FIGURE 8.12 Checking the balance with a clamp-on ammeter, commonly called an "amprobe."

This is dangerous for several reasons. First, we run the danger of overloading the neutral wire. Keep in mind that a neutral is never fused, so overloading it can have dire consequences. Second, even if our system can handle an overcurrent in the neutral, the transformer in the electric room or on the pole outside might fail as a result of the imbalance. In the realm of "things that will ensure you never get hired again by this company," melting down the transformer is near the top of the list.

The moral of the story is: balance your load. As you plug in or switch on, distribute the usage across all legs. Once everything is up and running, the load is checked with a clamp-on ammeter. Affectionately called an "amprobe" (after a major manufacturer of the devices), this type of meter is one of the most fundamental tools of the film electrician.

A good trick is to always read a load in the same order—for example, red, yellow, blue (RYB: "rib"). That way, you only need to memorize a set of three numbers. This will help you remember which legs are high or low.

In some cases, it may be necessary to run a *ghost* load. For example, you have a 100-amp generator but are running only one light, a 10K. Since there is only one light, the load would be entirely on one leg, deadly to a small genny. Plug unused lights into the other legs and point them away so that they don't interfere with the set lights. Don't set them face down on the ground or cover them. This could cause them to overheat and create a fire hazard or blow the bulb.

In a tie-in situation, don't forget that there may be other uses in the building. Check the load at the tie-in and on the building service itself. Even though your lights are in balance, there may be other heavy use in the building that is overloading the system or throwing it out of balance. This can be tricky—the worst offenders are, in fact, intermittent users: freezers, air

FIGURE 8.13 The "ring of fire" is a standard method of arranging electrical distribution on a set. It ensures that power will be available on all sides of the set without the need for cables to cross the set, disrupting dolly moves, actor's movements, or otherwise messing up the shot.

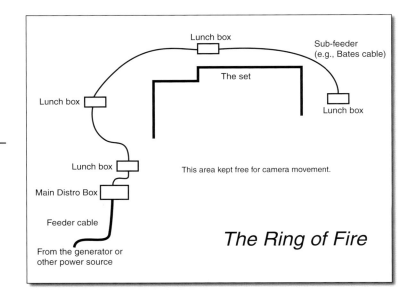

conditioners, etc., which might be off when you scout the location and check the load, but kick in just as you are pulling your heaviest load.

Working with AC and DC

DC is used much less than it was a few years ago. This is the tail end of a battle that has its origins in the earliest days of electricity. When electrical power was first being used outside of the laboratory—and proposals were being made to wire up parts of cities—both types of power had their champions. Thomas Edison felt that DC was the preferred form of power. Nikola Tesla, the other great electrical innovator of the era, favored AC for its ability to be run over greater distances by stepping the voltage up and down—higher voltages will carry over longer distances with less loss of power. In the end, of course, AC prevailed and now AC power grids cover entire continents, while DC power transmission is limited to a few miles at best.

DC has other disadvantages. Since all the current flows in one direction, it tends to eat the connectors by constantly eroding one side and depositing metal on the other. And, of course, modern electronics (such as those found in HMIs, xenons, and even variacs) are not possible with DC.

Still, it has its uses. Until recently, its major function on sets was for Brute arcs, which will run only on DC. Even today, if Brutes are planned, you must ensure that the generator or location is supplied with DC. Some generators will provide both AC and DC (some are switchable and will supply one at a time). This is a major consideration in ordering generators. Special ballasts are available that will run a DC on AC—most of them require three-phase.

Table 8.2 Calculating Voltage Drop

AWG	OHMS/Foot
#12	0.0019800
#10	0.0012400
#8	0.0007780
#6	0.0004910
#4	0.0003080
#2	0.0001940
#1	0.0001540
#0	0.0001220
#00	0.0000967
#000	0.0000766
#0000	0.0000608

Some older stages are still wired with DC. If this is true for your setup, the first thing the electricians must do is clearly label all DC boxes (white camera tape is usually used). DC can be deadly. If an HMI, compressor, computer, or any other AC device is plugged into DC, it will be cooked immediately. So, while tungsten lights (and most powered light stands, generically called "Molevators" or "Cinevators") will run on either AC or DC, few other devices are so nondiscriminating. Extreme caution is always paramount.

Calculating Voltage Drop

A problem with long cable runs is that the resistance of the cable itself will cause the voltage to drop. This has always been a problem, since each 10-volt drop creates a 100K drop in color temperature in tungsten bulbs. Now, with HMIs, voltage drops (VD) can lead to serious trouble. Many HMIs won't fire at all if the voltage is too low. Color temperature can be corrected with gels or in the lab, but a light that won't turn on can be fatal.

Voltage drop is a function of resistance. It can be cured in one of two ways: either shorten the cable run or reduce the resistance by increasing the size of the cable (thereby decreasing resistance).

Voltage drop should be dealt with in the planning stage. This means that the calculations must be done beforehand. The formula for voltage drop is

$$VD = C \times R$$

where VD is voltage drop, C is current in amps, and R is resistance in ohms. If you call voltage drop V, you can remember it as VCR.

VCR

The current is the total amperage of your expected load. Resistance is the resistance per foot of the cable times the total run (the distance in *both* directions). For example, we expect a 100-amp load at 1000 feet from the genny. We try #2 welding cable. Its resistance per foot is .000162.

R is thus 1000 feet times 2 (the run coming and going) times .000194 (see Table 8.2) times 100 amps:

$$1000' \times 2 \times .000194 \times 100 = 38.8$$

The voltage drop would be 38.8 volts. If we start with 120 volts, we would end up with 120 38.8 = 81.2 volts—way below acceptable.

Let's try it with #00 cable. The resistance per foot of #00 is .0000967 ohms per foot:

$$1000' \times 2 \times .0000967 \times 100 = 19.34$$
$$120 \ 19.34 = 100.66$$

FIGURE 8.14 A circuit tester is important not only for safety, it is also a quick way to check if a line is hot or not.

FIGURE 8.15 A cube tap and a 3-to-2, also known as a ground lifter, U-ground adapter, or pig nose.

Still not good enough. How about #0000?

$$1000' \times 2 \times .0000608 \times 100 = 12.16$$

This means that with 120 volts we would end up with 107.84. Almost there. But the generator has a trim adjustment! We can crank the generator up to 130 volts. This leaves us with 117 volts. More than enough. That's why we get the big bucks.

Electrical Safety

Electrical safety must be taken seriously. We can't cover every aspect of this complex subject here, but the following is a list of the most fundamental rules to remember on a set:

1. Ground all systems whenever possible.
2. *Always* tape your neutrals and *never* fuse the neutral.
3. Keep distribution boxes away from water and off of wet ground. Use half-apples and rubber mats.
4. Always ground HMIs with substantial wire; zip cord is not sufficient.
5. No one but an electrician should ever plug in a light or provide power.
6. Always use a fused disconnect near the power supply.
7. Check voltage before plugging anything in.
8. Tape over any loose hot connectors or energized metal.
9. Never overload distribution equipment.
10. The fuse should always be the weakest link of the chain. The capacity of any fuse should always be *less* than the ampacity of any part of the system.
11. Never bypass the fuses.
12. Cables should be routed sensibly and taped down or bagged if necessary. Never let loops of cable stick up to trip somebody. Use rubber mats over any cables where traffic is substantial.
13. The head cable of a light on a stand should always hang vertically. It should never come off a light at an angle so as to put sideways force on the stand.

FIGURE 8.16 Sizes of copper wire used for distribution and sub-distribution.

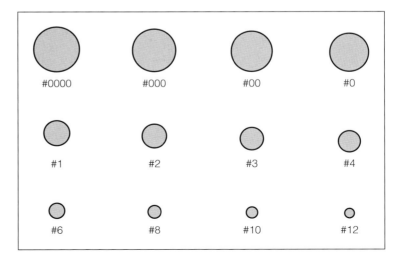

14. Keep your load balanced.
15. With large lights (5K and above in tungsten and some HMIs), the bulbs should be removed for transportation.
16. Hot lenses can shatter when water hits them. If rain or rain effects are a problem, provide rain hoods, plastic covered flags, or other rain protection.
17. Warn people to look away when switching on a light.
18. Never touch two lights or light stands at the same time.
19. Don't assume it's AC. DC can be deadly. Check it.

Wet Work

Because water triples conductivity, working in or near water is probably the most hazardous situation a crew can face. Extra precautions and constant vigilance are required. Saltwater-soaked beaches are particularly hazardous. Some things to keep in mind:
1. Keep all stage boxes and connectors dry by wrapping them in plastic and keep them on half-apple boxes. Remember that gaffer's tape is not resistant to water or cold; plastic electrical tape will work. Garbage bags are useful, but Visqueen or heavy plastic is better.
2. Ground everything in sight.
3. Keep HMI ballasts out of water and off damp sand.
4. Use waterproof shoes, rubber gloves, and waterproof suits if necessary. Place dry rubber mats liberally, wherever someone might be working with hot items such as HMI ballasts, distribution boxes, etc.
5. When equipment (including cable) has been around saltwater, wash it down if you can.

It is possible to run lights underwater. They must be immersed when turned on and cannot be taken out while hot or they will explode. If the connections are not completely sealed (with, for example, hot glue) the water will become electrically hot and may pose a danger.

HMI Safety

Owing to poor design and engineering, HMIs can be extremely hazardous. The startup voltage on an HMI can be 13,000 volts or more.
1. The ballast should always be grounded. The ground should be of substantial wire (at least #12 or larger) and attached to the ground metal with something that can take a large load—a Trico, vise grips, Anderson clamp, etc. Incredibly, few ballasts provide an attachment point for a ground wire. Usually, a screw must be slightly loosened or a bit of paint scraped off.
2. Read voltage from the ballast to a ground and from the head to a ground.

3. Never operate the HMI with the lens off. The lens filters harmful ultraviolet radiation.
4. Never attempt to defeat the microswitch, which prevents the unit from firing if the lens is open.
5. Don't let anyone lean on the stand or sit on the ballast.

Grounding Safety

The concept of safety grounds is simple. We always want the electricity to have a path that is easier to follow than through us. In general, any metal object that is in some way connected to the earth will serve as a suitable ground. A metal rod buried in the ground is the most basic and perhaps most reliable ground. Most permanently installed electrical systems are grounded. Many building codes require that the neutral and ground be bonded together at the box and that a direct ground be run from the box to the earth. This ground is then continued by the continuous metal contact of conduit and box to the metal housing of all devices.

Cold-water pipes are a reliable ground since they have a continuous metal-to-metal circuit connected to the supply pipes, which are buried in earth. Hot-water pipes are less likely because the metal-to-metal contact may be broken at the hot water heater.

Sprinkler system pipes are grounded, but it is considered unsafe (and in most cases illegal) to ground to them.

1. Always check for adequate ground with a voltage meter. Read the potential voltage between the ground and a hot source.
2. Remember that paint is an insulator. You will not get a good ground if you don't scrape down to bare metal.
3. A ground is not truly safe if it is not capable of carrying the entire load. A 200-amp load cannot be safely grounded with #20 wire.
4. When in doubt, ground it.

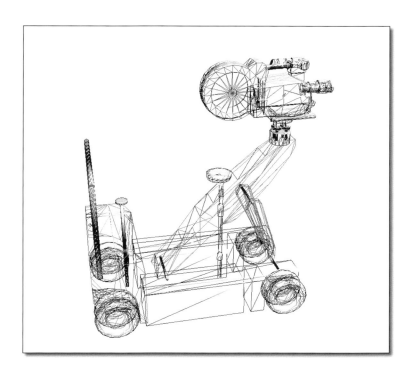

GRIPOLOGY

Grip work is an important part of the lighting process. An understanding of basic grip procedure and equipment is essential for any lighting professional. This chapter covers the tools and equipment of grip work, standard methods, and general set operating methods.

What is a grip? Grips do many jobs on a film set: they set up and push the dolly; they handle cranes and all rigging, including hanging lights from a wall, over the side of a cliff, or on the front of a roller coaster—anything that goes beyond simply placing a light on a stand or on the floor. They also handle any lighting control devices (such as nets, flags, and silks) that are not attached to the light. Anything that actually is attached to the light, such as diffusion clipped on with C-47s, is done by electricians. This is the American system; in most other countries, all lighting control is done by the electricians.

Definitions: *Baby* means a $\frac{5}{8}$-inch stud on a light or pin on a piece of grip equipment or female receiver. *Junior* and *Senior* refer to $1\frac{1}{8}$-inch stud or female receiver. Other standard sizes are $\frac{1}{4}$, $\frac{3}{8}$, and $\frac{1}{2}$ inch. These plus the $\frac{5}{8}$ inch are all found on most standard grip heads.

FIGURE 9.1 A combo head with both $\frac{5}{8}''$ baby stud and a $1\frac{1}{8}''$ junior receiver.

(a)

(b)

FIGURE 9.2 (**a**) A grip shaking it up—aiming a reflector right before they roll camera. (**b**) A soft-side reflector on the left and a hard-side reflector on the right.

Light Controls

Grip effects units modify the character or quantity of light—blocking, redirecting, feathering, and wrapping the light—in a word, control. The basic rule of thumb is that when the control is attached to a light, it is an electrical department deal; if it is separate from the light (on a grip stand, for example), it becomes a grip thing and, for the most part, different equipment is used to deal with it.

Reflectors

Reflector boards or shiny boards are venerable film equipment. On the B westerns of the 1940s and 1950s, they were practically the only piece of lighting equipment used, those being the times of day-for-night, a now largely abandoned technique. Traditionally, reflector boards are roughly 42 × 42-inch and are two-sided, a hard side and a soft side. The hard side is mirror-like, smoothed, highly finished, reflective material. The soft side is reflective material with just a bit of texture. This makes it a bit less specular and slightly softer. As a result, the soft side has considerably less punch and throw than the hard side, which is sometimes referred to as a bullet for its ability to throw a hard, specular beam of reflected sunlight amazing distances.

The soft side is important for balancing daylight exteriors. Because the sun is so specular, daylight exteriors are extraordinarily high-contrast. The problem is that the sun is so intense, most film lights are insignificant in relation

(a)

(b)

FIGURE 9.3 (**a**) A 4′ × 4′ floppy. (**b**) Some shots call for a lot of lighting control—a forest of C-stands can grow quickly. Here several cookies and nets shape the light for a greenscreen shot.

to it. Only an arc, 6K, or 12K makes much of a dent against direct sun. The answer is to use the sun to balance itself. This is what makes reflector boards so useful: the intensity of the reflection rises and falls in direct proportion to the key source.

A variety of surfaces are available for reflector boards. The hardest is actually glass—a mirror, which provides tremendous punch and control—but, of course, is delicate to handle. Easier to transport but less regular is artificial mirror, which can be silvered Plexiglas or silvered Mylar (which can be stretched over a frame).

Hard reflector is very smooth and specular and has very high reflectivity. The soft side is usually silverleaf, which is not as smooth and has leafy edges that hang loose. Boards are also available in gold for matching warm-light situations such as sunsets.

Beadboard is just large sheets of styrofoam. Beadboard is a soft reflector because of the uneven surface. But it is not rigid and seldom stays flat for very long. This is no problem for the soft side, but it makes it very difficult to focus and maintain an even coverage on the hard side. Beadboard is a valuable bounce material, but keep in mind that a single sheet of beadboard is the equivalent of thousands of styrofoam cups.

Rosco and Lee also make supersoft and other reflector materials available in rolls. They can be stretched on frames and made into 6′ × 6′s, 12′ × 12′s, etc. A good trick is to take a cheap glass mirror that is permanently mounted to a backing board (the kind of inexpensive full-length mirror available at a drugstore, for example) and smash it with a hammer in several places. With a semi-soft light, it provides a dappled bounce with nice breakup. With a hard light, it makes a sparkly reflection that can simulate reflection off buildings.

Operating Reflectors

The key rule in relation to operating a reflector is, of course, the old physics rule:

$$\text{angle of incidence} = \text{angle of reflection}$$

This is the problem with reflectors. Because the sun is constantly moving, the boards require constant adjustment. For fast-moving work, it is necessary to station a grip or electrician at each board (one person can handle a couple of boards if they are together). Before each take, the command "shake 'em up" means to wiggle the boards to check that they are still focused where they should be.

Reflector boards are equipped with a brake in the yoke to keep them properly focused. Other rules for using reflectors are:

1. Keep reflectors flat (parallel to the ground) when not in use. This keeps them from blinding people on the set and makes them less susceptible to being knocked over by the wind. It also serves as a reminder that they need refocusing.
2. If it's windy at all, lay the boards on the ground when they are not being attended by a crew member.
3. The reflection of direct sun is very intense. Try to keep it out of people's eyes.
4. Boards must be stabilized during the take. A moving reflection is very noticeable and obviously artificial.

Standard procedure for aiming a board is to tilt it down until the reflection of the sun is just in front of you. Once you have found the spot, it is easier to aim it where you want it to go.

Specialized stands known as reflector stands are usually used for shiny boards. Also called "combo stands," they feature junior receivers, leg braces, no wheels, and a certain amount of heft to help keep things in place. They are called combo stands because they are also used as light stands.

Flags and Cutters

Flags and cutters are basic subtractive lighting. Coming in sizes from 12×18 inches to 24×72 inches, they are used to cast shadows, control spill, and shape the light. They are constructed with $\frac{3}{8}$-inch wire and terminate in a $\frac{3}{8}$-inch pin that fits in grip heads. Flags come in the standard sizes: 12×18, 18×24, 24×36, and 48×48-inch ($4' \times 4'$). There are other, less common sizes as well.

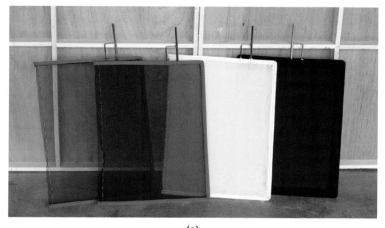

(a)

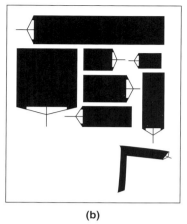

(b)

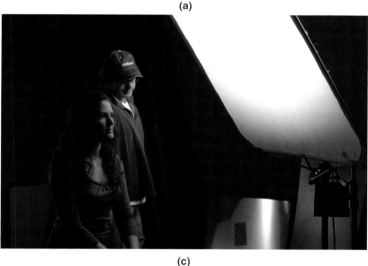

(c)

FIGURE 9.4 (a) A single grip net, a double, a silk and solid (or flag). These are 18 × 24 inches. (b) Various sizes of flags, cutters, and empty frames. (c) Grips handle any sort of lighting control that is not attached to the light, such as this 4′ × 4′ silk creating a soft light for the model.

Flag Tricks

The most basic rule about flags is that the farther away the flag is from the light source, the harder the cut will be—that is, the sharper the shadow will be. This is why flags are such an important adjunct to barndoors. Being attached to the light, barndoors can't be moved away from the light, and there is a limit to how sharp a cut they can produce. The flag can be moved in as far as the frame will allow, making the cut almost infinitely adjustable. For the sharpest cut of all, remove the fresnel, usually by opening the door of the light. This makes it sharper because the bare bulb is a smaller source than the fresnel lens.

The more flooded the light, the sharper the cut. For razor-sharp control of light (and for harder shadows) the light must be at full flood. The more spotted a light is, the softer the shadows will be, and the harder it is to control with barndoors and flags. Cutters are longer and narrower. Sizes include 10 × 42, 18 × 48, and 24 × 72 inches.

(a)

FIGURE 9.5 (**a**) A cuculoris (cookie) creates shafts of light in the smoke effect. (**b**) A branchaloris on a highboy.

(b)

Floppy flags have two layers of duvetyne (the black cloth covering material); one of them is attached on one side only and can be flopped down to make a 4′ × 4′ into a 4′ × 8′, for example. For additional shaping, it is possible to clip small pieces of showcard onto the flag. Just position the spring clip so that it doesn't cast an unwanted shadow. Except in rare circumstances, never mount a flag directly to the grip head on a C-stand. Always include at least a short arm so that the flag can be repositioned. As with any piece of equipment you set, always think ahead to the next step—you may have it where you want it now, but what happens if it needs to move? Don't get yourself too locked in. Leave some slack! Common terms are sider, topper, top chop, bottomer, and bottom chop, all self-explanatory.

Nets

Nets are similar to flags, but instead of opaque black duvetyne, they are covered with bobbinet, a net material that reduces the amount of light without altering its quality.

Nets come in two predominant flavors, single and double (there is a third, called a lavender; rare, but it reduces the light $\frac{1}{3}$ stop). Double nets are usually just a double layer of bobbinet. Each layer is rotated 90° from the layer underneath it. Nets are color-coded in the bindings that secure the scrim to the frame. Singles are white, doubles are red, and silk is color-coded gold. Net material comes in black, white, and lavender, but black is predominantly used.

A single net reduces light by a $\frac{1}{2}$ stop, a double by 1 stop, and a triple, $1\frac{1}{2}$ stops. A lavender reduces by $\frac{1}{3}$ stop. The values are, of course, approximate—the actual reduction depends on the light source, its distance from the net, and the angle of the net material relative to the direction of the light. The main difference between a flag frame and a net frame is that net frames are open-ended. That is, they have one side open, making it possible to orient the net so that there is no shadow of the bar where it might show.

Net Tricks

If you tilt a net so that it is at an angle to the light, it becomes thicker and cuts the light even more. This is an easy way to fine-tune the attenuation. As with a flag, the farther away the net is from the light source, the harder the cut will be.

To set a single source so that the f/stop stays constant over a long distance (to cover a walk, for example), nets can be stacked, overlapped so that the area nearest the light is covered by a single and a double, then a single only, then nothing.

To fine-tune very small areas, paper tape can be applied directly to a net. When the gaffer calls for a single or double net on a light, don't just bring the one s/he asks for, bring them both; it might save you a trip. (This goes for just about anything that you offer to a light: diffusion, scrims, etc.)

Cuculoris

No one knows the origin of the word, but a cuculoris (or cookie or cuke) is arandom pattern designed to break up the light either subtly (if close to the light) or in a hard shadow pattern (if far from the light).

Any flat device designed to cast a patterned shadow is a cookie. Standard cookies come in two varieties: wood, made from $1/4$-inch plywood, and celo, which is a layer of wire net covered with plastic-like material that has a random pattern burned into it to create a varying pattern of transparency and semi-opacity. Celos are much more subtle than a wood cookie. Leaf patterns, blinds, and stained-glass windows are common cookie patterns. Cookies of this type are also known as "gobos." Foamcore is easily cut, but rigid enough to be self-supporting. When actual branches and leaves are used as cookies, they are called "dingles." A small branch is a 1K dingle and larger ones are 2K or 5K dingles; another name is branchaloris. If they actually appear in the frame they are called "smilex".

As with flags, the farther away from the light, the sharper the cut. If a hard, sharp shadow pattern is needed, be sure to employ a light large enough to back way off and still get the stop. For maximum sharpness, take the lens off the light. This reduces the radiator to a point source which casts the sharpest possible pattern.

(a)

FIGURE 9.6 (**a**) A 4 × 4 cart holds 4 × 4 open frames "skinned up" with various gels and diffusion. Extra rolls of diffusion are stored on the side. (**b**) Grips "Hollywood" a quarter-stop silk to cover a walk. Since the actors are walking and the dolly moving, they can't set it on highboys. One of them rides the dolly for ease of movement. A full silk, which is a much heavier diffusion, would have been too much; the actors would have been significantly darker than their background and needed additional lighting, which would have been hard to do on a walking shot (a walk and talk) and even more difficult without shutting down the entire street—which is much more complex to get a permit for in most cities.

(b)

Grid

The use of grids came from still photographers, who used them to make nondirectional light directional. Honeycomb grids have very small openings and are one to two inches thick. They function in the same way as an eggcrate on a soft light.

Open Frames

Frames of all sizes come uncovered so that the grips can put on the diffusion of the day. A couple of open frames in each size are a must in any grip order. Paper tape can be used to apply gel to a frame, but double-stick tape is also useful. Snot tape is the more professional solution; it is double-sided transfer tape in a dispenser, which is an extremely quick way to gel up a frame—and the best way to accomplish the job.

Cookies and Celos

Nobody really knows why it's called a cuculoris, but it is. Cookies (or cuculoris) are flags made of plywood with random patterns cut out. They are used to break up the light and add texture. A soft version, called a "cello," is a wire mesh with a semi-transparent layer that has been burned into a random pattern. Another variation on the cuculoris is the "branchaloris" which is made from a real branch—usually held up by a branch holder.

Diffusers

Also known as silks, diffusers come in all the standard flag sizes and are covered with a white silk-like diffusion

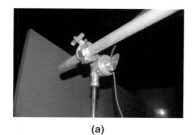
(a)

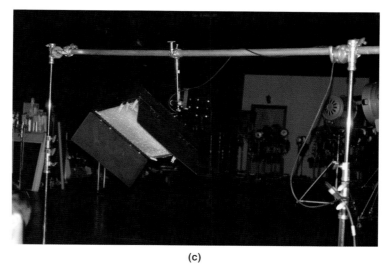
(c)

(b)

FIGURE 9.7 (a) A detail of the goalpost—two pipe clamps hold the Speedrail (aluminum pipe). (b) A sidearm is used to rig the Mole Biax to the Speedrail. (c) Two highboys and a piece of Speedrail are used to rig a goalpost to support a Biax light. This type of rigging would be done by the grip crew in collaboration with the electricians.

material. Originally, of course, it was real silk, and still is if you order China silk. More often, the silk is made of white nylon, which is easier to clean and doesn't turn yellow as readily. Silks soften the light and reduce it by about 2 stops. There is also a much lighter diffusion $\frac{1}{4}$-stop silk that reduces the light by about $\frac{1}{3}$ stop—go figure.

Butterflies and Overheads

Permanently mounted silks are seldom larger than the standard $4' \times 4'$. Six-by-sixes are called butterflies. They come in breakdown frames which are assembled on site and the covering is stretched and secured with ties.

Larger silks are called "overheads" and come in the standard sizes $8' \times 8'$, $12' \times 12'$, and $20' \times 20'$, commonly called 8 by, 12 by, and 20 by. The frames are transported disassembled with the covering off. Also available are $9' \times 12'$, $20' \times 40'$, and $30' \times 30'$, and even $40' \times 40'$. Butterflies (6×6) can be flown on one stand (usually a highboy).

Large frames are flown on highboys. The critical factor in flying a 20 by is knowing that it requires sufficient area to drive a sailboat at 12 knots; it can be powerful! Use extreme caution when a large silk is up. Don't fly a silk without an adequate size crew of knowledgeable grips.

(a)

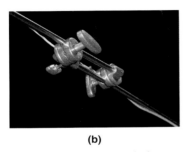

(b)

(c)

FIGURE 9.8 (a) A highboy (hi-hi roller stand) has a 4½-inch grip head which in this case holds a grip arm. The arm is doubled to get it out farther. (b) A detail of the doubled grip arm. (c) The right-hand rule. Note how, as you face the stand, the handles are on the right.

Overhead Rules

Never leave silks unattended when they are up in the air. One grip per stand is required at all times, and two or three more when moving it in anything but dead calm conditions. These things can do real damage if they get away from you. Bag liberally! Run your lines out at as shallow an angle as you can and secure properly. If possible, leave the top riser of the highboy unextended and leave it loose so it can take out any torsion that builds up in the system. Use a grip hitch on the anchor lines so they can be tensioned and readjusted.

Standard technique for the lines is to take a 100-ft hank of sash cord and find the center, which is then secured to one of the top corners. The excess line is then coiled and left to hang far enough down so that it can be reached, even if the frame is vertical.

Tying off to several heavy sandbags can make readjustment easier than tying off to something permanent. It is then possible just to drag the bags a bit, rather than having to adjust the knot. To attach the tie-lines to the bags, use a trucker's hitch knot. Attach the rag to the frame using a shoelace knot, which is quick to untie when it is time to change the rag. Set the frame up on apple boxes when attaching or removing the rag to keep it off the ground.

FIGURE 9.10 A studded C-clamp with two baby spuds.

(a)   **(b)**

FIGURE 9.9 (**a**) Everything about this C-stand setup is wrong. The right-hand rule is not observed, the arm is set at eye level in a way someone could poke his/her eye out, the weight is not over the high leg, there is no sandbag, and they have begun raising it not on the top riser. (**b**) A properly done C-stand. The right-hand rule is observed, the arm is set safely out of the way, the weight is over the high leg, and a sandbag is set also on the high leg.

Griffs

One more type of covering that can go on overhead frames is griffolyn (pronounced grif-lon). Originally produced as a farm product (it's really just a high-tech tarpaulin), griffolyn (or griff) is a reinforced plastic material. Its advantage is that the white side is extremely reflective and the whole unit is highly durable and waterproof.

Griffs come in all sizes from 4 × 4 to 20 × 20 or even larger, and also can be had in rolls for custom application. Matthews markets special tape, which can fuse sections together, and duck feet griff clips, which provide attachment points so that a custom-made piece can be quickly flown in a variety of situations—with or without a frame. Matthews offers griff in black-and-white, white-and-white, and clear configurations.

With all large overheads, ordering it complete means that it includes the silk, a solid (black duvetyne), a single net, and a double net, which gives you a wide variety of controls on the same frame. Bleached muslin (very white, about the consistency of a bedsheet) and unbleached muslin (yellowish white for a warmer look) can also be stretched on frames as a very heavy diffusion or bounce.

Griffs are versatile. Their most frequent use is as a large reflector, either for sun or for a large HMI as a bounce fill. A 12 × 12 or 20 × 20 white griff with a 6K, 12K, or 18K bounced into it is also a popular combination for night exteriors. It's soft enough to appear sourceless, but reflective enough to provide a good stop. A griff on a frame can also be used by turning the black side to the subject as a solid cutter or as negative fill. If it rains, the griff is waterproof so it can be an excellent rain tent. With the white side down, it even provides a bit of sky ambiance.

Holding

Grip Heads

Much of grip hardware is for just that—gripping stuff. A good deal of your job as a grip is getting things to stay where you want them.

The grip head is one of the most valuable devices in a grip's armamentarium for getting just about anything to stay just about anywhere. Holding stuff is the essence of gripping. The grip box is full of things that are designed only to hold something somewhere, firmly—but adjustably.

The grip or gobo head is one of the most important inventions of the twentieth century. Versatile, powerful, and stable, the grip head has been called upon to perform a mind-boggling array of tasks. It is a connector with two pressure plates and holes for pins of various sizes. It can also accept slotted flat plates (such as on the ears of an overhead mount), foamcore, show cards, plywood, etc. In place, it can hold a grip arm, a $\frac{5}{8}$-inch stud for a light, a baby plate, a small tree branch, armature wire, pencils, and just about anything else you can imagine; and if you put it there, it stays there.

A gobo arm is the same device but permanently mounted on a steel rod, which is 40 inches standard. Short arms are usually around 20 inches and are an important part of any order. A short arm with a grip head attached is known as a short-arm assembly. Always order at least a few of them; they are invaluable.

C-Stand Rules

As any grip will tell you, one of the most basic rules of gripology is the right-hand rule. The rule is always set a grip head so that gravity wants to tighten it. Remember: "Righty tighty, lefty loosey." It's simple when you think about it. Grip heads are friction devices. By tightening the screw in a clockwise direction, you are putting pressure on the arm (or whatever you're holding), and friction is what is both holding the arm in and preventing the pressure from releasing. If the item being held extends out from the stand, it exerts rotational force in the direction of gravity. If this rotational force turns the screw in a counterclockwise direction, it will release the pressure.

Make sure that the force of the load is trying to turn the head in the same direction that you used to tighten it.

FIGURE 9.11 A grip truck on location. Carts for C-stands and 4 × 4s stand ready. A four-step ladder makes it easier to get on and off the truck via the lift gate. Reflector stands are stored on the door.

Highboys

The highboy, also called a "high-high stand" is a roller stand used for holding large silks, making "goalposts," and rigging all manner of large items. It can extend very high, usually about 18 feet, and is heavy-duty construction. Most have a larger version of the grip head: the 4½-inch grip head.

Clamps

Studded C-Clamps

Studded clamps come in a range of sizes from 4 to 12 inches, with either baby (⅝ inch) studs or junior (1⅛ inch) receivers. They are used for rigging lights, grips heads, tie-off points, and other items to beams, trees, and anything else that can be fitted on.

C-Clamp Tips

- A properly mounted studded C can hold a substantial load securely. It is not good at resisting the turning load perpendicular to its axis. So don't try to make it do that.
- A C-clamp will definitely leave marks on just about anything. Standard procedure is to card it: put a small piece of showcard underneath the feet to protect the surface.
- ALWAYS put a safety line around the item being mounted and the C-clamp itself.

FIGURE 9.12 Tips for Grips. (Drawing by Brent Hirn, Master of Gripology).

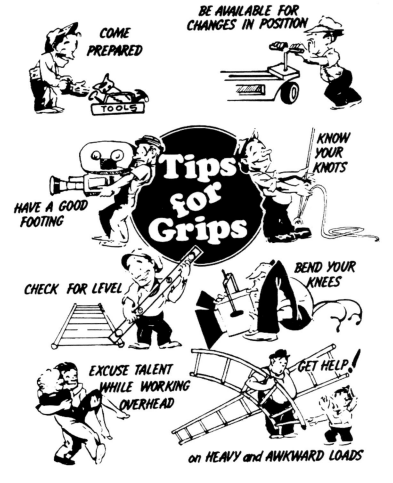

- Choose the appropriate size C-clamp. A clamp that is too large for the job will have to be extended too far. When this happens, the threaded bar can wobble and twist because it is too far from its support. This is an unsafe condition and should be avoided.
- If you are clamping to a pipe, you must use a C-clamp that has channel iron mounted to it (U-shaped steel feet). A flat C-clamp will not safely grab a pipe.

Bar Clamps

A variation on the studded C-clamp is the bar clamp, which is a furniture clamp with a 1K stud attached to it. Bar clamps can be extremely wide (up to several feet) and so can fit around items that would be impossible for a C-clamp.

Pipe Clamps

Pipe clamps are specialty items for mounting directly to pipes and grids. They are a theatrical item and see their most frequent use in studio work. If you are likely to be working in a studio or an industrial situation with a pipe grid, pipe clamps can free lights from stands.

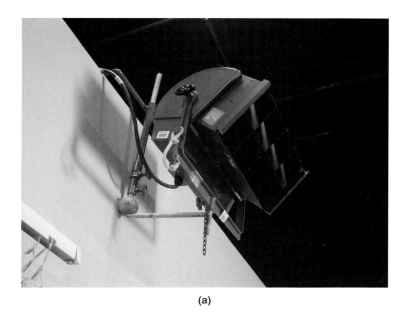

(a)

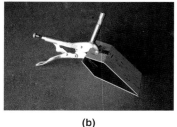

(b)

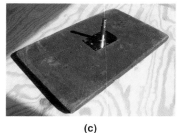

(c)

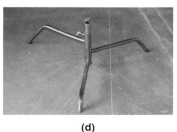

(d)

FIGURE 9.13 (**a**) A 2K ziplight rigged on a set wall with a set hanger. (**b**) A platypus—used for holding beadboard and foamcore in a C-stand or highboy. (**c**) A pigeon—baby plate on a pancake. (**d**) A 2K turtle base. This one is actually the bottom of a C-stand. Others are designed only as bases for lights or equipment (such as wind machines) which have a $1\frac{1}{8}$-inch (junior) stud.

Studded Chain Vise Grips

This is a grip's grip tool. Many grips carry chain vise grips in their personal kits, because they are oddball items not carried by some rental companies. Studded versions can mount lights to vertical pipes, beams, bumpers, and other odd places. Nonstudded chain vise grips are often used to secure two pipes together or to mount a light stand on a crane or a fire escape. They provide the kind of bite and stability that you just can't get from sash cord or clamps.

Cardellini and Mafer Clamps

Pronounced "may-fer," mafers clamps are indispensable: don't leave home without them. They can bite anything up to the size of a 2 × 4, and have interchangeable studs that can do anything from rigging a baby spot to holding a glass plate. They have dozens of other uses:

- Grips often clamp mafers onto the end of the dolly track so that they don't accidentally let the dolly run off the end.
- With the baby stud clamped into a grip head, a mafer can hold up a 6 × 6 frame.
- With a baby plate mounted in it, the mafer can be attached to pipe or board to hold a small reflector card. The uses are endless.

A Cardellini is similar, but a bit more versatile, and has tremendous holding power.

Platypus

A platypus is a studded vise grip with 5 × 6-inch plates for grabbing beadboard and foamcore with minimal breakage.

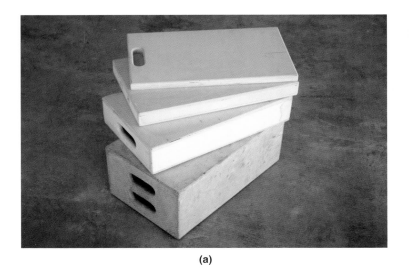

(a)

(b)

FIGURE 9.14 (**a**) Full apple, half-apple, quarter-apple and on top, a pancake. (**b**) Three full apples in the standard positions (from left to right): Number 3 (upright—full height), number 2 (on the side—medium height), and number 1 (laid down—lowest height).

Wall Plates, Baby Plates, and Pigeons

Although technically different things, the names—wall plates, baby plates, and pigeons—are used interchangeably. They are all basically baby studs with a flat plate attached. It can also be done with a junior ($1\frac{1}{8}$ inch)receiver. The plate always has screw holes. With a baby plate, some drywall screws, and a portable drill, a grip can attach small lights, grip arms, cutters, reflectors, and props to any wood surface.

A particularly popular combination is a baby plate mounted on a half-apple, quarter apple, or pancake—it is called a pigeon. This is the standard low mounting position for small lights. When you need to get even lower, a pancake (the slimmest form of apple box) should be used, although the depth of the screws is limited. When a half-apple is not enough, other apple boxes can be placed beneath for some degree of adjustability.

2K Receivers and Turtles

While a pigeon is generally a baby plate, a similar rig can be made with a 2K receiver. A variation on the 2K pigeon is the turtle, which is a three-legged low mount for any 2K studded light. The advantage of the turtle is that it is self-supporting with a sandbag or two. The T-bone is similar. It is a T made of two flat steel bars with a 2K receiver. It will mount the light lower than a turtle and can also be screwed to a wall. T-bones all have safety chains attached. The chains are constantly in the way and always seem to get under the T-bone or apple box when you try to get it to sit flat. They have no conceivable application, and yet they are permanently mounted. We can all hope that manufacturers will wake up and make T-bones without the chains.

Several manufacturers now make C-stands with a detachable base. When the vertical riser is removed, the legs are an independent unit with a junior hole. This makes an instant turtle. The riser can be clamped to a fire escape or mounted in other hard-to-get-to places as an extendable mount.

Side Arms and Offset Arms

Side arms (both 1K and 2K varieties) serve two functions:
1. They arm the light out a bit for that little extra stretch.
2. Because they can clamp onto the stand at any level, they are useful for mounting a light low but still on a stand.

Offset arms (both sizes) are similar, but fit into the top of a baby or junior stand, rather than on the side.

Miscellaneous

Apple Boxes

The term comes from the early days of Hollywood, when they used actual apple boxes. Now they are specially made items that are sturdily built. Simple boxes in four sizes, they have an amazing variety of uses. The sizes are full apple, half-apple, quarter-apple, and pancake.

Wedges

Wedges are simple wooden wedges used primarily for leveling; most often leveling dolly track. A box of wedges is a normal accessory for any work with dolly track. Smaller ones, called "camera wedges" are used for small jobs around the camera and dolly.

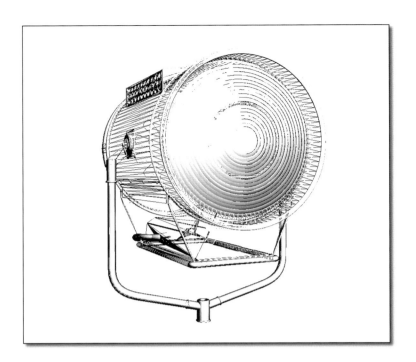

THE TEAM AND SET OPERATIONS

The way the camera and lighting team work together is fairly standardized; there are some regional variations, but the basics are the same throughout most of the world. The commonalities of technique and tools make it possible for a crew that has never worked together before to get the job done with a fair amount of efficiency, even when it includes members from other countries. In this chapter we examine the duties of each member of the team and how they work together on and off the set.

The DP

The person responsible for the lighting team varies, depending on the type of production. In feature films, single-camera television, and commercials shot on film (or in some cases HD or DV video), the team is run by a director of photography (DP; in other regions, DoP). The DP works with the director and has authority over the electric crew, camera crew, and grip crew. He or she will also consult directly with the production designer.

FIGURE 10.1 Film crews work together in a highly coordinated way. All know their individual jobs and cooperate closely with members of their own department and those of other departments.

Although directors differ in the amount of input they want concerning the frame (lens selection, camera position, angles, camera moves), it is the job of the DP to fulfill the director's vision of the scene. The DP implements this through the camera operator, the camera assistants, and the dolly grip.

The cinematographer's vision of the lighting is implemented by the gaffer (sometimes called Chief Lighting Technician) and the key grip. In video production (particularly television), the responsibility is split. The camera operator deals strictly with the video camera and framing the shot, and a lighting director (LD) takes full responsibility for lighting the scene. This is not unlike the English system (also used in many other countries) where the operator is responsible for working with the director on camera moves, placement, and lens choice, and the lighting cameraman devotes his full attention to the lighting, often never even looking through the lens.

As some HD and DV shoots become more and more like standard film production, with a DP instead of an LD, the traditional division of duties between the DP and gaffer will diminish and re-establish themselves. In addition, there may be a DIT (digital imaging technician; however, this person does not get involved in lighting—it is a camera crew position). In commercials there are many director/cameramen (or director/camerawomen). With their

(a)

(b)

FIGURE 10.2 (a) Don't forget to put a strain relief on all header cables on lights. (b) A C-47 (left, a wooden clothespin) and a C-74 (right)—a reverse clothespin for pulling scrims out of lights.

attention devoted primarily toward directing the scene, dealing with the client, and operating the camera, they have come to depend heavily on lighting gaffers, who light the scene based on a brief discussion of the board (storyboard of the commercial) with the director.

The Team

The Gaffer

First let's clear up an ancient controversy. By now, you will likely have heard many fanciful stories about the origin of the term "gaffer." Let's set the record straight—according to the *Oxford English Dictionary,* "gaffer" is a sixteenth-century term meaning "one whose position entitled him to respect," or, more directly, "the foreman or overman of a gang of workmen: a headman … a master, a governor."

The gaffer is, in traditional production, the DP's chief lieutenant for lighting. In the early days he was referred to as the chief electrician and director of the electric crew, although these terms are now seldom used. Recently the title has been changed to chief lighting technician. This more accurately reflects the job, since the gaffer rarely deals with electricity, which is the responsibility of the second electric.

The gaffer implements the DP's vision by issuing orders to the electricians and works in conjunction with the key grip. Responsibilities include a wide range of duties. The gaffer

- Scouts the location for lighting problems and opportunities and determines the availability of power, cable runs, etc.
- After consultation with the DP and the production manager, prepares the lighting and electrical order.
- Consults with the grip about rigging lights in the grid or ceiling, rigging lights on cars for running shots, silks or butterflies, diffusion frames, etc.
- Gives orders to the electricians concerning what lights to place, and where and what diffusion or color correction they will need.
- Meters the scene, directs the electricians in focusing and balancing the lighting, spot/flooding, adding or removing scrims or dimmers. Directs the grips in placing flags, nets, cutters, and diffusion frames.
- Alerts the DP and/or director to any potential problems. For example, the lighting may look great for a certain position, but the actor will burn up if he gets too close to a window.
- Depending on the DP, the gaffer may meter the scene to determine the camera aperture.
- Consults with the DP, operator, and AC about special conditions such as frame speed, practical monitors, HMI sync, filtration, etc.

- During filming, monitors the scene for changing conditions, shifting sunlight, or clouds. Particularly where the DP is also operating the camera, the gaffer functions as the eyes alert for trouble.

The DP and gaffer's tools include

- Incident meter
- Spot meter
- Color-temperature meter
- Digital or Polaroid camera
- Gel books
- HMI sync charts
- 18% gray card and perhaps a gray scale and color chart
- Viewing filter (gaffer glass)
- Compass
- Flashlight
- Sun charts

The Best Boy

The electrical best boy is the NCO in charge of the electric crew. He or she is the gaffer's or lighting director's key assistant. Some people don't like the term "best boy" (particularly with many women fulfilling the function these days) and the position is also called second electric or assistant chief lighting technician. The job covers:

1. Everything electrical: performing the tie-in or generator hookup, cable runs, load balancing, and electrical-equipment selection.
2. Direct supervision of the crew. On larger jobs the second will select and schedule electricians, see that their time sheets are filled out, and so on.
3. Equipment management. The second coordinates with production to ensure that all equipment requested is available and accounted for, and works out plans for swing trucks, rigging crews, and strike crews. The second should be ready at any time to tell the gaffer what lights are in use and what is still available.
4. Staging. The second should be ready to maneuver for a good staging area and then supervise off-loading the equipment and preparing it for use. At the end of the day, the second is responsible for making sure it all gets back on the truck safely and efficiently.

On larger productions, many of these functions will be performed by the third or fourth electric and the second electric will generally stay on the truck, taking care of the paper work.

Third Electric and Electricians

The third electric is the corporal of the crew. On smaller jobs the third is the lowest on the totem pole, but on a large feature, s/he may have some supervisory duties over the electricians and day players (hired for the day.)

(a)

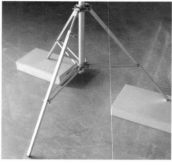

(b)

FIGURE 10.3 (a) Moving a large unit safely requires teamwork and coordination. Here the best boy and electricians get a hand from the grips in leveling the light: a half-apple and quarter-apple keep the light (an 18K with a Chimera) level while one leg extends off the sidewalk.
(b) A Rocky Mountain leg can help with leveling smaller units. It can be extended to adjust to uneven terrain, stairs, etc.

FIGURE 10.4 A hand-squeezer—a small dimmer for practical lamps, efx, and lights of 1000 watts or less.

In the early days when open arcs were the only lights, there were no motors to advance the carbons as they burned down. Instead, an electrician tended each light, slowly turning a crank to keep the carbons in trim. This required considerable skill and these people earned the title "lamp operators." Even today on the standard feature budget forms, you will see the category lamp operators.

Other Responsibilities

Equipment preparation: it is up to the third to make sure every piece of equipment is ready to go: every light has its barndoor and scrims, Bates extensions, and singles are standing by, and so on. In general, when the gaffer calls for a light, it is the third who actually brings the light, while at the same time the second brings power to the position so that the light is hot as soon as it hits the stand.

A best boy/electrician should carry on his/her belt or in pockets

- Cutter (usually a mat knife or razor knife; extra blades)
- Wooden clothespins
- Work gloves
- Crescent wrench 6
- Flashlight
- Volt/ohm meter (both AC and DC)
- Continuity tester
- Amprobe
- Slotted screwdriver
- Slip joint pliers
- Marking pens

FIGURE 10.5 The basics that every technician should have on the set: a cutter, some kind of multi-tool, a Swiss Army knife, and a flashlight. One additional essential for grips and electricians: work gloves.

In the tool kit
- Visegrips
- Channel lock pliers
- Phillips screwdrivers: #1, #2
- Set of hex wrenches
- Fuse puller
- Cube taps—heavy-duty
- Current taps
- 3-to-2s
- Electrical tape (black)
- Colored plastic marking tape (red, blue, yellow, white, green)
- Spare fuses: household, stage box, barrel fuses
- Heavy-duty staple gun
- Tape measure
- Wire nuts
- Zip cord

The Key Grip

The grips are an important part of the lighting team. Their responsibilities in regard to lighting include
- Rigging all lights hanging from the grid or from the set walls or ceiling.
- Rigging lights to vehicles for running shots.
- Setting of flags, cutters, nets, and cookies.
- Setting up and adjusting reflector boards.
- Rigging and adjusting silks, butterflies, and overheads.
- Seeing to any diffusion or gel not attached to the light, such as gel tacked to windows, on frames, or otherwise *tricked up*.
- Placing all sandbags, tying off tall stands with sash, grip chain, etc.
- Any hoisting or rigging of heavy equipment.

FIGURE 10.6 A grip Hollywooding (handholding) a courtesy flag for the camera operator. Note that the Fisher dolly is mounted on a track dolly which sits on the tracks.

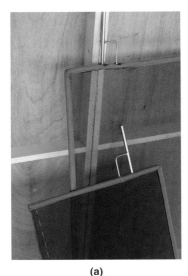

(a)

(b)

FIGURE 10.7 (a) Never do this. Stacking a smaller net against a larger one will most certainly cause damage; likewise with flags and silks. (b) A good trick with milk crates: the boxes that reams of paper come in exactly fit inside to prevent small objects from poking out and getting tangled.

- Helping out with heavy units or hard-to-reach situations.
- Providing ladders, lifts, cranes, scissor lifts, etc.
- Providing rain protection for lights.
- Leveling all tall stands such as Molevators and Crankovators and Cinevators with apple boxes, step-ups, and wedges.

If there is no dolly grip, the key grip usually tends to the dolly and the electricians deal with the second grip.

As described here, the responsibilities of the grips are strictly according to the American system, as it was developed in Hollywood in the first 50 years of the 20th century. To a certain extent, it is the result of union rivalries between electrics, grips, and prop people. In Europe, Japan, and elsewhere, different systems are used; typically, the electricians handle all lighting tasks, including rigging, sandbagging, and setting flags and cutters. Grips supervise when there is a heavy or complex rigging job, such as one involving cranes or pulleys.

This leaves the grips free to run the dolly, work with the set carpenters, attend to cranes, and perform other important duties. The division of labor under the American system can be a source of problems. It is possible for an electrician to set a light, focus, gel, and scrim it, then have to search for a grip to move the flag two inches. If it needs further adjustment, the electrician has to find the grip again, explain (with much discussion and hand waving) what the flag is supposed to accomplish, and then stand by while the grip adjusts the flag.

A great grip crew can be an invaluable support. But for many grips, working with the electricians is low-priority. Often they must wait while s/he sees to more pressing duties with the camera support, dolly, or crane. In the meantime, the electrician's job can grind to a halt while s/he stares at a piece of equipment that s/he knows perfectly well how to operate but is not allowed to touch.

Grips

The second grip works for the key grip, just as the best boy electric does for the gaffer. On larger jobs the duties become largely administrative, but as with the key, the grips might be called on to perform a variety of duties in lighting control, rigging, leveling, camera support, cranes, and safety.

Most grips carry a large assortment of tools including
- Mat knife and extra blades
- Hammer
- Tape measure
- Slip-joint pliers
- Channel lock pliers
- Work gloves
- Slotted screwdrivers

- Phillips screwdrivers
- Flashlight
- Heavy-duty staple gun
- Portable drill; drywall screws and drill bits
- Saw (a folding tree saw is handy; for big jobs, a circular saw)
- Bubble level
- 4′ level
- Crescent wrench
- Vise grips
- Chain vise grips
- Motorcycle straps (ratchet straps)
- Socket wrench set
- Set of hex wrenches
- S-hooks
- Speed square
- WD40 or silicone spray
- Marking pens (Sharpie)
- Chalk for marking the floor
- Squeegee and spray bottle for applying gel to windows
- Bailing wire
- Washers, including fender washers
- Camera wedges
- Chalk line
- Side cutters (dykes)
- $^3/_8″$—16 bolts of various lengths (camera tie-downs)

(a)

(b)

FIGURE 10.8 (**a**) Soldiering the lights in a studio keeps the work area organized and efficient. (**b**) C-Stands soldiered. It's not about aesthetics; it's about being able to get the equipment quickly and efficiently, knowing what's available, and quickly being able to assess if all units are complete and ready to go.

Other Crews

One of the great secrets of efficiency and speed in filming is prerigging. This means the crew (or a few members of the main crew) arrives on a set the day before to run power, position large lights, rig lights in unusual places, etc. It can make it much more efficient when the shoot crew arrives. A prerig (or prelight) crew may consist of a single electrician or grip, all the way up to a large crew with a rigging gaffer, rigging grip, and support services.

Set Operations

The difference between a smoothly run set and a chaotic one can be measured by the number of extra hours worked in a production day. The DP is in charge creatively, but it usually falls to the gaffer and second to run the lighting operation efficiently.

Load-In

One of the most critical decisions on many locations can be where to park the truck. Try to keep it as close as you can while retaining sufficient room behind the loading gate. One of the most fundamental mistakes is parking the truck where it will appear in a shot later in the day. Moving the truck

FIGURE 10.9 Block, light, rehearse, shoot: the standard methodology is not only efficient, but is also a safeguard against chaos and confusion.

during the shoot day can be a disaster. Pin down the AD on a safe location. If there is more than one truck, try to keep them together.

Staging

Arrive early and stake out a good staging area before other departments take out all the good ones. You will need room to line up all the equipment in an orderly fashion so each can be reached quickly. You will need room to line up lights and stands so they can be grabbed quickly. Depending on how the day is expected to run, it may be efficient to leave some items on the truck, but every shoot is different.

The Generator

Finding a parking place for the generator is even more critical than staging the trucks. A generator should be as close as possible in order to minimize time-consuming cable runs and voltage drop. On the other hand, even blimped generators make some noise. And if you are shooting sound, you will want to keep the genny back far enough to minimize sound problems. You will probably want to have the genny operator fire up the engine as soon as possible to allow time for warming up before applying a load. Voltage output and crystal sync must be checked at the beginning of the day and monitored periodically.

Cabling

A well-thought-out cable run from the power source can make an enormous difference in the day. It should be as direct as possible, but it should not go any place where it might appear in a shot—this is imperative.

Likewise, it should cross the path of traffic as little as possible, particularly with respect to the dolly, stands on wheels, and so on. It may be necessary to fly it to keep it out of the way of vehicles or dolly traffic. Sash cord is used to tie it off to beams, highboys, the truck, or whatever is available.

As the cable is run out, it is checked for proper color coding and adjusted if necessary. A quick visual check of connectors is a good idea. Then the neutrals are taped and distro boxes or lunch boxes are plugged in. The second tests each box for proper voltage and marks the boxes if AC and DC are being mixed.

The Process

Rough-In

Based on previous plans, the DP and gaffer might know some things about where they want the lights. As soon as they can, they start to rough-in. This is not really lighting; it is

FIGURE 10.10 Large rigging jobs such as these dozens of Kino Flo Image 80s for the film *X2* are tasks better handled by rigging crews: rigging gaffer, rigging grip, and as many electricians and grips as are needed to get the set prepped in time for when the shoot crew is scheduled to arrive. (Photo courtesy of Tony "Nako" Nakonechnyj.)

things like running power from the generator, pre-positioning cranes, getting the units to the set (or nearby), that sort of thing.

Running power is a big part of this. All power and distribution on a set is the responsibility of the best boy. With larger distro setups, the best boy should walk the line, inspecting the cabling, checking the connections, and making sure the right lines are plugged into the correct phases of the power source. Once lights are up and running the best boy will also use a clamp-on ammeter (commonly called an Amprobe) to verify that the load is in balance and no phase, line, or connector is loaded above ampacity.

Blocking

Really serious lighting can begin only when you know the frame—what area you are lighting and where the camera goes. You also need to know the actions. Are the actors standing or sitting? Does the car enter the alley from the left or right? Does the door stay open or does the actor close it? All this is critical information you will need to do lighting—and most of all, to do lighting efficiently. If you don't know the action and blocking of the actors (or cars or horses, or

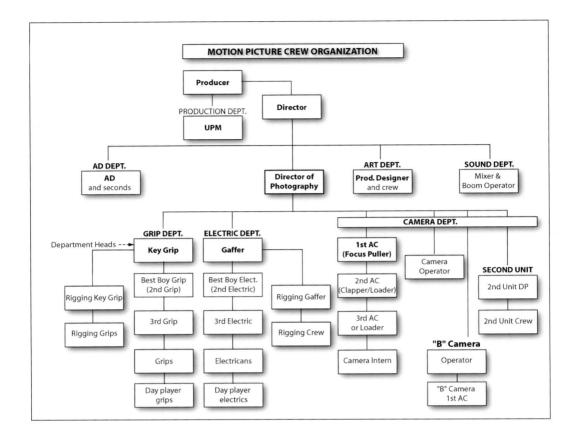

MOTION PICTURE CREW ORGANIZATION

- Producer
  - PRODUCTION DEPT. — Director
    - UPM

- **AD DEPT.**
  - AD and seconds
- Director of Photography
- **ART DEPT.**
  - Prod. Designer and crew
- **SOUND DEPT.**
  - Mixer & Boom Operator

GRIP DEPT.
Department Heads →
- Key Grip
  - Rigging Key Grip
  - Rigging Grips
  - Best Boy Grip (2nd Grip)
  - 3rd Grip
  - Grips
  - Day player grips

ELECTRIC DEPT.
- Gaffer
  - Best Boy Elect. (2nd Electric)
  - 3rd Electric
  - Electricans
  - Day player electrics
  - Rigging Gaffer
  - Rigging Crew

CAMERA DEPT.
- 1st AC (Focus Puller)
  - 2nd AC (Clapper/Loader)
  - 3rd AC or Loader
  - Camera Intern
- Camera Operator
- **SECOND UNIT**
  - 2nd Unit DP
  - 2nd Unit Crew
- **"B" Camera**
  - Operator
  - "B" Camera 1st AC

FIGURE 10.11 Crew organization

whatever), you may end up lighting air—making the set look beautiful but not really lighting the actors for the scene.

Even worse in terms of efficiency, you may end up lighting things that are not even going to be in the movie. You must insist on knowing what the frame is and what the blocking of the shot is. Directors may be otherwise preoccupied; in that case, the AD will usually be your ally in insisting on nailing down the frame and seeing a blocking rehearsal.

Light

Once the blocking is done, the AD will say two things. First, s/he will say, "Put them through the process," meaning start the actors in makeup, hair, and wardrobe. The second thing s/he will say is, "Lighting has the set," meaning that control of the set now belongs to the DP, the gaffer, key grip, and their crews. Everyone else should leave the set to make room for the lighting crew. Of course, the ACs will be prepping the camera, but whenever possible, they should do that in a place that won't interfere with lighting (and also protect the camera from any potential damage).

(a)

(b)

(c)

It is critical that the lighting team have the real actors or good stand-ins for this phase. Lighting is fine-tuned for a particular blocking and a particular facial shape and coloring. No stand-in—or one that does not match in height, coloring, or depth of eye socket—will often mean delays later on, when the director and the high-priced talent will be even more impatient. It is the AD's responsibility to provide for this. Insist on it. At this stage, the lights are positioned and focused. Scrims, nets, dimmers, or spotting and flooding are used to balance the lighting, and flags cast shadows where they are needed.

Rehearsal

With lighting complete, the lighting crew retires from the set and the DP and gaffer observe as the director rehearses the actors. This is probably the first time that they can see with finality the full scope of what they must do and any particular conditions that must be met. Rehearsal complete, the director and actors leave, and the DP may need to make a few fine-tuning adjustments, or tweaking. Hopefully it won't be necessary, but sometimes things come up that need to be taken care of.

Shooting

Time for coffee, right? Wrong. The lighting team (gaffer and grip) must be alert and ready. This is when fuses are short and everyone is impatient. Some items are standard and should be standing by as close to the set as possible and completely ready to go: two or three each of inkies, tweenies, and babies and usually at least one of each type of light that

(d)

FIGURE 10.12 (a) The absolute worst thing you can do when setting up a light—clotheslining the cable practically ensures that someone will trip over it and either be injured, damage the light, or worse. (b) A properly set up light. Most important of all, the cable is not clotheslined; it hangs down straight and is tucked in. Also the light has its barndoors and scrims, a strain relief on the cable, and a sandbag on the leg. (c) A detail of the strain relief on the header cable. It also keeps the switch handy. (d) Avoid letting any type of cable have ground loops, which create a tripping hazard.

you are using. These should be on stands with barndoors, scrims, snoots, and diffusion attached.

While shooting, the gaffer and electricians stay alert for changing conditions, bulb burnouts, etc.

Procedures

As the gaffer calls for a light the procedure is generally this: an electrician goes to get the light and the best boy brings power to it with a single, Bates extension, or whatever is appropriate. If necessary one of the group passes on to the grips any required rigging, bagging, flagging, or ladders.

The most important part of this process is communication. As the crew is set in motion, they announce what they are doing: for example, the third calls out "*Deuce flying in*" while the second says "Bringing power to you." The reason for this is to ensure that no task is duplicated (there is no more obvious proof of an amateur crew than watching three anxious-to-please electrics run—all in unison—for the same light), and the gaffer and best boy know that all the bases are being covered.

When bringing a light to the set, *it must be complete*; never bring a light to the set without barndoor and scrims. Diffusion and clothespins should come with the light or be readily available—*anticipate*. If called for (or anticipated), bring snoots, gel frames, etc. If the gaffer calls for a single scrim, don't go up the ladder with just a single scrim. Take the whole set with you; he may change his mind. The same goes for electrical equipment. If you need a stinger on the other side of the set, why not take two to stay ahead of the game?

Scrims should stay with the light, with scrim clips or scrim boxes if possible. Time permitting, a piece of each standard diffusion and gel can be precut and attached to the light. Cut the gel large enough to fit outside the doors; it can be trimmed down to fit inside.

LAMPS AND SOCKETS

In this chapter we look closely at the many different types of radiating sources that are available, examining their potential and learning what techniques are necessary to work with each of them successfully.

Types of Radiating Sources

Carbon Arc

The oldest type of radiating source is the open arc. All carbon-arc sources consist of a positive and a negative electrode. Current flows from the negative to the positive electrode. The high-current flow across the tip of the negative carbon gasifies the carbon/cerium metal electrode and creates a small flame, which is an extremely hot plasma produced by the arc. The output is intense and can be viewed only through darkglass viewing ports in the side and back of the unit.

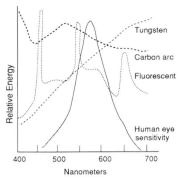

FIGURE 11.1 SED of typical sources.

FIGURE 11.2 Early tungsten bulbs were enormous, such as this 10K lamp (**a**) in a Mole–Richardson Solar Spot. The invention of tungsten–halogen bulbs (**b**) made the lamps themselves much smaller, allowing more compact, lighter, and more portable lighting units. (Photo courtesy of Mole–Richardson, Inc.)

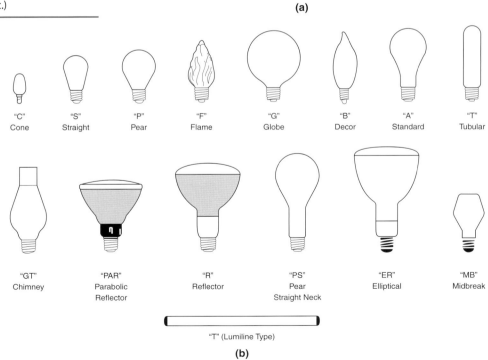

(a)

"C" Cone "S" Straight "P" Pear "F" Flame "G" Globe "B" Decor "A" Standard "T" Tubular

"GT" Chimney "PAR" Parabolic Reflector "R" Reflector "PS" Pear Straight Neck "ER" Elliptical "MB" Midbreak

"T" (Lumiline Type)

(b)

As the arc burns, the electrodes are consumed and must be moved forward to maintain optimal operating distance. In modern arcs this is performed by geared motors, but requires constant attention by an operator. In addition, the positives must be replaced roughly every half-hour and the negatives last about twice as long.

Tungsten

The incandescent lamp was invented by Thomas Edison and patented in 1879. It works on the principle of incandescence—the greater the current passing through the filament, the brighter the bulb will burn. Tungsten is used because it has the highest melting point of any material suitable for forming a filament. Even in the partial vacuum inside the globe, the tungsten atoms boil off and accumulate on the relatively cooler glass envelope, where they form a sooty coating that gradually dims the bulb and affects its color temperature. To slow this evaporation, the globe is filled to about 80% atmospheric pressure with the nitrogen and the inert gas argon.

Tungsten–Halogen

The accumulation of soot on the bulbs was solved by the introduction of the tungsten–halogen bulb. The idea for a tungsten–halogen bulb originated with Edison, but at the time there was no glass that could withstand the temperature. In general use, the term "tungsten" refers to any incandescent bulb. Quartz refers to tungsten–halogen bulbs.

Table 11.1

Designation	Wattage	Type	Size	Base	Color Temp
25 watt	25 W	household bulb	A-19	medium screw	2600K
40 watt	40 W	household bulb	A-19	medium screw	2600K
60 watt	60 W	household bulb	A-19	medium screw	2600K
75 watt	75 W	household bulb	A-19	medium screw	2600K
100 watt	100 W	household bulb	A-19	medium screw	2600K
150 watt	150 W	household bulb	A-21	medium screw	2800K
200 watt	200 W	household bulb	A-23	medium screw	2800K
ECA	250 W	photoflood bulb	A-23	medium screw	3200K
ECT	500 W	photoflood bulb	PS-25	medium screw	3200K
BBA (#1 flood)	250 W	photoflood bulb	A-21	medium screw	3400K
EBV (#2 flood)	500 W	blue photoflood	PS-25	medium screw	4800K
BCA (#B1 flood)	250 W	blue photoflood	A-21	medium screw	4800K
EBW (#B2 flood)	500 W	blue photoflood	PS-25	medium screw	4800K
211	75 W	enlarger bulb	A-21	medium screw	2950K
212	150 W	enlarger bulb	A-21	medium screw	2950K

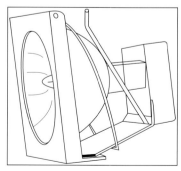

FIGURE 11.3 An MR-16 in a holder.

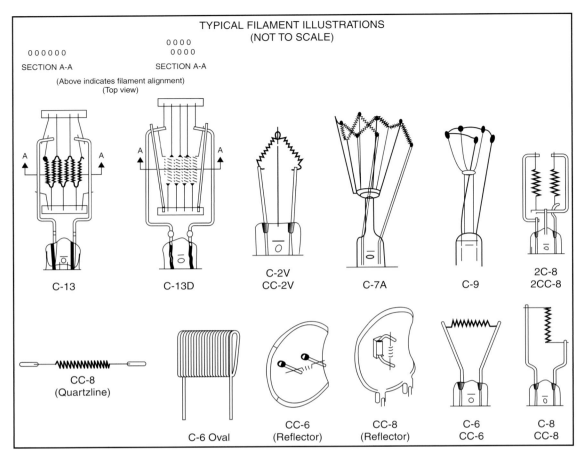

TYPICAL FILAMENT ILLUSTRATIONS
(NOT TO SCALE)

000000
SECTION A-A

0000
0000
SECTION A-A

(Above indicates filament alignment)
(Top view)

C-13

C-13D

C-2V
CC-2V

C-7A

C-9

2C-8
2CC-8

CC-8
(Quartzline)

C-6 Oval

CC-6
(Reflector)

CC-8
(Reflector)

C-6
CC-6

C-8
CC-8

FIGURE 11.4 Common incandescent filament forms. (Courtesy General Electric.)

Tungsten–halogen bulbs operate on a gas cycle that works to redeposit the evaporated metal back onto the filament. As the tungsten atoms leave the filament, they chemically combine with the iodine and bromine gases in the bulb. The resulting tungsten halide migrates back to the filament, where the very high temperature decomposes it back into tungsten, iodine, and bromine.

The halogen cycle will fail if the lamp is operated below 250°C. If operated for a prolonged period with a bulb wall temperature of less than 250°, blackening may occur, with a loss of output and a reduction of lamp life. Obviously, dimming the light may result in an operating temperature lower than this limit, but if the lamp is dimmed to low levels, the evaporation of tungsten is also minimized and usually there is no problem. In an incandescent lamp a 1% change in voltage results in a $3\frac{1}{2}$% change in output.

Enclosed Metal Arc: HMI

HMIs generate three to four times the light of tungsten–halogen, but consume up to 75% less energy for the same

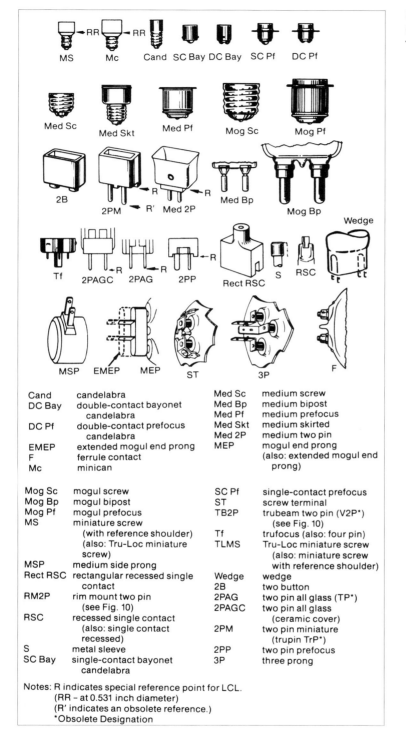

FIGURE 11.5 Bulb base codes. (Courtesy of General Electric.)

Cand	candelabra	Med Sc	medium screw
DC Bay	double-contact bayonet candelabra	Med Bp	medium bipost
		Med Pf	medium prefocus
DC Pf	double-contact prefocus candelabra	Med Skt	medium skirted
		Med 2P	medium two pin
EMEP	extended mogul end prong	MEP	mogul end prong (also: extended mogul end prong)
F	ferrule contact		
Mc	minican		
Mog Sc	mogul screw	SC Pf	single-contact prefocus
Mog Bp	mogul bipost	ST	screw terminal
Mog Pf	mogul prefocus	TB2P	trubeam two pin (V2P*) (see Fig. 10)
MS	miniature screw (with reference shoulder) (also: Tru-Loc miniature screw)		
		Tf	trufocus (also: four pin)
		TLMS	Tru-Loc miniature screw (also: miniature screw with reference shoulder)
MSP	medium side prong		
Rect RSC	rectangular recessed single contact	Wedge	wedge
		2B	two button
		2PAG	two pin all glass (TP*)
RM2P	rim mount two pin (see Fig. 10)	2PAGC	two pin all glass (ceramic cover)
RSC	recessed single contact (also: single contact recessed)	2PM	two pin miniature (trupin TrP*)
S	metal sleeve	2PP	two pin prefocus
SC Bay	single-contact bayonet candelabra	3P	three prong

Notes: R indicates special reference point for LCL.
    (RR – at 0.531 inch diameter)
    (R' indicates an obsolete reference.)
    *Obsolete Designation

luminous flux. When a tungsten bulb is corrected to daylight, the advantage increases to seven times because they are more efficient in converting power to light; moreover, they give off less heat than a tungsten lamp.

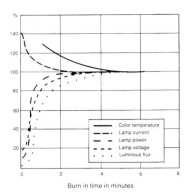

FIGURE 11.6 The HMI startup cycle. Incandescent lamp bulb shapes. (Courtesy General Electric.)

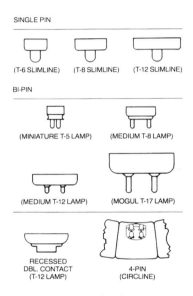

FIGURE 11.7 Bases for fluorescent lamps. (Courtesy of GTE-Sylvania Lighting).

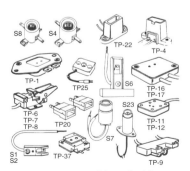

FIGURE 11.8 Typical lampholders for fluorescent lamps. (Courtesy GTE-Sylvania Lighting.)

The term HMI is an abbreviation for the basic components. "H" is from the Latin symbol for mercury (Hg), which is used primarily to create the lamp voltage. "M" is for medium-length arc. "I" stands for iodine and bromine, which are halogens. The halogen serves much the same function as in a tungsten–halogen lamp and ensures that the rare earth metals remain concentrated in the hot zone of the arc.

HMI lamps are manufactured from high-temperature–tolerant quartz glass. They have two axial electrodes made from tungsten that project into a cylindrical or ellipsoidal discharge chamber. Power is supplied via molybdenum foils with a special surface profile. The foil is sealed in the quartz glass lamp shaft and provides the electrical connection between the base and the electrodes in the discharge chamber. Color temperature, as derived from a black-body Planckian radiator, does not directly apply to HMIs because they are not continuous-spectrum radiators. HMI lamps produce a quasi-continuous spectrum that is very similar to that of the sun.

In an HMI lamp the basic mercury discharge spectrum is very discontinuous and concentrated in a few narrow bands. The output of the rare earths fills out the spectrum and produces an SED very close to daylight. For most HMIs the color rendering index is greater than 90, and thus above the minimum for film. When first developed, HMIs were not dimmable. Lamps have now been developed that can be dimmed to 40% of their rated output, which corresponds to 30% of their luminous flux. There is some slight shift of color temperature under these conditions.

All HMIs require a ballast. As with a carbon arc or an arc welder, the ballast includes a choke that acts as a current limiter. The reason for this is simple. An arc is basically a dead short. If the current were allowed to flow unimpeded, the circuit would overload and either trip the breaker or burn up. Original ballasts for HMIs were extremely heavy and bulky. The invention of the smaller and lighter electronic ballast was a major improvement. They also allow the unit to operate on a squarewave, which solves the flicker problem. The squarewave also increases light efficiency by 6 to 8%.

Voltages of 12,000 VAC or more are needed to start the arc, which is provided by a separate ignitor circuit in the ballast. The typical operating voltage is around 200 V. When a lamp is already hot, much higher voltages are needed in order to ionize the pressurized gap between the electrodes. This can be 20 kV to more than 65 kV. For this reason, older HMIs could not be restruck while hot; most now have a hot restrike feature. Owing to devitrification, which increases as the lamp ages, the color temperature falls by about 0.5K to 1K per hour burned, depending on the wattage.

Household and Projector Bulbs

Ordinary household bulbs and photographic bulbs also play a part in film and video lighting. They are used in these instances:

1. Specially built rigs such as large soft boxes that use ordinary photographic or household bulbs as the source.
2. Practicals, such as lamps and sconces, that appear in the frame.

All bulbs have a coded letter designations known as ANSI codes, coordinated by the American National Standards Institute. These three-letter codes designate the basic bulb wattage, configuration, and socket of a bulb, and are used by all manufacturers. This ensures that bulbs from different makers are interchangeable. For example, the ANSI code for a 2,000 watt tungsten–halogen bulb to fit in a studio baby is CYX. A 5K bulb is a DPY, and so on.

Practical Bulbs

Practical bulbs are needed for just about any desk lamp, floor lamp, wall sconce, or hanging light that appears in a scene. It is important to order a variety of sizes that will fit these units. Note also that many modern lamps use specialized miniature bulbs that are not commonly available.

A practical bulb kit is a must on any production that involves on-camera practicals. It is common practice for any company to have a box of bulbs always available. (All of these bulbs are medium screw base, which is the most common socket in household lamps, sconces, and ceiling-mounted lamps, followed closely by the smaller candelabra base.)

One of the most important things to understand about household and photo-flood bulbs is that they come in different sizes. The fiddles of many table or floor lamps may not be large enough to accommodate a large 200-watt household bulb, which is an A-23. A BBA, on the other hand, is an A-21 bulb and measures only $4^{15}/_{16}$, small enough to fit in most lamp housings.

Other popular bulbs include the 211, 212 series of enlarger bulbs. These feature a special bonded ceramic coating for even and soft light. The 211 is 75 watts, the 212 is 150 watts, and 213 is 250 watts; all are medium screw base.

Fluorescent Tubes

Not surprisingly, fluorescent bulbs work on the principle of fluorescence, which was discovered by Sir George Stokes in 1852. Alexandre Bequerel used the principle to develop the first fluorescent tube, which is not much different from

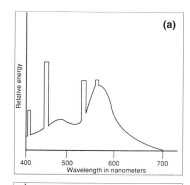

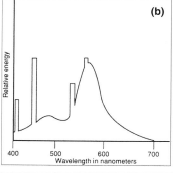

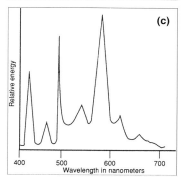

FIGURE 11.9 (**a**) SED (spectral energy distribution) of a cool white fluorescent. (**b**) Warm white fluorescent SED. (**c**) Warm white deluxe fluorescent.

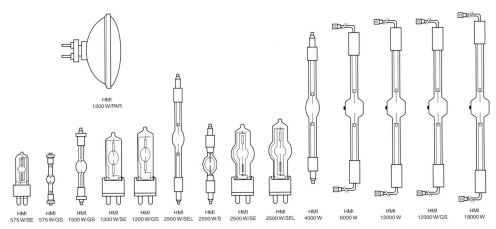

FIGURE 11.10 Typical HMI bulbs.

those in use today, although low-voltage lamps were introduced by General Electric in 1938.

Fluorescent tubes have electrodes at each end of the tube. The electrodes propel electrons into the mercury vapor in the tube. The impact of an electron on a mercury atom dislodges an electron from its orbit. When it returns to its orbit, ultraviolet radiation is produced. The ultraviolet rays strike the phosphor coating around the interior of the tube, causing it to fluoresce in the visible spectrum. The color of fluorescent tubes is a result of the chemical makeup of the phosphor coatings.

All fluorescents operate with a ballast that limits current flow and raises the voltage for initial firing. Ballasts may emit an audible hum that can interfere with sound filming. Some bulb types have special phosphors added that change their spectral output. Bulbs have been developed that closely simulate daylight and tungsten-balanced light and have color-rendering indexes high enough for reliable color filming. Continuous-spectrum bulbs have few of the color rendition problems of standard fluorescents but have about 35% lower output.

Because a fluorescent is an AC gas discharge lamp, its output varies as the AC current rises and falls. With 60-Hz current, the light pulses 120 times per second. Fortunately, the phosphor coating, which is what is producing the visible light output, decays more slowly. Once it is excited into producing light by the ultraviolet, it does not extinguish immediately when the current drops. This moderates the flicker effect, but does not eliminate it completely.

Fluorescents can cause flicker problems, just like HMIs. When using fluorescents as the sole source of lighting, it is best to put some of them on different legs so that the flicker effects of each phase of the AC cancel each other out.

Exposure time, and hence shutter angle, is an important factor in preventing flicker. It is wise to use the widest shutter angles you can (to achieve the longest exposure time) and to avoid, if possible, high-speed shooting, which dramatically increases the possibility of flicker.

Other precautions include using a crystal motor if at all feasible and using other types of lighting (such as appropriately filtered tungsten) as part of the set lighting.

Fluorescents can be dimmed, with the following caveats:

- Only autotransformer or solid-state dimmers will work on fluorescents.
- They cannot be dimmed all the way out. At a certain point they flicker and spiral inside the bulb.
- There is usually no color shift when fluorescents are dimmed, but lamps that have been dimmed will appear warmer.
- While being dimmed, the cathodes should remain heated at the standard current.

Bulb Handling and Safety

- Never touch a bulb with your bare fingers—to do so shortens its life.
- Don't move a light with the bulb on. Excessive vibration can damage the filament. Also avoid rapid flood-spotting or other sudden moves.
- Use extreme caution installing and removing bulbs, especially double-ended bulbs like the FCM and FHM, which have very delicate and damage-prone porcelain ends.
- Note and follow the recommended operating positions of bulbs, particularly large bulbs like DTY and 6K/12K HMI bulbs, which are not only sensitive to position, but also extremely expensive.
- Try to minimize on-and-off switching. Dimmers are an excellent way to control the light, reduce the heat

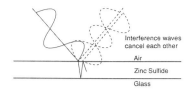

FIGURE 11.11 Dichroic filter operating principles.

FIGURE 11.12 Dichroic filter on FAY bulbs.

level on the set, and reduce total energy consumption, which helps save the planet.

- Make sure all lamps are securely seated in their sockets.
- Large bulbs (5K and above) must be removed from the light and placed in a foam-padded box for shipment. This does not usually apply to HMI bulbs, which means that added caution is called for when handling HMIs.

Dichroics

Some bulbs have built-in conversion filters, primarily for converting tungsten to daylight balance. Generically called FAYs or faylights, they are a reliable old standby for daylight fill.

Technically, FAY is the ANSI code for a 650-watt PAR 36 with ferrule contact terminals and a color balance of 5000K. This occurs most commonly in PAR clusters, such as the nine-light, although one- and two-lamp units are common for just a touch of fill on cloudy days or for hood-mounted rigs for running shots. Some units take a similar bulb that has screw terminals, the FBE/FGK. They may look quite similar from the outside, so check carefully before ordering bulbs.

Both of these bulbs have dichroic filters for conversion to approximate daylight color balance. Dichroic filters operate on the principle of interference. Glass is coated with a number of layers that are one-quarter or one-half the thickness of the wavelength of the color they are to filter. As that wavelength enters these layers, it creates a series of interior reflections that cancel out the color. Dichroics have been developed to the point where they are very stable.

PAR 64 1000-watt dichroic bulbs are also available for MaxiBrutes for high-intensity uses. They come in narrow spot (NSP), medium flood (MFL), and wide flood (WFL). Their rated life is only 200 hours, so be sure you have spares.

Although dichroics (often called dykes) are generally an integral part of the lamp, they are sometimes a separate filter that clips onto the lamp and can be swung in and out for instant changeover from daylight to tungsten balance. These rigs have become standard equipment for ENG video news crews.

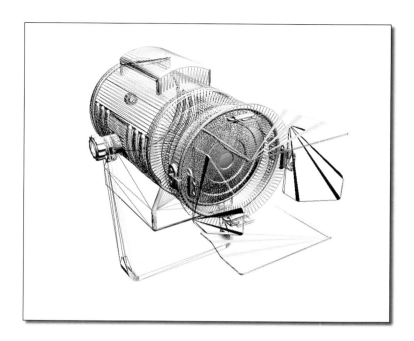

TECHNICAL ISSUES

As more high-tech equipment becomes available, lighting becomes more complex. A solid grounding in the theory and practice of using tools for lighting is essential not only to complete the day successfully, but also to avoid disaster in the screening room. In this chapter we examine these issues and review the basic operating techniques associated with them.

Shooting with HMI Units

Shooting with HMIs (as well as fluorescents and other AC-powered nontungsten lights) always presents the danger of *flicker*. Flicker appears on film or video (if not shooting at 30P or 60i) as a rhythmic change in exposure. It is caused by uneven exposure from frame to frame as a result of a mismatch in the output waveform of the light and the framing rate of the camera. Flicker can be serious enough to render an entire shoot unusable.

To understand the reason for flicker, we must look at how an HMI generates light. Except for Brute arcs and studio

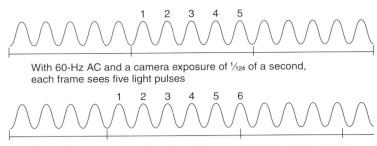

With 60-Hz AC and a camera exposure of $\frac{1}{124}$ of a second, each frame sees five light pulses

When the camera speed is not stabilized, each frame sees a slightly different number of pulses, which creates unequal exposure

situations in which tungsten lamps are run on DC, most filming situations utilize alternating current. The fundamental nature of alternating current is, of course, that it alternates. The output of an AC generator varies constantly as a sine wave. When the current flow is at the maximum (top of the peak) or minimum (bottom of the trough), the output of the light will be maximum. The light doesn't care whether the flow is positive or negative. At the moment when the sine wave crosses the axis, however, the current flow is zero. At that instant, the electron flow is static—the light can generate no output. Since the light is on for both the positive and negative side of the sine wave, it reaches its maximum at twice the rate of the AC: 120 cycles per second (cps) for 60-Hz current and 100 cps for 50-Hz current.

This applies to any source powered by AC, but with tungsten filament lamps, the result is negligible because the tungsten stays glowing hot, even when the current is momentarily zero. There is some loss of output, but it is minimal, usually only about 10 to 20%.

With enclosed arc lamps (HMIs as well as CSI and CID lamps), the variation is greater. For an HMI with a standard reactance ballast, the minimum output may be as low as 17% of total output. At first glance it would seem that we might just average the maximum and minimum output (58%) and take this as the total average output of the light.

In a crude way, this is exactly what does happen. In film, however, there is another complication. The shutter is opening and closing at a rate that may be different from the rate at which the light output is fluctuating. As illustrated in Figure 12.1, when the relationship of the shutter and the light output varies with respect to each other, each film frame sees different amounts of the cycle. The result is unequal exposure. This problem can occur in three ways:

1. The frame rate of the camera varies unevenly.
2. The frequency of the electrical supply varies unevenly.
3. The frame rate of the shutter creates a mismatch in the synchronization of the shutter and the light output.

The first two are intuitively obvious. If either the shutter rate or the light output is random, it is clear that there will be different amounts of exposure for each frame. The third is a bit more complex. Through experimentation, engineers have found that only certain combinations of shutter speed and power supply frequency can be considered acceptably safe. Deviations from these combinations always entail the risk of noticeable flicker.

The danger of HMI flicker will always be greatest when there are no other nonflicker sources (tungsten, DC arcs, daylight) and when all HMIs are being run on the same electrical phase. The risk will be reduced by combining other sources or by powering the HMIs on all three electrical phases. None of these, however, completely eliminates the risk of at least a small amount of noticeable exposure variation.

To prevent flicker, four conditions are absolutely essential:
1. constant frequency in the AC power supply
2. constant framing rate in the camera
3. compatible shutter angle
4. compatible frame rate

In practice the first two conditions are met with either crystal controls on the generator and camera or by running one or both of them from the local AC mains, which (in most countries) are considered reliable in frequency.

The shutter angle and frame rate are determined by consulting the accompanying charts. The relationship of AC frequency to shutter is generally crucial only in high-speed cinematography and is not usually a factor in most filming situations.

At 24 fps camera speed, if a stable power supply is assured, shutter angle can be varied from 90 to 200° with relatively little risk. Theoretically, the ideal shutter angle is 144°, since this results in an exposure time of $\frac{1}{60}$ of a second and thus matches the frequency of the power supply. In practice, there is little risk in using a 180° shutter if the camera is crystal-controlled and the power supply is regulated. At 180°, the camera is exposing $2\frac{1}{2}$ pulses per frame (rather than exactly 2 pulses per frame, as you would get with 144°), so exposure can theoretically vary by as much as 9%.

The Power Supply

Any variation in the frequency of the power supply will result in an exposure fluctuation of approximately .4 f/stop. The time for one cycle of fluctuation to occur will depend on how far off the power supply is. (See Table 12.2.)

When working with a generator, it is essential that it be crystal-controlled. Governor controls are never sufficient for the accuracy demanded. Even with a crystal-controlled generator, a frequency meter should be used and constantly monitored. As a general rule, plus or minus one-quarter of a cycle is considered acceptable.

Flicker-Free HMIs

The newest generation of HMIs uses flicker-free ballasts, thereby minimizing the danger of exposure fluctuation.

The ideal shutter angle for shooting at 24 fps with 50 Hz per supply is 172.8°.

A simple way to think about it is to divide 120 by a whole number, e.g.,

$$^{120}/_4 = 30$$
or
$$^{120}/_8 = 15$$

With electronic ballasts, there is less likelihood of a mismatch from frame to frame. The major disadvantage of this method is an increase in the noise level of the light. Some flicker-free units are switchable from normal to flicker-free operation. Flicker-free units are now available in every size of HMI.

Some caution is required when using flicker-free ballasts. Because they convert the normal sine wave of AC current to a series of sharp peaks, the load on different phases does not cancel out. This means that you cannot balance the load in the normal manner: whatever comes out on the hot legs goes back on the neutral.

For this reason, it is essential that you use an oversize neutral when running large loads at near capacity. Because it is not a normal sine wave, the load can only be read with a true root-mean-square (RMS) amp meter, such as the Fluke 87 with a clamp-on accessory.

Flicker-free ballasts have the advantage of being able to run on either AC or DC; they are also less susceptible to variation in frequency and can operate effectively from 47 to 63 Hz on AC. They will generally fire on 100 to 132 volts. They have a color temperature adjustment that will vary the output roughly plus or minus 500K.

Because they generate less firing voltage, flicker-free ballasts may sometimes fail to fire heads that are not well maintained or that have the ignitor box spark gap set improperly. With properly maintained heads, there should be no problem.

Dimmers

There are a number of ways we control the intensity of light output at the unit itself:

- flood-spot
- wire scrims
- grip nets
- diffusion

- neutral density filters
- aim (spilling the beam)
- switching off bulbs in multi-bulb units (soft lights)

The alternative is to control the power input to the light with dimmers. The advantages are

- fine degree of control
- ability to control inaccessible units
- ability to look quickly at several different combinations
- ability to do cues
- ability to preset scene combinations
- ability to save energy and heat buildup by cooling down between takes

The disadvantages are

- lights change color as they dim
- some lights cannot be dimmed, particularly some HMIs
- necessity of additional cabling

SCR dimmers do not alter the voltage. They work by clipping the waveform so that the voltage is heating the filament for a shorter period of time. The result is that the output of this type of dimmer cannot be read with an ordinary voltage meter. Only a VOM that reads root-mean-square voltage (RMS), such as the high-end Fluke meters, will work—there must be a load to read the output. The shorter rise time can sometimes cause filament sing and create RF (radio frequency) and AF (audio frequency) noise. The RF interference can be transmitted back along the power line and cause problems, particularly for unbalanced high-impedance sound systems. In most cases, with properly grounded audio systems, there should be no problem, but a portable radio can be used to test.

When using an SCR dimmer with a generator, the genny must be frequency-controlled—the loss of sync will cause flicker. Also, since most dimmers are voltage-regulated, raising the voltage of the generator will not increase the output. An anomaly of these systems is that the neutral load can, in some cases, be higher than the hot leg.

SCR dimmers are basically theatrical equipment, so their connectors will often not be compatible with the rest of your equipment. As a rule, the outputs will be theatrical three-pin connectors, either 60 amp or 100 amp. It is important to order adaptors compatible with your plugging system.

The first dimmers invented were resistance units. They operate by placing a variable resistance in the power line. The excess energy is burned off as heat. Resistance dimmers, which are still available up to 10K, are heavy and clumsy, but cheap. The major problem with resistance dimmers is that they must be loaded to at least 80% of their capacity in order to operate. If you put a 5K on a 10K dimmer, for example, the

FIGURE 12.2 A dimmer system controls Kino Flo units for a large blue screen shot. (Photo courtesy of Kino Flo, Inc.)

dimmer will reduce only a small amount of the output. You won't be able to dim all the way down—a dummy load may be necessary to operate.

Auto transformers were the next generation of dimmers. They operate as variable transformers and alter the voltage. They don't have to be loaded to capacity and don't generate excess heat, but they do operate only on AC. Known as "variacs" (for variable AC), they are still standard equipment, particularly in the 1K and 2K sizes.

For larger applications, silicon-controlled rectifiers are used. Known as "SCRs," these are electronic devices that are small, quiet, and relatively low-cost. They can be controlled remotely by dimmer boards, which means that the dimmer packs can be near the lights. This saves cabling, since only a small control cable needs to run from the board to the dimmer packs.

Table 12.1

Type	Lamp Color Shift	CCT Direction	Degree of Shift
Tungsten	Orange-red	Lower	Marked
Fluorescent	Not discernible	Negligible	Negligible
Metal halide	Blue	Higher	Drastic
Mercury	Not discernible	Negligible	Negligible

Dimmer Systems On The Set

It is increasingly popular to run entire sets from a central dimmer board. While this calls for additional cabling, it has enormous advantages in speed and efficiency. This is always a premium on a working set, especially when many lights are somewhat remote or difficult to reach, rendering it harder to make quick adjustments in level. Since a dimmer board makes it possible to radically alter the balance of the load, it is often a good idea to run a double-size neutral cable as an imbalanced load on the hot legs sends more amperage back on the neutral.

Working with Strobes

There are several types of strobe lighting for cinematography, the most widely known being Unilux. Clairmont Camera also has strobe units that are widely used. Frame rates of up to 500 fps are possible. The strobes are fired by a pulse from the camera, which signals when the shutter is open. Any camera that provides such a pulse is compatible with the system. In some cases, a pulse contact is added to a moving part of the camera, and this provides the sync signal.

Strobe lighting in film is used for several reasons:

1. To light cooler (strobes produce substantially less heat than tungsten heads), which can be a tremendous advantage when shooting ice cream, for example.
2. To produce sharper images. The exposure duration for each flash can be as short as $1/100,000$ of a second. As a result, the image is frozen and appears sharper than if photographed on moving film at standard exposures.
3. To provide sufficient exposure for high-speed photography with a small power input.

Strobe lighting is often used in spray shots of soft drink cans being opened: the strobe effect captures each droplet of spray crisply. In fact, it can be too sharp. Consider shower scenes for shampoo commercials: the shower can appear as a series of razor-sharp drops rather than as a soft spray.

As a result, for beauty applications, it is common practice to combine strobes with tungsten lighting. In most cases, the strobe light is balanced with an equal amount of tungsten within a range of plus or minus one stop. This presents an interesting exposure problem.

Most strobes run about 6000K in color temperature. When combining strobes with other sources, appropriate filtration is required. When mixing with tungsten, use an 85 to obtain 3400K and an 85B to reach 3200K. To maximize the strobe light, use 80A or CTB on the tungsten lights. Most people prefer to light only the moving object with strobe and the rest of the scene with tungsten. Strobes are fan-cooled and so are not useful for sync-sound shooting.

Strobe Exposure

Suppose you are shooting at 96 fps with equal amounts of tungsten, and strobe lights are desirable. Every time you increase the frame rate of the motion picture camera, you are decreasing the amount of time the shutter stays open—you are decreasing exposure. Ninety-six fps is four times faster than normal; therefore, the shutter speed is $1/200$ of a second instead of the normal $1/50$. This is an exposure loss of two stops. This is simple enough. To achieve an f/5.6, for example, you light to an f/11.

But the same is not true of the strobe lighting. The strobe is instantaneous. It fires for only a few thousandths of a second at some time while the shutter is open. As a result, it is completely independent of the frame rate. It doesn't matter whether the film is moving at 6 frames a second or 600, the exposure will be the same.

Here's the problem. We read the tungsten and have to compensate. We then read the strobe with a strobe meter and we don't have to compensate—clearly, we can't read them at the same time. How do we arrive at a setting for the lens?

The answer is intuitively obvious, but mathematically a bit complex. We read them separately and then add the two exposures. As it turns out, adding an f/stop is not especially simple.

Let's take the simplest case first. We read the strobe by itself (and it is very important to turn off all tungsten lights when we do this) and find that it is f/5.6. We have to balance the tungsten to that. As we know, at 96 fps, we have to set the tungsten lights for f/11, which will be f/5.6 at 96 fps.

The logical temptation might be to average them, which would result in a very incorrect exposure—therefore, we must add them.

What is f/5.6 plus f/5.6? In effect, we are doubling the amount of light. The tungsten is providing f/5.6 and the Unilux is supplying an entirely different illumination that is also f/5.6. Twice as much light as f/5.6 is f/8. Recall that each f/stop represents a doubling of the amount of light.

Now it gets a bit stickier. Let's say that the the strobe is f/8 and the tungsten is f/5.6. Think of it this way: if f/8 is a base of 100%, then the tungsten light is 50% (one stop less equals one-half the amount of light). We then have 150% of the base light. One hundred fifty percent of f/8 is one-half stop hotter than f/8, f/8 and one-half.

If one of the sources is f/8 and the other is f/4, the correct exposure is f/8 and ¼. f/4 is only 25% the amount of light of f/8, 125%.

Although a flashmeter is the preferred method, many ordinary electronic light meters can read high-speed strobes. The reason is that at 60 flashes per second, it is perceived as continuous by many meters—not really much different from fluorescents, for example.

Exposure for Macrophotography

Most regular prime lenses and zooms have a minimum focus; they can't focus on anything closer than a certain distance.

Extreme closeup photography has a set of problems all its own. The most critical aspect of macro work is the degree of magnification. A magnification of 1:1 means that the object will be reproduced on film actual size, that is, an object that is ½ inch in reality will produce an image on the negative (or video tube) of ½ inch. 1:2 will be ½ size, 1:3 will be ⅓ size, and so on.

In film, the 35 mm academy frame is 16 mm high and 22 mm wide. In 1:1 reproduction, a 22-mm object will fill the entire frame. Most lenses of ordinary design can focus no closer than a ratio of 1:8 or 1:10.

When a small image is being spread over a large piece of film, it naturally produces less exposure. With reproduction

FIGURE 12.3 Spacelights create an ambient base for a snorkle rig shot; some Source Four lekos add the highlights. Macro and snorkle shots almost always require a high f/stop and thus must be lit to a fairly high level. (Photo courtesy of Mark Weingartner.)

ratios greater than 1:10, exposure compensation is necessary. The formula is

$$\text{Shooting stop} = \frac{\text{f/stop determined by light meter}}{1 + \text{magnification ratio}}$$

Example: Meter reading is f/8. Your reproduction ratio is 1:2 or $\frac{1}{2}$ size. The calculation is $8/(1+.5)=5.3$.

Depth-of-Field in Closeup Work

There are many misconceptions associated with macro-photography; perhaps the most basic is that wide-angle lenses have more depth-of-field. Frequently, this prompts the DP who is having a depth-of-field problem to ask for a wider lens. Sorry: it doesn't help.

Depth-of-field is a function of image size, not focal length. Yes, it is true that wide-angle lenses have more depth-of-field—a look at any depth-of-field chart confirms this. The problem is that once you have put a wider lens on, you still want the same image you had before, and in order to accomplish this, you must move the camera closer to the subject. Once you do this, the depth-of-field is exactly the same as it was before, since focus distance is also an important determinant of depth-of-field.

The important aspects of closeup photography are:
- Depth-of-field decreases as magnification increases.
- Depth-of-field decreases as focus distance decreases.
- Depth-of-field is doubled by closing down the lens two stops.

Lighting for Extreme Closeups

There are two basic considerations in lighting for extreme closeups. The first is that, owing to extremely small depth-of-field (which is inherent in close focusing) and the need to stop down for improved optical performance, very

FIGURE 12.4 Kino Flo in an underwater housing. (Photo courtesy of Kino Flo, Inc.)

Table 12.2

Magnification Ratio	Exposure Increase in Stops
1:10	$\frac{1}{3}$
1:6	$\frac{1}{2}$
1:4	$\frac{2}{3}$
1:3	1
1:2	$1\frac{1}{3}$
1:1.4	$1\frac{1}{2}$
1:1.2	$1\frac{2}{3}$
1:1	2

high light levels are needed. Particularly in conjunction with high-speed photography, an uncorrected stop of f/64 and higher is often called for. Since the area being lit is usually very small, this generally poses no problem, although in dealing with large units (such as 10Ks) it can be quite a job just to get them close together and all focused on a small subject.

The other problem is caused by the fact that the lens is so close to the subject. In some cases, the front of the lens may be no more than an inch away from the subject. This makes it difficult to achieve any kind of front lighting or fill, as the lens and the camera are in the way. A further difficulty is introduced when the subject is reflective. In this case, no matter how much light is poured on the subject, what you will see in the reflective surface is a mirror image of the lens itself, looking like a large black circle.

There are two solutions. One is to cut a hole in a reflector card just large enough for the lens. Sometimes it is not even necessary for the hole to cover the entire front optic. You will find by experimenting that the actual working area is smaller and that the hole can be smaller without interfering with the image. This is a form of ring light and a number of subtleties are possible with a little imagination. Black strips of tape can put some modulation into the reflective surface, and slightly bending the card can create a pattern of highlights and shadows.

The other solution is a half-silver mirror. The mirror is placed between the lens and the object and angled slightly to reflect the image of the light source onto the subject in axis with the lens. Don't forget that the mirror has an exposure factor that you can measure with a spot or incident meter.

Ring lights, which comprise any type of unit that fits around the lens, may be useful in lighting for extreme closeup, if they are small enough.

Underwater Filming

Water—even fresh water—acts as a filter, absorbing the red wavelengths first, on down the spectrum, until all frequencies

FIGURE 12.5 Low-lying fog in the studio adds to the atmosphere on this music video scene. In most cases, dry ice is used to keep the fog close to the ground.

are absorbed. This is why there is no light at all below a certain depth, which varies according to the clarity of the water.

There are several underwater lighting units available. Most of them are smaller sungun, battery-operated units. Observe the manufacturer-rated maximum depth carefully, as exceeding it may lead to an implosion and short circuit.

Tungsten–halogen PAR 64s (1000 watt) and PAR 36s (650 watt) are also available in watertight housings. The PAR 36 can be configured for use with an underwater battery pack that can run two lights for an hour. In the tungsten units, the bulbs can be changed to alter the beam from wide-flood to narrow-spot and for daylight or tungsten balance.

The SeaPar® by HydroImage is built around a 1200-watt Sylvania HMI PAR bulb, encased in a watertight container, which can withstand depths of up to 220 feet in salt water (110 pounds per square inch). The fresnel is permanently bonded to the front of the bulb to reduce the amount of glass so instead of changing lenses, it is necessary to change lights.

Effects

Rain

Rain is the province of the prop department, but it does have implications for lighting. To be visible, rain must be back-lit. Frontlighting will not work with anything but the most intense downpours—and even then, the result will be anemic.

Even with the most carefully controlled rain effect, water gets everywhere. Several precautions are necessary:

- Raise all connectors, especially distribution connectors, off the ground on apple boxes. Wrap them in plastic and seal with tape. Use electrical tape, as gaffer's tape won't withstand water.

FIGURE 12.6 This scene combines a moon effect (created with ½ CTB on a MaxiBrute) and fire effect—flicker box through ¼ CTO.

- Ground everything you can.
- Put rain hats on all lights. Protect the lenses of all large lights; water on a hot lens will shatter it, whereupon glass can fly everywhere.
- Cover light carts and other spare equipment with heavy plastic.
- Crew members should wear insulating shoes and stand on rubber mats whenever working with hot equipment.
- Observe all electrical safety rules religiously.

Smoke

Many types of smoke are available for use on sets: incense in bee-smokers, smoke cookies, smoke powder, hazers, and others. Cracker smoke is atomized oil, such as baby oil, cooking oil, and other types of lightweight oil. The oil is atomized by forcing compressed air or nitrogen through extremely small holes. The smoke has the added advantage of hanging for an extremely long time, which can be a tremendous time-saver in production. Other types of smoke require smoking it up before every take, followed by wafting it around, and then waiting for it to dissipate—a laborious, boring process.

Smoke machines and hazers are available in many types and sizes, from small hand-carry units up to big industrial-size crackers with compressors that are moved on dollies.

Fire

Fire is established by a low-key orange-flickering effect. CTO can be used to warm the light and the flicker can be accomplished in a variety of ways. Silver foil, waving hands, and rotating mirror drums are used, but the simplest and most convincing effect is usually to place the source light on a dimmer and have an electrician with an eye operate it.

A more high-tech method is the use of a flicker generator. Two kinds are available. One is a random generator that can be programmed for various rates of random flicker. The other uses an optical sensor to read the light of a candle or fire and drives a dimmer in sync with it. This is particularly effective for scenes where the dimmer or fire is the primary source and is visible in the scene. Large lamps don't do well with flicker boxes, as they remain glowing too long after the current is reduced.

Small hand-held candles or oil lamps can be executed with an inky socket and a small bulb. They can be AC-powered with a wire running up the actor's sleeve or DC-powered with a battery hidden on the actor's body. In a pinch, flashlight bulbs can be used, although the socket will be a bit more difficult to rig.

TV and Projector Effects

Like fire effects, the look of a flickering TV is best accomplished with dimmers or, even better, a flicker box. The source, which might be a fresnel or practical bulbs in porcelain sockets with some diffusion, is usually placed in a snoot box to confine the light in a realistic pattern. In general, one half or full CTB cools the light to simulate the blue look of black-and-white television. This is a convention even though most people watch color TV, which projects a variety of colors. Here again, it is important that the person operating the effect have some sensitivity to the mood of the scene and keep it random. Actual television flickers considerably less than is usually portrayed, but the activity helps sell the effect.

Projection effects can be accomplished the same way with the addition of bouncing the light for a softer look. Film projection is bounced off a large screen, while television is a smaller direct source. Projection can also be simulated by running actual film through a projector and aiming it at the audience. Obviously, it is necessary to defocus the projector or remove the lens so the image won't appear on the faces.

Day-for-Night

With the advent of high-speed film and electronic boost for video cameras, speed lenses, high-efficiency HMIs, and sunguns, day-for-night is hardly ever done anymore. In the early days of black-and-white, infrared film was used for night effects, generally in conjunction with a filter such as a Wratten #25. Traditionally, day-for-night is done around noon since long shadows would give away the fact that it is day. Of course, showing the sky is strictly forbidden.

In color (both film and video), it is possible to achieve a reasonably convincing effect by underexposing from $1\frac{1}{2}$ to $2\frac{1}{2}$ stops. Moonlight blue can be simulated by removing the 85 filter with tungsten-balanced film or white balancing the video camera for tungsten. Subtleties of color balance can be achieved with color-correcting filters, depending on the feel that is desired.

If reflectors are used, gold reflectors are a better choice to preserve the correct color balance. Silver reflectors without an 85 will probably be cold. Harrison and Harrison makes a series of day-for-night filters. The #1 is blue–red; the blue gives the night effect while the red component helps hold the skin tones in balance. The #2 is the same color but also lowers the contrast, which can help maintain the night illusion. The #3 filter offers a greater degree of contrast control. They all have an exposure factor of 2 stops.

(a)

(b)

FIGURE 12.7 (a) The Thundervoltz unit by Lightning Strikes is battery-run but a powerful lightning unit. (Photo courtesy of Lightning Strikes) (b) A very accurate compass is essential for daylight shooting, especially on the location scout and for setting up sunrise and sunset shots.

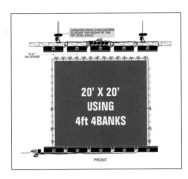

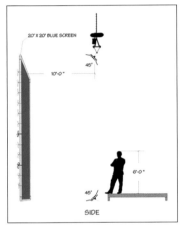

FIGURE 12.8 Kino Flo's recommendations for lighting process shot backgrounds; a 20 x 20 background is just an example. It is important to have the largest background possible for any particular shot. This keeps the foreground subject as far away from the background as possible in order to prevent backsplash, which gets the background color onto the edges of the subject—a real problem. (Courtesy of Kino Flo, Inc.)

Moonlight Effects

As you recall from our discussion of the Purkinje effect, it is a widely accepted convention that moonlight is blue. The use of blue for moonlight is controversial and many purists insist on using no more than $\frac{1}{2}$ CTB for the effect. More common is full CTB or double blue. Of course, these are all in addition to whatever blue is used to establish basic color balance.

Water Effects

The dapple of light reflected on water can be a beautiful and subtle effect. It can be achieved in a number of ways. Some people use broken mirrors or crumpled aluminum foil to reflect a strong directional light (usually a fresnel or a PAR). These tend to be somewhat stilted and artificial. The best effect is always achieved by actually using water. In a shallow pan with a black backing (black visqueen or a garbage bag is effective) water itself can be highly reflective if you use a strong enough unit.

Lightning

Because lightning must be extremely powerful to be effective, it generally calls for a specially built rig. Most lightning rigs are based on carbon arc technology. They consist of an arc ballast and a set of carbons, which can be pushed together, and then rapidly withdrawn with a levered handle. The resulting arc produces a powerful and momentary blast of light that is very convincing.

A Brute arc can be used by reversing the polarity of the DC so that it is wrong and then throwing the striking lever. The carbons will produce a brief, powerful arc but won't strike because the polarity is wrong. Understandably, these effects can be very hard on a generator, so be sure you have plenty of headroom before attempting them.

Sometimes, flashbulb rigs are used for the effect. M-Type flashbulbs, which have a long burn time, are most effective for this purpose. Regular flashbulbs fire very quickly, and they might burn while the shutter is closed.

Most of these methods have fallen into disuse, however, as purpose-built lightning machines such as those by Lightning Strikes are becoming very popular for this type of effect. They make several different units of various sizes and also units which recreate the flashbulbs of paparazzi and similar effects. They also make a battery-powered unit, the Thundervoltz, which is surprisingly powerful.

Using Daylight

Daylight is an important resource in film and we are often in the position of maximizing its effectiveness. Keep in mind that local weather conditions can seriously affect the

FIGURE 12.9 Kino Flo Image 80s hung on a truss light the greenscreen for this water shot. (Photo courtesy of Kino Flo, Inc.)

amount of usable light. Software is available that will predict the exact altitude and azimuth of the sun for any time on any date. A good compass is essential in being able to predict sun conditions, the exact spot where the sun will rise or set, etc.

Lighting for Process Photography

Chroma Key

Chroma key, also known as greenscreen, bluescreen, or process photography, is a method of producing mattes for compositing. The basic principle is simple: we place what we want to be the foreground object (typically an actor) in front of a uniformly colored background. Software later on makes that background color transparent. It is then replaced with a different background scene. Process photography based on photochemical means has been around since the earliest days of film.

The color of the background can theoretically be anything that does not appear as a color in the foreground, but for film, blue has been found to work well, while in video, green is best as it is the strongest channel.

Greenscreen

Blue and green are the most widely used colors, but any color that is different from the foreground object may be used. Other recommendations:

- Use the lowest grain film possible; grain introduces noise into the image. In video, don't add gain; with film don't push in processing.
- Do not use diffusion over the lens. Do not use heavy smoke effects.
- In film, use a pin-registered camera.
- Always shoot a grayscale lit with neutral light (3200K or 5500K) at the beginning of each roll. Shoot the grayscale (or chip chart for video) in a place where it will not be contaminated by splashback from the background or floor.
- Whenever possible, use a polarizing filter to eliminate specular glare.

(a)

(b)

(c)

FIGURE 12.10 (a) Two Mole Biax four bank lights illuminate the greenscreen evenly. (b) Tracking marks (the black crosses) help the compositor keep the correct orientation as the camera moves. Tracking marks are absolutely essential whenever there are camera moves in a process shot. (c) The final result.

(a)

(b)

(c)

(d)

FIGURE 12.12 The steps of the process. (**a**) The greenscreen, (**b**) the holdout matte, (**c**) the background plate, and then (**d**) the final composited shot.

FIGURE 12.11 (**a**) A typical greenscreen setup. (**b**) Kino Flo Flathead 80s on a pipe in the grid illuminate the background evenly. Two more fill in the floor behind the actor and also give the actor some definition around the edges while another Flathead gives him a good backlight/hairlight. (**c**) A 2K fresnel gives him a bit of a kicker. Finally another large Kino gives him a soft ¾ front key. The ramp is for his walk toward the camera.

(a)

(b)

(c)

(a)

(b)

(c)

FIGURE 12.13 Poor man's process.
(**a**) The whole setup. In the front, two bounce lights (a 2K and a Tweenie) add some soft moonlight for inside the car. A Tweenie is operated by an electrician in front to simulate passing headlights.
(**b**) Extended out on a C-stand is a Tweenie that simulates the car passing under street lights—important for creating a sense of movement. Behind the car are two small lights that add car headlights coming up from behind and the red taillights of cars that have just passed (this is coordinated with the passing headlights in the front).
(**c**) The end result. This is only a single frame, of course. What is important about this rig is that the lights are moving, which is what convinces viewers that the car is in motion, even though they don't see any movement in the background of the shot.

FIGURE 12.14 A compact 12-volt Kino Flo unit is perfect for car shooting as it can easily run off the car battery and fits into small places. In this position it simulates the glow of dashboard lights.

- With a zoom lens avoid shooting with the lens wide open. The reason for this is that many zoom lenses vignette slightly when wide open, which can create problems with the mat.
- The video camera should be color-balanced for the foreground subject.
- To match the depth of focus of the foreground, shoot the background plate with the focus set at where it would be if the foreground object was actually there.
- Carefully plan the screen direction and perspective of the background plates. It is essential that it match the foreground.

Digitial video (DV) is particularly difficult to use for process or compositing work. The reason for this is that it is highly compressed: while most professional video (such as Betacam) and most HD is at least 4:2:2; DV is only 4:1:1.

Lighting for Process Photography

A few basic principles apply to lighting for greenscreen and bluescreen photography:

- Light the background as evenly as possible. Within one-third of a stop from edge to edge and from top to bottom is ideal.
- Keep the subject as far away from the background as possible to prevent backsplash, which will put green or blue onto the subject at precisely the worst possible place: along the edges.
- Unless the post-production supervisor or compositor says otherwise, exposure on the background should match the exposure on the foreground objects. Check this by reading the background with a spot meter (reflectance meter) and the foreground with an incident meter. Note, however, that some compositors prefer that the background be slightly hotter than the subject and some prefer the opposite. Always check with the person who will be doing the compositing to see how s/he prefers it.

Nothing will undermine the believability of a composite more than a mismatch of lighting in the foreground and background. Careful attention must be paid to recreating the look, direction, and quality of the lighting in the background plate. For this reason, it is often better to shoot the foreground first, although in some cases it may be more convenient to work with existing background plates and adjust the foreground subject to match; it all depends on the particular circumstances of the job.

Again, this underscores the importance of careful co-ordination of all efx work in advance; particularly as it is quite common for different crews to be working on different elements of the shot: often the first unit will be shooting the foreground subjects, a second unit crew might be doing the background

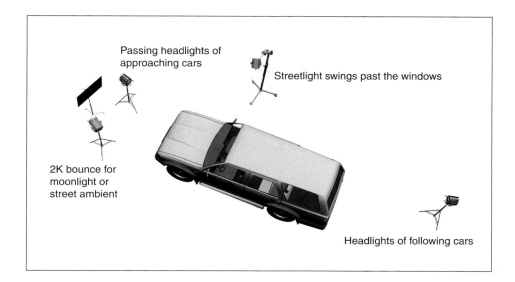

FIGURE 12.15 A typical setup for the poor man's process. The key to this effect is that all of the lights (except the ambient bounce) move by being panned past the windows in a way that imitates the changing lights of real traffic. It is the sense of movement that sells the gag (as these types of effects are called). Many people use a small interior light mimicking dashboard glow instead of or in addition to the ambient moonlight or city lights (see Figure 12.14 for an example.

plates and there will be additional CGI (computer generated graphics) elements to be composited in as well.

When a compositing shot gets this complex, an overall co-ordinator is essential. This function is usually performed by a post-production supervisor or a special effects supervisor; however, on smaller jobs, it might just be the editor who tries to keep everything running smoothly. As always, there is simply no substitute for working out the details before a single frame is shot. It is not merely a matter of matching the lighting and movement, but overal questions of formats, file types and workflow as well. The days when it was all done on film were much simpler; today, a single shot might involve three or four different types of digital files.

Greenscreen/Bluescreen Tips

- Guard against backsplash.
- Block off any background screen not in use.
- Don't use a complementary color as a backlight.
- Ask if they need to see the floor, as you will need to deal with the shadows if they do, and plan accordingly.
- Don't use diffusion.
- Don't use smoke.
- Don't include the matte color in the scene.
- Try not to have anybody lying on the floor or on a table. Sometimes a mirror on the floor will help by eliminating shadows.

Appendix

Brute Arc Operation

Arc operation is not difficult, but it is not something to be attempted by the uninitiated. Injury and damage to the equipment are very possible. Hands-on training from an experienced set electrician is a must. We can, however, provide some basics that will assist the electrician in preparation.

Make sure you have the right carbons. White-flame carbons (daylight-balanced shooting) are marked with a white dot. Yellow-flame carbons (tungsten-balance shooting) have a yellow dot.

Negative carbons are copper clad and about 10 inches long with a conical nose. Positives are 20 inches long with a crater at one end: this is the business end of the carbon.

The necessary tools are screwdriver, pair of pliers, and good leather work gloves. You will also need positive and negative electrodes and a can of arc lubricant. A dousing can full of water or sand is also useful if you are removing the glowing hot electrodes from a recently operating arc.

If DC is not available, it is possible to use a rectifier to convert AC. Special units are available for this.

Cautions

1. Never use cracked carbons. The sound when lightly tapped against metal will reveal their condition. The crack will cause a flicker at the point of the crack, possibly ruining a take.
2. Strike arcs one at a time. Striking too many arcs at a time creates a huge strain on the generator.
3. Warn the gaffer or cameraman when carbons are burning low. It is your job to make sure they don't burn out in the middle of a shot.
4. Never burn an arc at more than 45° tilt either way.
5. Get lots of help when mounting a light on the stand.
6. Do not lubricate a hot head.
7. Not all arc guts require lubricating. Some companies run their brutes as dry guts, which means they never lubricate them. Check with the rental house. Oiling a dry guts arc can cause trouble.
8. The units do exhaust gases and this should be taken into account in enclosed spaces.

Operating Steps

1. Make sure the power is off.
2. Release the latch and tilt the guts out for access.
3. Press the dimpled negative carriage release lever. The carriage will drop to its lowest position. Always use the pliers or screwdriver to operate anything inside

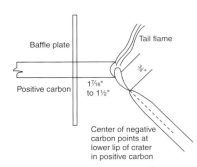

Baffle plate

Tail flame

Positive carbon

$1\frac{7}{16}$"
to $1\frac{1}{2}$"

$\frac{3}{4}$"

Center of negative carbon points at lower lip of crater in positive carbon

FIGURE A.1 Proper spacing of the carbons in an arc light.

the arc. If it has been operating, these parts will be hot enough to burn right through work gloves.

4. Depress one side of the negative holder. This lifts the roller and allows you to place the carbon in the V-block holder.

5. Rotate the positive electrode camming lever clockwise to release the positive electrode. If there is a used positive, remove it. You can then slide a new one in with its cratered end forward, protruding from the carrier about $1\frac{1}{2}$ inches.

6. Depress the striker lever (outside lower rear of the housing) to bring the negative up to its striking position. Push the positive gently forward until it touches the negative.

7. The ideal positioning is for the tip of the negative to just contact the lower lip of the positive. Adjust the manual positive handcrank if necessary.

8. Rotate the positive carbon camming lever counter clockwise to lock the rod in.

9. Tilt the guts back into the housing and lock in place.

10. Attach the power lines to the grid and then run cables from the grid to the light.

11. Check polarity. Correct polarity—the negative side of the DC source connected to the negative electrode— is essential to arc operation. Power on at the head and look at the polarity light; if it is ON, then the polarity is wrong. Reverse the cables to correct.

12. To strike the arc, gently depress the striking lever to bring the two electrodes into contact. Immediately release it. The arc should be working. If it's not, check your electrode positioning and try again.

13. Trimming during operation is a skill that can only come from practice. There are three basic trim functions: the external rheostat that controls the speed of the feed motors, the positive handcrank advance, and the negative handcrank advance. It is the job of the arc operator to view the flame through the viewing ports (never look at the flame with the naked eye; the intensity and ultraviolet will cause immediate eye damage) and make adjustments to maintain the optimal $\frac{3}{4}$-inch gap and proper relationship of the carbons.

Table A.1 International Voltage, Frequency, Plugs, and Sockets

Country	Type of Plug/Socket	Voltage	Frequency	Notes
Afghanistan	C, D, F	240 V	50 Hz	Voltage may vary from 160 to 280
Albania	C, F	220 V	50 Hz	
Algeria	C, F	230 V	50 Hz	
American Samoa	A, B, F, I	120 V	60 Hz	
Andorra	C, F	220 V	50 Hz	
Angola	C	220 V	50 Hz	
Anguilla	A (maybe B)	110 V	60 Hz	
Antigua	A, B	230 V	60 Hz	
Argentina	C, I	220 V	50 Hz	Live and neutral are wired backward
Armenia	C, F	220 V	50 Hz	
Aruba	A, B, F	127 V	60 Hz	
Australia	I	240 V	50 Hz	
Austria	C, F	230 V	50 Hz	
Azerbaijan	C	220 V	50 Hz	
Azores	B, C, F	220 V	50 Hz	
Bahamas	A, B	120 V	60 Hz	
Bahrain	G	230 V	50 Hz	
Balearic Islands	C, F	220 V	50 Hz	
Bangladesh	A, C, D, G, K	220 V	50 Hz	
Barbados	A, B	115 V	50 Hz	
Belarus	C	220 V	50 Hz	
Belgium	C, E	230 V	50 Hz	
Belize	A, B, G	110 V and 200 Hz	60 Hz	
Benin	C, E	220 V	50 Hz	
Bermuda	A, B	120 V	60 Hz	
Bhutan	D, F, G, M	230 V	50 Hz	
Bolivia	A, C	220 V	50 Hz	La Paz and Viacha 115 V
Bosnia	C, F	220 V	50 Hz	
Botswana	D, G, M	231 V	50 Hz	
Brazil	A, B, C, I	110 V and 220 V	60 Hz	Dual-voltage wiring is common
Brunei	G	240 V	50 Hz	
Bulgaria	C, F	230 V	50 Hz	
Burkina Faso	C, E	220 V	50 Hz	
Burundi	C, E	220 V	50 Hz	
Cambodia	A, C, G	230 V	50 Hz	
Cameroon	C, E	220 V	50 Hz	
Canada	A, B	120 V	60 Hz	Standardized at 120 V. For heavy-duty applications 240 V/60 Hz are used

(Continued)

Country	Type of Plug/ Socket	Voltage	Frequency	Notes
Canary Islands	C, E, L	220V	50Hz	
Cape Verde	C, F	220V	50Hz	
Cayman Islands	A, B	120V	60Hz	
Central African Republic	C, E	220V	50Hz	
Chad	D, E, F	220V	50Hz	
Channel Islands	C, G	230V	50Hz	
Chile	C, L	220V	50Hz	
P.R. China (mainland only)	A, C, I, G	220V	50Hz	Most outlets support types A, I, and C
Colombia	A, B	120V	60Hz	
Comoros	C, E	220V	50Hz	
Congo-Brazzaville	C, E	230V	50Hz	
Congo-Kinshasa	C, D	220V	50Hz	
Cook Islands	I	240V	50Hz	
Costa Rica	A, B	120V	60Hz	
Côte d'Ivoire (Ivory Coast)	C, E	230V	50Hz	
Croatia	C, F	230V	50Hz	
Cuba	A, B	110V	60Hz	
Cyprus	G	240V	50Hz	
Czech Republic	C, E	230V	50Hz	
Denmark	C, E, K	230V	50Hz	
Djibouti	C, E	220V	50Hz	
Dominica	D, G	230V	50Hz	
Dominican Republic	A, B	110V	60Hz	
East Timor	C, E, F, I	220V	50Hz	
Ecuador	A, B	120V	60Hz	
Egypt	C	220V	50Hz	
El Salvador	A, B	115V	60Hz	
Equatorial Guinea	C, E	220V	50Hz	
Eritrea	C	230V	50Hz	
Estonia	F	230V	50Hz	
Ethiopia	D, J, L	220V	50Hz	
Faroe Islands	C, K	220V	50Hz	
Falkland Islands	G	240V	50Hz	
Fiji	I	240V	50Hz	
Finland	C, F	230V	50Hz	
France	C, E	230V (formerly 220V)	50Hz	
French Guiana	C, D, E	220V	50Hz	
Gaza Strip	C, H, M	230V	50Hz	
Gabon	C	220V	50Hz	

(Continued)

Country	Type of Plug/ Socket	Voltage	Frequency	Notes
Gambia	G	230V	50Hz	
Germany	C, F	230V (formerly 220V)	50Hz	
Ghana	D, G	230V	50Hz	
Gibraltar	C, G	240V	50Hz	
Greece	C, F	230V (formerly 220V)	50Hz	
Greenland	C, K	220V	50Hz	
Grenada	G	230V	50Hz	
Guadeloupe	C, D, E	230V	50Hz	
Guam	A, B	110V	60Hz	
Guatemala	A, B	120V	60Hz	
Guinea	C, F, K	220V	50Hz	
Guinea-Bissau	C	220V	50Hz	
Guyana	A, B, D, G	240Hz	60Hz	
Haiti	A, B	110V	60Hz	
Honduras	A, B	110V	60Hz	
Hong Kong (S.A.R. of China)	G, D, M	220V	50Hz	
Hungary	C, F	230V	50Hz	
Iceland	C, F	230V	50Hz	
India	C, D, M	230V	50Hz	
Indonesia	C, F, G	127 and 230V	50Hz	Type-G socket/plug is less common
Iran	C	230V	50Hz	
Iraq	C, D, G	230V	50Hz	
Ireland	F, G, D, M	230V (formerly 220V)	50Hz	
Isle of Man	C, G	240V	50Hz	
Israel	C, H, M	230V	50Hz	Same plugs and sockets also used in Palestine
Italy	C, F, L	230V (formerly 220V)	50Hz	
Jamaica	A, B	110V	50Hz	
Japan	A, B	100V	50/60V	Eastern Japan 50Hz; Western Japan 60Hz. Sockets and switches fit in American-sized standard boxes
Jordan	B, C, D, F, G, J	230V	50Hz	
Kenya	G	240V	50Hz	
Kazakhstan	C	220V	50Hz	
Kiribati	I	240V	50Hz	
Korea, North	C	220V	50Hz	

(Continued)

Country	Type of Plug/Socket	Voltage	Frequency	Notes
Korea, South	C, F	220V	60Hz	
Kurdistan	A, B, C, D, E, F, G	230V	50Hz	
Kuwait	C, G	240V	50Hz	
Kyrgyzstan	C			
Laos	A, B, C, E, F	230V	50Hz	
Latvia	C, F	220V	50Hz	
Lebanon	A, B, C, D, G	110 and 200V	50Hz	
Lesotho	M	220V	50Hz	
Liberia	A, B, C, F	120 and 220V	50Hz	
Libya	D	127V	50Hz	Barce, Benghazi, Derna, Sebha, and Tobruk 230V
Lithuania	C, F	230V (formerly 220V)	50Hz	
Liechtenstein	C, J	230V	50Hz	Swiss standards
Luxembourg	C, F	230V (formerly 220V)	50Hz	
Macau S.A.R. of China	D, F, M, G	220V	50Hz	
Macedonia (FYROM)	C, F	220V	50Hz	
Madagascar	C, D, E, J, K	127 and 220V	50Hz	
Madeira	C, F	220V	50Hz	
Malawi	G	230V	50Hz	
Malaysia	C, G, M	240V	50Hz	Penang 230V
Maldives	A, D, G, J, K, L	230V	50Hz	
Mali	C, E	220V	50Hz	
Malta	G	230V	50Hz	
Martinique	C, D, E	220V	50Hz	
Mauritania	C	220V	50Hz	
Mauritius	C, G	230V	50Hz	
Mexico	A, B	120V	60Hz	Voltage can vary from 110 to 135V. Split phase is commonly available
Micronesia	A, B	120V	60Hz	
Monaco	C, D, E, F	127 and 220V		
Mongolia	C, E	230V	50Hz	
Montenegro	C, F	220V	50Hz	
Montserrat	A, B	230V	60Hz	
Morocco	C, E	127 and 220V	50Hz	
Mozambique	C, F, M	220V	50Hz	Type M in some areas
Myanmar/Burma	C, D, F, G	230V	50Hz	Type G found in some hotels
Namibia	D, M	220V	50Hz	
Nauru	I	240V	50Hz	

(Continued)

Country	Type of Plug/ Socket	Voltage	Frequency	Notes
Nepal	C, D, M	230V	50Hz	
The Netherlands	C, F	230V (formerly 220V)	50Hz	
Netherlands Antilles	A, B, F	127 and 220V	50Hz	
New Caledonia	F	220V	50Hz	
New Zealand	I	240V	50Hz	
Nicaragua	A, B	120V	60Hz	
Niger	A, B, C, D, E, F	220V	50Hz	
Nigeria	D, G	240V	50Hz	
Norway	C, F	230V	50Hz	
Okinawa	A, B, I	100V	60Hz	Military facilities 120V
Oman	C, G	240V	50Hz	Many voltage variations
Pakistan	C, D	220V	50Hz	
Palestine	C, H, M	230V	50Hz	
Panama	A, B	110V	60Hz	Panama City 120V
Papua New Guinea	I	240V	50Hz	
Paraguay	C	220V	50Hz	
Peru	A, B, C	220V	60Hz	Talara $^{110}/_{220}$V; Arequipa 50Hz
Philippines	A, B, C	220V	60Hz	Some type-C sockets deliver 110V/60Hz. Sockets and switches fit standard American-sized boxes
Poland	C, E	230V	50Hz	
Portugal	C, F	220V[3]	50Hz	
Puerto Rico	A, B	120V	60Hz	
Qatar	D, G	240V	50Hz	
Réunion	E	220V	50Hz	
Romania	C, F	230V	50Hz	Identical to German standards
Russian Federation	C, F	220V	50Hz	Former USSR: GOST sockets with 4.0-mm pins instead of the 4.8-mm standard
Rwanda	C, J	230V	50Hz	
St. Kitts and Nevis	D, G	230V	60Hz	
St. Lucia (Windward Is.)	G	240V	50Hz	
St. Vincent (Windward Is.)	A, C, E, G, I, K	230V	50Hz	
Saudi Arabia	A, B, F, G	127 and 220V	60Hz	
Senegal	C, D, E, K	230V	50Hz	
Serbia	C, F	220V	50Hz	
Seychelles	G	240V	50Hz	
Sierra Leone	D, G	230V	50Hz	
Singapore	G, D, M	230V	50Hz	
Slovakia	C, E	230V	50Hz	

(Continued)

Country	Type of Plug/ Socket	Voltage	Frequency	Notes
Slovenia	C, F	230V	50Hz	360V used for heavy applications
Somalia	C	220V	50Hz	
South Africa	M	220V	50Hz	Some areas 250V
Spain	C, F	230V (formerly 220V)	50Hz	
Sri Lanka	D, M, G	230V	50Hz	
Sudan	C, D	230V	50Hz	
Suriname	C, F	127V	60Hz	
Swaziland	M	230V	50Hz	
Sweden	C, F	230V	50Hz	
Switzerland	C, J	230V	50Hz	
Syria	C, E, L	220V	50Hz	
Tahiti	A, B, E	110 and 220V	60Hz	
Tajikistan	C, I	220V	50Hz	
Republic of China (Taiwan)	A, B	110V	60Hz	
Tanzania	D, G	230V	50Hz	
Thailand	A, B, C	220V	50Hz	Standard American form factor
Togo	C	220V	50Hz	Some 127V
Tonga	I	240V	50Hz	
Trinidad & Tobago	A, B	115V	60Hz	
Tunisia	C, E	230V	50Hz	
Turkey	C, F	230V	50Hz	
Turkmenistan	B, F	220V	50Hz	
Uganda	G	240V	50Hz	
Ukraine	C, F	220V	50Hz	
United Arab Emirates	C, D, G	220V	50Hz	
United Kingdom	G	240 and 220V	50Hz	D and M seen in older buildings
United States of America	A, B	120V	60Hz	Voltage ranges from 105 to 130 V, depending on location. 240V/60Hz used for heavy-duty applications
Uruguay	C, F, I, L	230V	50Hz	Neutral and live wires are reversed, as in Argentina
Uzbekistan	C, I	220V	50Hz	
Venezuela	A, B	120V	60Hz	
Vietnam	A, C, G	220V	50Hz	Type G found in some hotels
Virgin Islands	A, B	110V	60Hz	
Western Samoa	I	230V	50Hz	
Yemen	A, D, G	230V	50Hz	
Zambia	C, D, G	230V	50Hz	
Zimbabwe	D, G	220V	50Hz	

International Plug and Socket Types

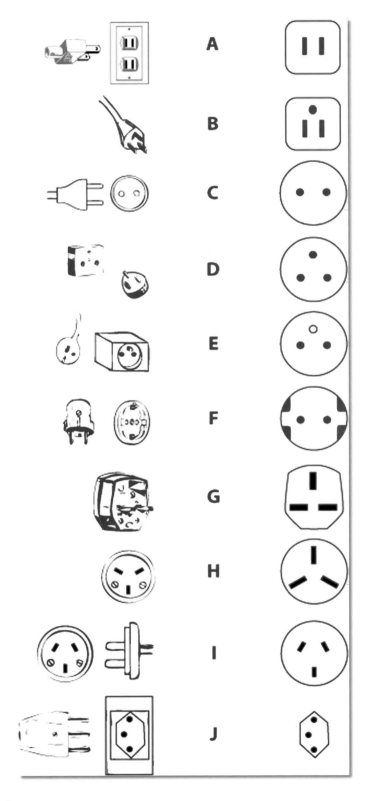

Building Your Own Hand Squeezer

Hand dimmers, known as hand squeezers, are standard equipment on a film set. Often, the gaffer and electricians bring their own or build them with materials supplied by the production company; they are seldom rented. Ordinary household dimmers are available at hardware stores, but they usually carry the more common 600-watt dimmers (not really adequate for use on the set). Electrical supply houses or online is likely a better source of 1000- or 2000-watt dimmers, which are what is used on film and video sets.

You will want to enclose the whole rig in some sort of box. The most common method is to use a standard electrical box, such as might contain a dimmer or switch when it is installed inside a wall. Be sure to use proper connectors and electrical tape, and be sure to make it so there are no loose wires or exposed copper, which might cause a shock hazard. Always be careful with electricity!

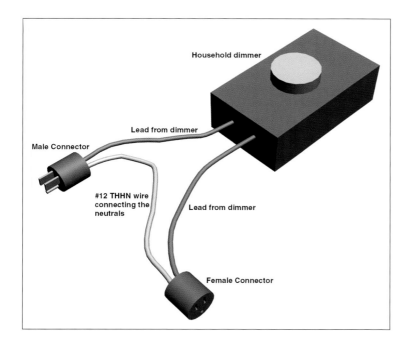

Typical Lighting Order for a Small Independent Film

This is a typical lighting order for a night exterior on a low-budget independent film. All lighting orders are different, depending on the budget, the circumstances of the shoot, the type of scene, etc. This one is shown as an example only; you must adapt every lighting/grip order to your particular budget, location, and type of production.

POWER
1—Generator, 450 amps, three-phase with Camlok connections

LIGHTS
2—MaxiBrutes with barndoors, barndoors, gel frames and stands
2—9-light FAY with tungsten NSP bulbs with barndoor and stand
4—Mightie Mole, open-face 2K, with barndoor, scrims, stands
2—Mickie Mole, open-face 1K, with barndoor, scrims, and stands
2—Baby Junior with barndoors, scrims, and triple riser stands
2—Baby Baby with barndoors, scrims, and stands
2—Tweenie with barndoors, scrims, and stands
4—Inkies with barndoors, scrims, and snoot set
4—1K zip soft lights (worklights for craft service, makeup, wardrobe, etc.), stands
2—2K zip soft light with eggcrates and stands

DISTRO
500'—Five-wire banded feeder cable—Camlok
50'—Five-wire #00 feeder cable—Camlok
10—Camlok tees
6—100', 100-amp Bates extensions
5—Bates 100- to 60-amp splitters
8—50', 60-amp Bates extensions
2—3-Phase distribution boxes
4—Lunch boxes
4—Bates to 6-outlet Edison
25—50' single extension (stingers)
20—25' single extension (stingers)
2—Flicker boxes
2—2K Variac
2—12K electronic dimmer

GRIP
25—C-stands
40—Sandbags
6—Cardellini clamps
4—Mafer clamp
14—Full apple boxes
10—Half-apple boxes
10—Quarter-apple boxes
10—One-eighth apple boxes
10—Pancakes
2—12' 2×12 dolly boards
6—4 × 4 floppy
6—4 × 4 open frames
2—4 × 4 cuculoris
2—4 × 4 single
2—4 × 4 double
2—4 × 4 silk
6—24 × 36 flags
4—24 × 36 single nets
4—24 × 36 double nets
6—18 × 24 flags
6—Highboys
2—Shiny boards soft/hard
4—Baby offset arm
2—Baby sidearm
2—Baby double header

DOLLY
Fischer 11 with seats, sideboards, pork chop
2—12" risers
5—Pieces straight track
3—Pieces wide circle track (45º)
Box of wedges

EXPENDABLES
Black wrap
Full CTB
$\frac{1}{2}$ CTB (about a half roll)
$\frac{1}{4}$ CTB (about a half roll)
CTS
$\frac{1}{4}$ CTS ($\frac{1}{3}$ roll)
$\frac{1}{8}$ CTS ($\frac{1}{3}$ roll)
Rosco Opal
Rosco 3026 (216)
Rosco 3027 ($\frac{1}{2}$ 216)
3 Yards bleached muslin

Sash cord 400' #8
Trick line (mason's line)—black
Dulling spray—black
Streaks' Tips—black

Lighting Order for a Large Studio Film

This lighting order is for the film *Mr. and Mrs. Smith* and was supplied by Chief Lighting Technician Tony "Nako" Nakonechnyj, a top Hollywood gaffer and an accomplished cinematographer in his own right. This is the "truck package"—the basic order which is carried on the truck (a 40′ semi-trailer) to all locations and stages. Other packages covered specific stages, 2nd unit, special locations, etc. Every order is different, depending on the location, the type of shot, the look, the budget, etc.

HMI

(All ballasts must be electronic and flicker-free)
- 1—18 Fresnel Complete w/2 50′ Head Feeders (LTM)
- 1—6K Pars Complete w/2 50′ Head Feeders (LTM)
- 2—4K Pars Complete w/2 50′ Head Feeders (LTM)
- 2—2500 Pars Complete w/2 50′ Head Feeders (LTM)
- 2—1200 HMI Pars Complete w/2 50′ Head Feeders (LTM)
- 2—575 HMI Pars Complete w/2 50′ Head Feeders (LTM)
- 1—575/2-K Hybrid Par Complete (CMC)
- 2—200-watt Joker Bug Lights Complete

TUNGSTEN

- 2—20K Mole Complete
- 4—MaxiBrutes Complete: 4 w/FFN & 4 w/FFR Globes
- 2—9 Lite Complete w/FCX Globes
- 3—Baby 10 K Complete w/4-way doors
- 3—Baby 5 K Complete w/4-way doors
- 3—Baby Junior Complete w/4-way doors
- 3—Baby Complete w/4-way doors
- 6—Tweenie Complete w/4-way doors
- 6—100 Peppers Complete w/4-way doors (w/200 w Globes)
- 2—2K Zips Complete w/eggcrate
- 2—750 Zips Complete w/eggcrate
- 8—Par 64s Complete (w/narrow, medium, wide globes)
- 16—Par Cans w/Baby Spuds (FFN)
- 2—Source Four Focal Spots
- 6—Blondes Complete
- 6—Red Heads Complete

KINO-FLO

- 1—Image 80 w/Kino55 and Kino32 tubes
- 4—4′ 4-Tube Kino w/Kino55 and Kino32 tubes
- 4—4′ 2-Tube Kino w/Kino55 and Kino32 tubes
- 4—4′ 1-Tube Kino w/Kino55 and Kino32 tubes
- 2—2′ 4-Tube Kino w/Kino55 and Kino32 tubes
- 2—2′ 2-Tube Kino w/Kino55 and Kino32 tubes
- 4—2′ 1-Tube Kino w/Kino55 and Kino32 tubes
- 2—Mini Flo Kit

STANDS

- 4—Roadrunners
- 2—Super Crank-a-vator
- 4—Mini Crank-a-vator
- 8—3-Riser Jr. Combo (American)
- 6—2-Riser Jr. Combo (American)
- 24—3-Riser Baby (American)
- 8—Junior low stands
- 8—Baby low stands

DIMMERS

- 4—6×12 kw Electronic Dimmer Packs (DMX)
- 4—12×2.4 kw Electronic Dimmer Packs (DMX)
- 2—Spare DMX Brains
- 1—Expressions 3 Control Board (1200ch)
- 1—ETC 48/96 Control Board
- 1—Gray's DMX combiner
- 2—Opto splitter
- 10—100′ DMX control cable
- 10—18″ DMX jumper
- 4—12K CD-80 Independent Electronic Dimmer (DMX)
- 2—20K CD-80 Independent Electronic Dimmer (DMX)
- 4—2K Variacs
- 4—1K Variacs
- 8—100′ Socoplex 6-channel cables
- 8—50′ Socoplex 6-channel cables
- 10—Male Break-ins (20-amp M-Bates to F-Soco)
- 10—Female Break-outs (M-Soco to 20-amp F-Edison)

HARDWARE

- 2—Trapeze
- 4—T-Bones
- 4—Turtles
- 4—Baby pipe hangers
- 4—Baby plates
- 4—Junior pipe hangers
- 4—Junior plates
- 4—Baby off-sets
- 4—Junior off-sets
- 12—Chain vise grips
- 6—Candlesticks

SPECIAL

- 1—Electrician's 7-crate cart
- 1—Kino cart
- 1—Chimera cart
- 2—Distro cart
- 2—Tungsten head carts
- 2—HMI head cart
- 4—Cable carts
- 2—4′ Ladder [note: other ladders would be supplied by the grip dept.]
- 1—Case of Tota-Lights

1—Case of Stick-ups
1—K5 Kit
2—13″ JEM Paper Lantern Harp and Ball
2—19″ JEM Paper Lantern Harp and Ball
4—22″ JEM 1000-watt Muz Ball
4—30″ JEM 1500-watt Muz Ball
2—19″ JEM Bug Light Grid Ball
4—Mini Space Lights
1—Tweenie Chimera Ring—Extra Small Quartz Plus w/Soft Eggcrate
1—1K Baby Chimera Ring—Small Quartz Plus Bag w/Soft Eggcrate
1—1K Red Head Chimera Ring
2—2K Baby Chimera Ring—Small Quartz Plus w/Soft Eggcrate
2—2K Blonde Chimera Ring
2—5K Baby Chimera Ring—Medium Quartz Plus w/Soft Eggcrate
1—10K Baby Chimera Ring—Medium Quartz Plus w/Soft Eggcrate
2—575 HMI Par Chimera Ring
2—1200 HMI Par Chimera Ring
1—2500 HMI Par Chimera Ring
1—4K HMI Par Chimera Ring
1—6K HMI Par Chimera Ring
6—100 Pepper Snoot
2—Tweenie Snoot
2—Baby Baby Snoot
2—Baby Junior Snoot
2—Baby 5K Snoot
1—Baby 10K Snoot

CABLE
5—100′ 4/0 CAM [Camlok connectors]
5—50′ 4/0 CAM
10—100′ 2/0 CAM
5—50′ 2/0 CAM
12—50′ 2/5 CAM Banded (Three-Phase)
20—6′ 4/0 CAM Jumpers
12—Male CAM to Lug adapters
12—Female CAM to Lug adapters
8—Male CAM Suicide adapters
8—Female CAM Suicide adapters
8—Male CAM to Female Pin adapters
8—Female CAM to Male Pin adapters
24—CAM Soft Three-fers
12—CAM Ground Squids
4—600-amp Pin through CAM Distro Box
8—100-amp Lunch Boxes

4—100-amp Gang Boxes
4—60-amp Gang Boxes
8—100-amp M-Bates to 2 100-amp F-Bates Splits
8—100-amp M- Bates to 2 60-amp F-Bates Splits
4—60-amp M-Bates to 2-60-amp F-Bates Splits
12—100-amp M-Bates to F-CAM (Reverse Snake-Bite)
4—100-amp F-Bates to M-CAM 5-wire (Triple Snake-Bite)
4—100-amp F-Bates to M-CAM 3-wire (Single Snake-Bite)
4—220-volt M-Bates to F-CAM Pin (220 Reverse Snake-Bite)
4—220-volt F-Bates to M-CAM Pin 3-wire (220 Snake-Bite)
50—25′ Stingers
50—50′ Stingers
8—50′ 220-volt Bates
6—25′ 220-volt Bates
2—100′ 100-amp Bates
8—50′ 100-amp Bates
6—25′ 100-amp Bates
8—50′ 60-amp Bates
6—25′ 60-amp Bates
12—Cable Crossovers
5—Female CAM Suicide adapters
24—CAM Three-Fers
12—CAM Ground Squids
4—600-amp CAM-through distribution boxes
4—100-amp Lunch Boxes
4—100-amp M-Bates to 2 100-amp F-Bates Splits
4—100-amp M-Bates to 2 60-amp F-Bates Splits
4—220-volt M-Bates to F-Mole Pin (220 Reverse Snake-Bite)
4—220-volt F-Bates to M-Mole Pin 3-wire (220 Snake-Bite)
20—25′ Stingers
20—50′ Stingers
4—50′ 220-volt Bates Extension
2—25′ 220-volt Bates Extension
6—50′ 100-amp Bates Extension
4—25′ 100-amp Bates Extension
4—50′ 60-amp Bates Extension
2—25′ 60-amp Bates Extension
12—Cable Crossovers

GENERATOR
1—1200-amp tow plant

Acknowledgments

Special thanks to the following for their assistance in helping with this book.

The Los Angeles Film School
www.LAFilm.com

Mole–Richardson Lighting, Larry Parker, Vice-President
www.mole.com

DSC Laboratories
www.dsclabs.com

ETC—Electronic Theater Controls (Source Four lights)
www.etcconnect.com

Gossen Foto
www.gossen-photo.de

Bogen Imaging
www.bogenimaging.us

Barger BagLites, Ed Barger
www.barger-baglite.com

Yuri Neyman, Gamma and Density
gammadensity.com

Everyone at Cinematographer's Mailing List created by Geoff Boyle
www.cinematography.net

Magic Film and Video, telecine and negative cutting
www.mfvw.com

Elinor Actipis, Editor, Focal Press
www.focalpress.com

Cara Anderson, Focal Press

Pampa Lites, Owen Stephens
www.pampalite.com

Luminaria/Ruby 7, Charles Libin, David Skutch
luminaria.net

Kino Flo, Freider Hochheim
www.kinoflo.com

Rosco
www.rosco.com

Tony "Nako" Nakonechnyj, Gaffer and Director of Photography

Tom Denove, Director of Photography

Special Thanks

Special thanks to all those who helped me with this book and helped me be a better teacher of cinematography, with additional thanks to those who helped me to better understand the art of motion picture and video lighting:

Joe Byron, Director of Education, Los Angeles Film School

Ariel Levy, Head of Production, Los Angeles Film School

Dave Dailey, Los Angeles Film School

Faculty, staff, and students of the Los Angeles Film School, including Barbara Dunphy, Karen Thompson, Patrick Olmstead, Nesdon Booth, Paul Balbirnie, Matt Villines, Gina Tucker, Greg Filkins, Charlie Rose, Kevin Atkinson, and everyone else.

Larry Mole Parker and John Clisham at Mole–Richardson. Gaffer and D.P. Tony "Nako" Nakonechnyj; gaffer and D.P. David Chung.

Special thanks to Brock D. Lafond, 3D Modeler, for creating the 3D models of motion picture lights used in the illustrations: brock@ateires-media.com

About the Author

Blain Brown has worked in film and video production for more than 20 years as a cinematographer. He has also been a director/writer on feature films, commercials and music videos, as well as a line producer and producer.

Currently working in Los Angeles as a Director of Photography and writer/director, he teaches cinematography at Los Angeles Film School in Hollywood. His other books include *Cinematography: Theory and Practice*, which is used as a textbook at many film schools. He can be reached at his website: www.BlainBrown.com

Index

photographic films and, *see*
Photographic films
reflectance meters for, 118
reflectances and, 102
zone system and, 119–127
exposure index (EI), 103, 117, 144
and camera filters, 144
exposure time, of camera, 100, 125–126,
211
extreme closeup photography, *see*
Macrophotography
exteriors in studio, creation of, 81–85

F
faylights (FAY), 21, 211, 212
FAY lights, *see* Faylights
filaments, incandescent, 206
film production, early, 3–5
films, *see* Photographic films
flags, 16, 176
and cutters, 176–179
tricks, 177–178
flicker-free ballasts, 216
flicker-free HMIs, 216
flickering , 61–62
in HMIs, 213–214
problems, 210–211
fluorescent bulbs, 209–212
lampholders, 208
fluorescent lighting, 146–147
shooting with, 147
fluorescent lights, 139
fluorescent tubes, *see* Fluorescent
bulbs
foot-candle (fc), 99, 102
fresnel lens, 6, 10
650, Betweenie, and InBetweenie, 12
Inkie, 12
juniors, 12
1K, 12
5K, 11
10K and 20K, 11
tungsten fresnel lights, 11
f/stop scale, 100, 101

G
gaffer, lighting, 191, 192–193
Gamma, 98, 109–111
generators, 42, 152, 153–154, 162, 168,
198, 215
AC generator, 153, 214
DC generator, 153
operation, 154
grayscales, 120
greenscreen photography, 175, 227, 228,
230, 231
grids, 180

griffolyn, *see* Griffs
griffs, 183–184
grips, 85, 195–197
grip works, 173
butterflies and overheads, 181–182
clamps, *see* Clamps
cookies and celos, 180
C-stand rules, 184
cuculoris, 179
diffusers, 180–184
flags and cutters, 176–177
grids, 180
griffs, 183–184
grip heads, 184
highboys, 185
holding, 184–185
light controls, 174–176
nets, 178–179
net tricks, 179
open frames, 180
overhead rules, 182
grounding, 150
safety, 172

H
Hand dimmers, 241, *see also* Dimmers
hairlight, 45
H&D (Hurter and Driffield) curve,
107–110
heavy antimony batteries, 158–159
highboys, 181, 182, 185
high-high stands, *see* Highboys
HMIs, 6, 145, 148, 153
flicker-free, 9, 216
lamps, 206–218
bulbs, 210
HMI PARs, 21–22, 76
safety, 171–172
shooting with, 213–215
units, 12
caring and feeding of, 15
failures, 14–15
6K and 8K, 13–14
12K and 18K, 12–13
4K & 2.5K, 14
smaller units, 14
xenon, fluorescent, and LED sources,
8–9
household bulbs, 209
hue, color quality, 132

I
incident meters, 117–118, 122, 193
industrial lamps, 148
inertia point, 104–105, 110
ISO, 103
speed and exposure, 100, 102